MOTHER

Born in Paris on February 21, 1878, in a very materialistic, upper middle class family. She completed a thorough education of music, painting and higher mathematics. A student of the French painter Gustave Moreau, she befriended the great Impressionist artists of the time. She later became acquainted with Max Théon, an enigmatic character with extraordinary occult powers who, for the first time, gave her a coherent explanation of the spontaneous experiences occurring since her childhood, and who taught her occultism during two long visits to his estate in Algeria. In 1914, she visited the French colonial city of Pondicherry in India and met Sri Aurobindo who had sought refuge there from the British. She returned permanently to Pondicherry in 1920 via Japan and China, and when Sri Aurobindo "withdrew" to his room in 1926 to devote himself to the "supramental yoga," she organized and developed his "Ashram," and tried in vain to awaken the disciples to a "new consciousness." In 1958, after Sri Aurobindo's departure, she in turn withdrew to her room to come to terms with the problem—in the cells. From 1958 to 1973, she slowly uncovered the "Great Passage" to the next species and a new mode of life in matter, and narrated her extraordinary exploration to Satprem. This is the *Agenda*.

SATPREM

Born in Paris in 1923. Spent much of his childhood sailing off the coasts of Brittany. Arrested at the age of 20 by the Gestapo, he spent a year and a half in German concentration camps. His quest for a "deeper meaning of life" led him to Egypt, to the forests of Guyana, and finally to India where he discovered the "new evolution" heralded by Sri Aurobindo: "Man is a transitional being." This is the theme of his first book, *Sri Aurobindo or the Adventure of Consciousness*. After a few years as a wandering monk on the roads of India *(By the Body of the Earth)*, he became Mother's confidant and for some 20 years recorded the account of her cellular experiences, which gave rise to an insightful biography of Mother and a lively personal account of his years near her in a trilogy, MOTHER: (1) *The Divine Materialism*, (2) *The New Species*, (3) *The Mutation of Death*. His latest work, *The Mind of the Cells*, distills the essence of Mother's discovery: the change of the genetic programming and another view of death.

AGENDA
OF THE SUPRAMENTAL ACTION
UPON EARTH

MOTHER'S AGENDA

XIII

1972 – 1973

Translated from the French

INSTITUTE FOR EVOLUTIONARY RESEARCH
200 Park Avenue, New York

Library of Congress Cataloging in Publication Data

La Mère
    Mother's Agenda
    Half-title: Agenda of the Supramental Action upon earth.
    Translation of L'Agenda de Mère.
    Journal and correspondence.
    Vol. 13 — published in New York.

     1. La Mère.   2. Hindus — correspondence.
I. Institut de Recherches Évolutives.   II. Title.
BL1175.L35A413 1979 294.5'5 [B] 80-472990 AACRI
ISBN 0-938710-00-1 (13-volume set)
ISBN 0-938710-07-9 (Volume 13)

For subscriptions and information write to:

- *For the U.S.A. and Europe:*

      INSTITUTE FOR EVOLUTIONARY RESEARCH,
    200 Park Avenue, Suite 303 East, New York, NY 10166

- *For India and Asia:*

      MIRA ADITI CENTRE
    Aspiration, Auroville, Kottakuppam 605 104 (T.N.)

Manufactured in the United States of America

FIRST EDITION

*This Agenda . . . is
my gift to
those who love me*

MOTHER

In truth, no system can on its own effect the change humanity desperately needs; for that change can only occur by developing the possibilities of one's higher nature to the fullest. And this development depends on an inner growth, not on an external change.

However, external changes can at least prepare favorable conditions for that more substantial improvement, or on the contrary lead to such conditions that Kalki's sword alone can purify the earth of the burden of an obstinately asuric humanity.

The choice depends on the species itself; for as it sows, so shall it reap the fruit of its Karma.

Mother

The Last Path

As I begin this thirteenth volume, I look once again.

One morning in 1956, twenty-five years ago, Mother was telling me her first vision of the supramental world. She was seated in a tall straight-backed chair of carved wood that reminded me of Egypt, reminded me of so many other times before lost in forgotten ages. This was the first time this time that she was telling me about the fantastic adventure—the "transformation," the "new species"— and it seemed so familiar and yet was the same old mystery. During these last twenty-five years hardly an hour has gone by—and now hardly a minute or a second—without my poring over that Mystery. Twenty-five years is a lot of minutes in a man's life. And now, on this day of the year nineteen hundred and eighty-one, on this fifteenth of May, I look at it once more—it has become very burning. I look through the veil of that "stupid death," as she called it, I look at what is no longer visible to our physical eye and yet throbs with a compelling presence—how I wish I could take that cool hand again, so soft and yet so strong, and say: WHAT IS IT?

What is it?

It's so familiar, and yet totally unknown. All that the mind can know is known and yet nothing is known. All her words have been lived with almost excruciating intensity, understood from the depths of the soul, from the depths of a thousand lives spent tracking down the same secret, the same question, and yet nothing is understood. In the end, there remains only love, that's all. But there remains also this WHAT IS IT? Perhaps not so much personally as for the earth: what is it? For all this pain-racked humanity. The earth is indeed very miserable. Perhaps she is even at the end of her rope.

The day after she left, eight years ago, I scribbled two lines on a scrap of blue paper: "She left so that we would find something."

"We," human beings, that is.

I did not believe in death, not for a single second of those nineteen years spent near her, up till the very last day I did not believe in it—it didn't even occur to me she could leave. That morning of November 18, 1973, I was thunderstruck—numb, like a stone. Profoundly mute. And that intense question which has not left me since. A wordless question. Something burning within, like love, like the whole question of the earth. What is it?

Find what?... The passage?

I have plumbed each of her words for a clue, I have lived since then in the powerful vibration that enveloped her small white frame and extended far, far away into an infinity of snow and fire. Each second, perhaps, of these eight years, with each look, I have pored over an indefinable something. I have even written books, written again and again in an attempt to ferret out the mystery—in a transparent, suspended breath, so terribly still, I have tried to capture the pure little vibration, the slightest ripple from beyond that would fall upon the mirror of my soul and reveal the secret: the passage, the process.

But the only answer I got was a mounting flame. A mounting question. More and more infinity packed into one burning point. Like an imploding star.

It was a simple prayer—wordless, pure. A prayer for the pain of the earth. A prayer for the beauty of the earth.

Once again I am going to follow Mother's last path, her halting little breath—1972-1973—wade upstream to the source of that pure little prayer, as if to the farthest reaches of love and death, and ... I don't know, but something tells me that the earth will find it—this time the earth will find her own secret. Precisely there where nothing is left but love or death.

But only at that point.

We are being led, the entire earth is being led to LIVE that: to the point where all of a sudden the secret will come alive.

An hour of fire and prayer when nothing is left but "that."

Mother's Agenda is perhaps simply that prayer coming alive—and we are in the secret ... without knowing it. We will know it only when we have passed through death without dying from it.

For the hour WILL come when the earth stands on the threshold.

At the farthest reaches of love, death will vanish into an earthly glory.

Land's End
May 15, 1981

CONTENTS

1972

CHRONOLOGY OF WORLD EVENTS

1972

January 10   – Bangladesh becomes a sovereign state; Sheik Mujibur Rahman is named prime minister after returning from Pakistan, where he was in jail since March 1971.

February 21   – *Mother is ninety-four.*
              – Death of Eugène Cardinal Tisserant.
              – 21-28: President Nixon visits China; "normalization" of relations between the U.S. and China.

March 10   – Coup in Cambodia; Marshal Lon Nol takes complete control of the Cambodian government.

March 19   – Signing of a friendship treaty between India and Bangladesh.

March 30   – Following years of violence between Catholics and Protestants, Britain imposes direct rule on Northern Ireland; 467 Northern Irish killed during the year.

April 16   – Resumption of American bombing of North Vietnam.

May 9   – President Nixon announces the mining of North Vietnamese ports.

May 22   – President Nixon visits Moscow; signing of SALT.
              – Ceylon becomes a republic and changes its name to Sri Lanka.

May 30   – Gunmen shoot up Lod airport near Tel Aviv; twenty-four killed.

June 1   – The terrorist Andreas Baader is arrested in West Germany.

June 10   – Tropical storm Agnes strikes the eastern United States. It is called "the worst natural disaster in U.S. History."

June 17   – The District of Columbia police arrest five men inside the Democratic headquarters of Watergate. Beginning of the "Watergate" affair.

June 29   – The death penalty is declared unconstitutional by the U.S. Supreme Court.

July 3   – India and Pakistan sign the Simla Agreement to reduce tension over Kashmir.

July 18	– President Sadat ends the Soviet presence in Egypt.
July 19	– Kissinger and Le Duc Tho, the Vietnamese representative, hold secret talks in France.
July 21	– Violence in Belfast by the Irish Republican Army.
July 27	– China officially acknowledges the death of Lin Piao in September 1971 in a plane crash, while he was trying to escape to the Soviet Union after failing to overthrow Mao Tse-tung.
August 7	– The discovery of an important British oil field in the North Sea is confirmed.
August 21	– President Nixon is triumphantly renominated by the Republican party to run for president.
August 25	– China vetoes the admission of Bangladesh to the U.N.
September 5	– Eleven Israeli athletes are killed by Arab terrorists at the Olympic Games in Munich.
September 10	– A severe cyclone strikes the State of Orissa in India.
September 25	– China and Japan establish diplomatic relations for the first time since 1937.
November 18	– President Nixon is triumphantly reelected president of the United States.
December 7	– Armistice between India and Pakistan in Kashmir; retrocession of the territories occupied during the 1971 war.
December 21	– Fiftieth anniversary of the Soviet Union.
December 23	– Earthquake in Nicaragua; 10,000 are killed.
December 26	– Death of former U.S. President Harry S. Truman.
December 30	– President Nixon announces the resumption of the Paris peace talks, negotiations with Vietnam, and a halt to the bombings of North Vietnam.

January

January 1, 1972

Happy New Year, mon petit!

(Mother takes Satprem's hands. He offers her a "Divine Love."[1] She then distributes some presents.)

You saw Indira's letter, I showed it to you. . . .

Yes, Mother, I noted it down.

They're becoming conscious up there, some very interesting things are happening.

You mean at the Centre, in Delhi?

No, at the front, in Bangladesh.
That fellow who returned from America[2] says he doesn't want to end the war—we'll see. . . . But we're plainly heading for the breakup of Pakistan.

(long silence)

The Force is working very strongly, it's very very strong.
And you, how is it going?

Trustingly.

Ah, good! That's all we need. All we need.

(silence)

The power of "that" is stupendous. But human bodies aren't used to it, so it's hard for them to bear it. But that doesn't matter.

*(Mother takes Satprem's hands
meditation)*

---

1. Pomegranate flower.
2. This certainly refers to Bhutto who had gone to America as Pakistan's Minister of Foreign Affairs and was called back last month to be nominated President of Pakistan.

*
* *

(Message of January 1)

Without the Divine, we are limited, incompetent and helpless beings; with the Divine, if we give ourselves entirely to Him, all is possible and our progress is limitless.

A special help has come onto the earth for Sri Aurobindo's centenary year; let us take advantage of it to overcome the ego and emerge into the light.

Happy New Year.

January 2, 1972

(Message from Mother)

When Sri Aurobindo left his body he said that he would not abandon us. And in truth, during these twenty-one years, he has always been with us, guiding and helping all those who are receptive and open to his influence.

In this year of his centenary, his help will be stronger still. It is up to us to be more open and to know how to take advantage of it. The future is for those who have the soul of a hero. The stronger and more sincere our faith, the more powerful and effective will be the help received.

January 5, 1972

How are you?

It still drags.

> *(Mother gives Satprem her latest message:)*

> "Sri Aurobindo does not belong to any one country but to the entire earth. His teaching leads us towards a better future."

(Then Mother listens to Satprem read a letter from a disciple who had felt a specially strong descent of force and was asking if it was related to the new year.)

It is related to the year of Sri Aurobindo.
Sri Aurobindo's Force will exert a pressure this year. I felt it immediately, on the very first of January. A strong pressure from his force, his consciousness, like this *(Mother lowers both arms).*

> *(silence)*

Well then?

Won't you say something?

No.... I have trouble speaking.
But the experience continues; it is getting increasingly stronger and more precise.... But expressing myself is difficult.
The Consciousness is VERY active, but in silence. As soon as I speak....

> *(Mother goes into contemplation*
> *until the end)*

What time is it?

It's eleven o'clock, Mother.

The atmosphere is very peaceful, very clear.

January 8, 1972

What's new?... Feeling better?... No?...

I don't know. I don't quite understand what course we're following.

Why, I myself don't understand it at all! Simply ... *(Mother opens her hands in a gesture of surrender).*
It isn't easy.
It isn't easy, but it's what I was telling you: both extremes. It isn't easy, but all of a sudden, for a few seconds, everything becomes wonderful, and then again.... So I'd rather not speak about it.

(silence)

Now that I am here like this, in seclusion, the lowest nature of everyone comes out. They do things, thinking "Oh, Mother won't know." That's how it is. So this "Mother won't know" means there's no more restraint. I would say it's rather disgusting.
People to whom I have said, "You can't stay in the Ashram" move in anyway. And nobody stops them. Not only that, but they go to the Auroville offices and try to direct things. I tell you ... it has become really, really disgusting.
Because I am here, because I don't see so clearly anymore and my hearing isn't so good—so they take advantage of it.
People say that I am no longer in control in the Ashram, that those around me direct and do exactly as they please.

!!!

But it's not true.

24

Of course, it's not true![1]

It's not true.

In terms of consciousness, the consciousness is FAR superior to what it was—that I know—but my expression is.... I no longer have any power of expression. And then, I never go out of this room, so they are all convinced that I won't know what's going on.

I prefer to.... You see, I would like to abolish this personality as much as possible, leaving only an external form. All the time, I would be ... only a transmitting channel, like this *(gesture of something flowing through Mother).* And I don't even ask to be conscious of it.

I feel the Divine Presence all the time—all the time—very strongly, but....

(long silence)

And this is what happens: at times, in some cases, the Power is so tremendous, so potent that I myself am flabbergasted, while at other times I sense, not that the Power has gone, but ... I just don't know what happens.

I don't know how to explain it.

And naturally people tell me, "You have cured me, you have saved so-and-so, you...." I almost perform miracles, but.... They think it's me, but there's no "me"! There's nothing, there's no "me" here; it's only ... *(gesture of something flowing through Mother)* the Force flowing. I try, I only try not to block, not to check or diminish anything, that's my sole effort: let it go through me as impersonally as possible.

You're the only one I can say these things to—to the others I say nothing, absolutely nothing.

But you, I don't even know if you feel the same thing.... I don't know if you feel that the Power is here. Do you feel it?

Oh, yes! The Power, I feel it tremendously! Certainly. It is tre-men-dous.

But what is it that you don't feel, then? You seem to have a reservation. Tell me.

---

1. How blind I was! In fact, I remained blind almost till the end. I could not bring myself to believe in the evidence.

25

It all depends whether I am with you or away from you. When I'm away from you, possibly.... Well, my complaint has to do with a lack of presence, a presence that's ... what's the word?

Tangible?

No, not that. I feel the Power, but ... if I could feel something more in the heart, you understand, something more ... intimate, something more vivid, less impersonal as a matter of fact.

Oh, that! Yes, I agree. But everything tends to insist on that impersonalization.

In my consciousness it is like a transitional condition (not a final condition, a transitional one) required to attain immortality. That's what it is. There is something—something to be found. But what, I don't know.

> *(long silence*
> *Mother shakes her head as if at a loss)*

Well, the old way of seeing things (I don't mean the ordinary way), the old way of seeing things has sort of dissolved leaving the place for ... everything to be learned anew *(Mother opens her hands, attentive to what comes from above).*

> *(silence)*

It's in the consciousness of the physical body, you know. A sort of ... not even an alternation of states, it's as if both were constantly together: the sense that you know nothing and are completely impotent in terms of, well, the "present" way of doing and knowing things; and at the same time—at the very same time (not even one behind the other, or one in the other or beside the other; I just don't know how to put it in words)—at the same time, the sense of an absolute knowledge, an absolute power. And the two states are not in one another, not behind one another, or beside one another, they're ... I don't know.... Both are there *(simultaneous gesture).*

I could almost say that it depends on whether I am according to others (by "I," I mean this body), according to other human beings, or according to the Divine. That's it. And both states are ... *(same simultaneous gesture).*

26

It's very concrete. Take food, for example ... the best example is food. The body needs food to live, yet everything in the body is a stranger to food. So meals are becoming an almost unsolvable problem.... To put it in a simplistic way, it's as if I no longer knew how to eat, although another way of eating comes spontaneously when I don't observe myself eating. Do you understand what I mean?

Yes, yes, Mother.

And the same applies to seeing, to hearing. I feel all my faculties diminishing. In that respect, it is true, I don't know what people are doing, saying or anything, but at the same time—at the same time— I have a MUCH TRUER perception of what they are, of what they think and do: of the world. A truer perception, but so new that I don't know how to describe it.

So ... I am no longer this, but I am not yet the other. It's like this *(gesture in between)*. Not easy.

No!

And people's reactions *(Mother holds her head between her hands)* are so utterly false! ...

(Mother plunges in)

January 12, 1972

Do you happen to remember where I wrote the twelve attributes of the Mother (the symbol with twelve petals)? There's one, four, and twelve.

Yes, I think it was for Auroville.

For Auroville? But I said it years ago....

I saw it recently.

The twelve?

(Sujata goes out in search of the paper)

On this one there aren't any details.

(Mother extends a note in English)

The Mother's Symbol

The central circle represents the Divine Consciousness.
The four petals represent the four powers of the Mother.
The twelve petals represent the twelve powers
of the Mother manifested for Her Work.

January 24, 1958
The Mother

(silence)

Recently, between your last visit and this one (two or three days ago), I suddenly had a revelation of the purpose of creation—what it signifies and the why of it: the meaning of creation. It was so clear! So clear. The vision of its reason and where we are going— simply impossible to describe it in words.

Some words came *(Mother shows Satprem a piece of paper)*, but then they had a very special meaning. Here:

> The result of creation is a
> detailed multiplication of consciousness.
> When the vision of the whole and the
> vision of all the details join together
> within an active consciousness, the creation will
> have attained its progressive perfection.

"Progressive" means ... *(expanding gesture)*. No word, no image can convey the experience. It was a real comprehension, a real vision of the thing. This *(Mother points to her note)* seems hollow in comparison. To use a very childlike metaphor, it's as if the creation unfolded on a screen, were projected on a screen. Or rather, the Supreme Consciousness is projecting itself on a sort of infinite screen.

The experience was ... it was obviousness itself! That was IT. But it lasted only a moment. Then, I tried to put it in words. And these words had meaning, a special meaning.

To a child, you could say that the Supreme unfolds himself before his own consciousness, like someone unreeling an endless film. He projects what is here *(gesture pointing within, at heart level)*, in front of him, like that. And since the supramental being would have the capacity to be consciously one with the Divine, he would at once be the seer and the seen.

There are just no words to say it.

(silence
Sujata enters with a piece of paper)

Did you find it?

There aren't any details.

Oh! No details....

You simply say:

> The dot at the centre represents unity, the Supreme.
> The inner circle represents the creation,
> the conception of the city [Auroville].
> The petals represent the power of expression,
> the realisation.[1]

No that's not it.

I wrote something, or rather I told Sri Aurobindo, who wrote down what the twelve petals were (the four petals are the four main aspects of the Mother, and the twelve are the twelve qualities or "virtues" of the Mother, her powers). I said it one day, and Sri Aurobindo wrote it down; that's when we were living in

---

1. Original English.

the other house.[1] I put it in a drawer among other papers of mine, but the drawer disappeared when we moved here, someone took it. Who, why, how, I have no idea. But the drawer disappeared. Then, I remember writing the twelve names again on a piece of paper which I kept with me, but now I can't find that one either. . . . Strange.[2]

When you made the sketch for Auroville, you said there would be twelve gardens, each one with a particular meaning.

That's Auroville—that's not what I am talking about.

But don't those twelve gardens correspond to the twelve qualities you mentioned?

No, no. No, I wrote it at least twenty-five years ago, at the very least—oh, even more than that! I don't remember when we moved here, when was it? . . .

In 1927 . . . forty-five years ago!

It's the same with the four. What are the four?

They must be Mahakali, Maheshwari, Mahalakshmi, and Mahasaraswati.

Yes, but I don't mean the popular deities. Sri Aurobindo gave each one a special significance.

Yes, you mean what he wrote in "The Mother."

But that's a long text.
What are these four? . . . *(Mother tries to remember, in vain).* How strange, I've forgotten.

(silence)

Did you read in the *Cosmic Review* about the "cosmic square":

---

1. "Library House," or west wing of the Ashram, which they left on February 8, 1927, to move to "Meditation House," in the east wing. These two houses, along with two others ("Rosary" and "Secretariat"), form the Ashram compound.
2. According to Sri Aurobindo, "The twelve powers are the vibrations necessary for the complete manifestation." (Cent. Ed., XXV.359)

1, 2, 3, 4, and one in the center? The cosmic square was conceived by Théon, and I know he put Love in the center. But the four sides ... what are the four sides? I don't remember anymore. I used to know all that so well; it's all gone. I know there was Light, Life, and Utility—the fourth was Utility, but the first? Utility was the last. What was the first?.... It's all gone.

That would have given me a clue.

I remember writing down the twelve. Yesterday I even recalled three of them, but now I don't remember. The first one was Sincerity....

I don't know anything anymore.

(silence
Sujata goes out to look for another text)

When it comes, it doesn't come as a thought: it comes as a vision. So when it's gone, it's gone.

I know there was Perseverance.

When it's there, it's clear, it's obvious. It's like a vision, you know. But then when it's gone, it's really gone.

What sort of clue would it have given you?

(Mother remains engrossed)

It's like that paper I gave you ["The result of creation"]. When I was in the experience, it was evident, the total key to understanding how everything works—why and where it is all going and how. It was clear, thoroughly clear. But you see the paper, it looks like nothing. Yet when the experience was there, it was so evident! It was wonderful. The key to understanding everything—the key to ACTION. The secret uncovered. As if it gave you the power. And then it left.

I remember when I wrote the note, the words had a special meaning for me, a depth they don't usually have. Well....

(Sujata returns with
"Words of Long Ago")

Mother, here in "Words of Long Ago" you have written the twelve "Virtues."[1] First you mention Sincerity.

---

1. "The Virtues," written in 1904.

Yes.

Then Humility.

Yes.

Then Courage. Then Prudence, Charity, Justice, Goodness, Patience, Sweetness, Thoughtfulness.... And then Gratitude.

Yes.
The first is Sincerity; the second, Humility. Yes, that's how it came back to me the other day—Sincerity, Humility.

And Courage.

Perseverance came first, then Courage followed. Sincerity, Humility, Perseverance and Courage. That I remember. But there were twelve.

Next you mention Prudence.

That's not it.

Charity.

No.

Goodness.

No.

Patience, Sweetness, Thoughtfulness....

No.... That was written before I met Sri Aurobindo.[1]

(silence)

Had you been there when it came[2] (it came in connection with a

---

1. Mother later ordered the list of the twelve powers or "qualities" in the following sequence: Sincerity, Humility, Gratitude, Perseverance, Aspiration, Receptivity, Progress, Courage, Goodness, Generosity, Equanimity, Peace.
2. The experience of joining the vision of the whole together with the vision of all the details.

32

question T.J. asked me), you would have understood it from what I wrote, because the consciousness was there. But I never know when it comes—it doesn't come at will. I remember when I had the experience, all at once I felt I understood, everything became clear. But when I tried to formulate it, it had already receded into the background.

You told me once in an "Agenda" about a similar experience you had.

Oh?

You said that the goal of creation is to join within the individual the total Consciousness (the consciousness of the whole) and the individual consciousness—the two together.[1]

Yes, something like that, but here it was clearer, more precise.... It's not that I "think," mind you.

Of course!

That's not how it works. I am as though bathed in it and start seeing ... I don't know. It isn't something I "see" (something foreign to me that I see), it's ... suddenly I AM it. There's no longer any person, any.... I can't find words to describe these experiences.

Everything I say or write gives me the feeling of something cast into an inert substance—like a photograph, if you will.

Yes, of course! When you talk with me, for instance, well, I feel the whole world of consciousness behind, your words are merely a prop for all that I sense in the background, which you make me perceive.

Yes, exactly.

So obviously, when there's nothing but words on paper, a whole depth is gone.

Yes, exactly, gone.... And unfortunately, it doesn't always come back.

---

1. See *Agenda XII*, October 30 and December 25, 1971.

Well, too bad.

(silence)

I remember, the experience is still very vivid. As I told you, T.J. has a very childish consciousness, so I said to her: you see, it's as if the Whole (not the Divine separate from the creation: the Whole) projected itself on a screen in order to see itself. Therefore it's infinite, it's "forever"—it's never the same and it never ends. It's like a projection to visualize the details and be conscious of oneself in another way.[1]

The metaphor is quite childlike, of course, but very evocative—that's how I saw it then. Exactly the impression of an infinite Whole projecting itself endlessly.

(Mother remains absorbed a long time)

For instance, the memory mechanism is gone, but I feel it's on purpose. My vision of things would be much less spontaneous and sincere (possibly) if I remembered.

Yes, I get it.

Things always come as a new revelation—and not in the same manner.

That's it—you BECOME the thing, you become it. You don't "see" it; it's not something you see or understand or know, it's ... something you ARE.

When I had that experience of the world, it was the experience itself, conscious of itself. It wasn't something I "knew," it was something that WAS.

But language, words are inadequate.

---

1. Mother later added the following clarification to her note: "No two consciousnesses are alike among human beings in time and space. The total sum of all these consciousnesses is a partial and diminished manifestation of the Divine Consciousness. That is why I said 'progressive perfection,' because the manifestation of the consciousness of details is infinite and will never end."

34

January 15, 1972

(Mother gives Satprem her latest notes.)

Do you have all these papers?... I had given this message [in 1966]: *Let us serve the Truth,[1]* and someone asked me *(in a childlike tone)*, "What is the Truth?" So I answered:

> Put yourself at the service of Truth,
> and you will know the Truth.

*
* *

Is it possible to develop in oneself a capacity for healing?

By consciously uniting with the Divine Force, all is possible in principle. But a procedure has to be found, depending on the case and the individual.

The first condition is to have a physical nature that gives energy rather than draws energy from others.

The second indispensable condition is to know how to draw energy from above, from the one impersonal and inexhaustible source.

January 12, 1972

*
* *

Sincerity, humility, perseverance and an insatiable thirst for progress are essential for a happy and fruitful life, and above all, to be convinced that the possibility of progress is limitless. Progress is youth; one can be young at a hundred years.

January 14, 1972

*
* *

---

1. Italics indicate words Mother spoke in English.

I would like to ask you about a physical problem.

Ah?

Whether or not I should have an operation.

An operation for what?

My whole right leg is in bad condition—all the veins are sclerotic.

Oh!

It's the result of an operation I had five years ago. I was operated on at the hospital here five or six years ago, they opened me up....

(Mother laughs)

And for five or six days I was fed intravenously ...

Oh, they ruined your veins!

Yes, completely! And it has kept getting worse ever since.

And now they want to operate again?

One possibility is to wear a bandage, but Dr. Sanyal says the bandage won't help much; it won't stop the veins from deteriorating.... But it's quite a radical operation, you know: they open up the leg all the way from top to bottom and rip out your veins.

And?

And they leave you only with the main vein. All the others are ripped out.

Oh, but then they may immobilize your leg! ...
With bandages, at least you can walk. Personally, I would choose the bandage, I am not in favor of these....

Yes, it's pretty radical.

But if you could—if you could call the Force.

Take the bandage. I myself have been wearing one for months. Put the bandage on and then concentrate. When you go to sleep and before you get up in the morning concentrate and call the Force on it. I am confident that this is a much better solution— much better.

Yes, Mother.

Personally I am not in favor of those things.
No, don't do it.

I'd rather avoid it if I can!

Absolutely. It's better even to limp a little than....

And if you concentrate the Force.... Just offer your leg to the Divine, morning and evening! *(Laughing)* I have more confidence in that method!

Yes, Mother.... There are so many obstinate obscurities in me. One offers them, of course, but they just don't budge.

Yes, but you can do what I just told you.

*(silence
Sujata comes up to Mother)*

(Sujata:) Mother, he is always so depressed. He always says he has many obscurities. But I feel that even our obscurities are part of our nature, we have been made that way by the Divine, so it's up to Him to change us, no, Mother?

(Mother laughs) Yes, but you must want to change.

(Sujata:) Yes, of course, Mother, we want to. But why get all upset when it's not changed immediately?

What I am telling him is to want it—to want it morning and evening. When you're in bed, concentrate for a moment *(laughing),* with as much faith as possible!

(Satprem, coughing:) Yes, Mother.

37

You're coughing?

I don't know, some dust caught in my throat.

The obscurity is going out!

If it were only true....

(Mother laughs) It is going out!

I have a feeling the problem of my leg is quite symbolic.

Yes, yes.

There are two beings in me.

Yes.

Besides, I see the "other one" more and more distinctly. And I find it has a totally self-contained and independent existence....

Aah!...

Nothing seems to have any influence over it.

(silence)

.We really have two beings in us.

Yes, I have noticed that. I noticed. But that doesn't matter. It makes things a little more difficult, that's all.

Yes, difficult.

(silence)

I don't know what could have power over that being.... What could sway it.

(silence)

Well, that's the reason. That's what I meant—offer that being to the Divine. You who know (the part of you that knows), offer it, just

offer it. . . . Never mind if it protests, don't pay any attention—offer it OB-STI-NATELY to the Divine, morning and evening, morning and evening . . . using your leg as a symbol. And we will see.
We will see.

As you say, Mother.

That's the only way.
The Divine knows.

Yes.

He knows what to do.
You just give it to Him, you understand. Even if it protests, even if it is skeptical, it doesn't matter at all, you give it anyway—you follow?

(silence)

In fact—in fact, there's a BIG change.

??!!

A big change. But these are its last attempts to remain what it is. So it goes all out—you just have to outdo it, to put a special pressure. And the only way to do that is: "Here, take it." Give that being, give it to the Divine! Tell Him, "Here, I give it to you *(laughing)*, I don't want it anymore, take it!" Just like that.

But you do find there's a change?

YES—yes, oh, yes! There's a big change! A big change. Only, the resistance has sort of *(Mother clenches her fist)* crystallized a little to resist, so it's become more evident. That's all. You have to be more obstinate. More obstinate. I tell you, just offer that being; you are conscious of it, you offer it to the Divine morning and evening: "Do whatever You want with it, do whatever You want. . . ." You understand? Using your leg as a practical reference.

Yes, Mother.

We'll succeed.

Yes, Mother, yes.

(concentration)

*
* *

(A little later, Satprem reads to Mother some passages from the "Agenda" for the next "Bulletin," in particular the conversation of December 18, 1971, in which she said, "At each minute you feel you can either live eternally or die.")

That experience is more and more constant. It's become very.... Sometimes it's for one thing, sometimes for another (the practical things of life like eating, walking, etc.). It has become very intense. But at the same time, there's the knowledge *(Mother raises her forefinger):* "Now is the time to win the Victory." Which comes from the psychic, from above. "Hold on ... hold on, now is the time to win the Victory."

Quite interesting really.

I am experiencing a pain (physical pain), which becomes almost insurmountable and suddenly ... something happens ... the offering, the offering of oneself ... the sense that the Divine alone exists. Well ... the pain disappears almost miraculously.

But it can return the next second. It's not yet.... My body is in the middle of living the process.

It's only when I am immobile, in a sort of cellular contemplation ... then—then it's magnificent. Time vanishes, everything ... everything is changed into something else.

(silence)

When the body became conscious of what was happening, its prayer, the prayer of the body was: "Let me know when the time for dissolution comes, if dissolution is necessary, so that everything in me will accept the dissolution, but only in that case." Well.... Oh, it's so strange, the states of consciousness are strong, limpid, precise, but they can't express themselves. There are no words.

One day it's one thing, another day another thing.

(silence)

So, no operation.

Yes, Mother.

Offer, offer your leg to the Divine, day and night! *(Mother laughs.)*

(Satprem rests his head on Mother's knees)

You should be able to cure it.

January 19, 1972

Last time I told you I was looking for the twelve attributes *(Mother takes out a sheet of paper)*. Here they are, someone found this.

Sincerity,	Humility,	Gratitude,	Perseverance
Aspiration,	Receptivity,	Progress,	Courage
Goodness,	Generosity,	Equanimity,	Peace

The first eight concern the attitude towards the Divine, and the last four towards humanity.

And we also found a text from Sri Aurobindo *(with a colored chart of the twelve petals):*

> Centre and four powers, white.
> The twelve all of different colour
> in three groups: top group red,
> passing to orange towards yellow.
> Next group, yellow passing through green
> towards blue. And third group, blue passing
> through violet towards red.
> If white is not convenient,
> the centre may be gold (powder).

> March 20, 1934

The center is gold.

But what did you need these twelve attributes for?

They're going to build twelve rooms around the Matrimandir, at ground level, and R. wanted each room to have a name: one of the twelve attributes of the Mother, and the corresponding color.[1]

* *
*

A little later.

Nirod is reading me his correspondence with Sri Aurobindo. Strangely enough, there are all sorts of things that I said much, much later, I had no idea he had written them! Exactly the same things. I found that very interesting.

In the correspondence, he tells Nirod in one of his letters (he repeated it several times), "I may take a fancy to leave my body before the supramental realization...."[2] He said that a few years before he died. He had sensed it.

(silence)

But he did speak of a transformation preceding the appearance of the first supramental being. That's what he had told me. He told me that his body wasn't capable of withstanding the transformation, that mine was more capable—he says it there too.

But it's difficult. As I told you the other day.

Especially, especially for food ... it's become a real labor.

---

1. It may interest the reader to know that according to Sri Aurobindo, these colors generally have the following significances, though the exact meaning may vary "with the field, the combinations, the character and shades of the colour, the play of forces": red = physical; orange = supramental in the physical; yellow = thinking mind; green = life; blue = higher mind; violet = divine compassion or grace; gold = divine Truth; white = the light of the Mother, or the Divine Consciousness. (See also *Agenda IV*, May 18, 1963.)

2. March 30, 1935. *(Question:) Sri Aurobindo is bound to be wholly supramental and is being supramentalised in parts. If that is true—and it is—well, he can't die till he is supramental—and once he is so he is immortal.* (Answer:) "It looks very much like a *non-sequitur*. The first part and the last are all right—but the link is fragile. How do you know I won't take a fancy to die in between as a joke?" *(Question:) Some people say that yourself and the Mother would have been supramentalised long ago if only we had not kept you down. Is it really true?* (Answer:) "I can't say there is no truth in it." (Cf. *Bulletin*, August 1975.)

January 22, 1972

(Two days earlier, as Pranab was leaving Mother's room late, he had remarked to Sujata, "Usual trouble. Heart, giddiness.")

The work is going on with increasing clarity. But it's difficult.... On its own, the physical is terribly pessimistic. It is steeped in atavistic habits of helplessness, contradiction, and also catastrophe —it is terribly pessimistic. What a work it is.... Only gradually, by constantly turning to the Divine, can it start to hope things will improve a little.

Can't eat, you know, not a morsel.... This physical world is terrible, terrible, terrible.

It's the mind and vital that make it bearable and permit us to go on, but once they're gone—awful!

(silence)

Yesterday was detestable all day; this morning it started to get a little better ... but then I don't know how things work out, I don't understand.... The body feels it has lost all control over time.[1]

(Mother plunges in)

*
* *

(Then Mother proceeds to sort out some papers.)

There's a great need to file, to put things in order.... Perhaps it's simply the Force pressing down, that wants everything to be in order (I think that's what it is) ... or else it may be that the body knows it is going to leave.

No, no! No, no, no—that is not possible!

(Laughing) No, of course not!

It does feel a process of transformation taking place. But sometimes it feels it's impossible—it's impossible, you simply can't go on existing like this—but then, just at the last minute, something comes, and then it's ... it's a Harmony totally unknown to this

----

1. Mother was more than half an hour late that day.

physical world. A Harmony—the physical world seems appalling in comparison. But that doesn't last.

> *(Mother touches her chest,*
> *she is always short of breath when she speaks)*

I am finding it more and more difficult to speak.

But my perceptions are clearer and clearer *(Mother draws a sort of picture in front of her),* clear, luminous. My perceptions are getting clearer and clearer, more and more luminous—vaster and vaster.

It's really like a new world that wants to manifest itself.

In silence, I am comfortable.

> *(Mother goes into contemplation.*
> *After a few moments,*
> *a blissful smile spreads over her face.)*

January 26, 1972

What's new?

Nothing. Nothing to say.

How are you?

I don't know.

> (silence)

The doctor who took care of my leg and had gone to Delhi has returned. He looked at my leg today and said it was a miracle the way it healed. It's almost all better—not completely, but almost.

> (silence)

What I told you is continuing—but it's continuing *with an improvement*. I mean, it's taking a turn for the better. But speaking is still difficult—speaking and eating are the two most difficult things.

January 29, 1972

(Mother listens to Satprem read a letter from Msgr. R., the friend of P.L., who is intently turning to Mother to start a new life. Mother concentrates on him for a quarter of an hour.)

Is he ill?

He had several very serious operations in a row, and I think he had a lung removed in the last one.

Ooh!

He's a man who has been severely stricken. He went through a record number of operations.

What's the time difference between here and France?

Five or five and a half hours.

Which means?

Which means, it is now five-thirty or six in the morning there.

Note the time it is now.

It's eleven o'clock.

Could you ask him if.... What's the date today?

The 29th.

Ask him whether on the 29th at eleven o'clock (put it in local time there) he felt something.

And if he did feel something—whatever it is, an impression (I don't want to define it), something, a Force, some phenomenon—if he felt something at that hour, we could agree on a particular day and time, and try: I would do a special concentration on him.

If he could send a photo, it would be easier.

That's all I can do.

Send it registered.

(silence)

It would be better if he set a time when he can be free and quiet a little.

(silence)

What did I say to ask him?

First, if he felt something ...

Better not say "felt": ask whether he was CONSCIOUS of something—because "felt" may suggest a vital or physical sensation —if he was conscious of something.

(Mother plunges in till the end,
then Sujata approaches her)

Mother, I would like to tell you about a rather strange occurrence. The night before last, independently, Satprem, F. and I had similar dreams.

Ah! And what was it?

Violent attacks.

By whom?

I don't know, Mother. As for me, I was in a large group of Ashram people, and we were about to be executed. But I had a tremendous faith: "It's not possible," I thought, "a miracle is bound to happen at the last minute ..."

Yes.

"... and stop this." I was saying this to someone who was greatly worried and depressed.

Who?

I can't say. I don't remember. Someone who was also going to be executed. There were also many children. Then I heard a sort of great chant (many people were gathered there, it was time for the execution), like a mantra rising up from each of us, like this: OM Namo Bhagavate Sri Arabindaye.

Ah!

And everybody was chanting it—everybody was chanting. And the threat withdrew.

Who else had this dream?

Satprem saw himself heavily attacked by bombs and grenades.[1] F.'s dream: she was trying to see you, but she was locked in a room. She wanted to feed you, and she was told, "No, no, Mother doesn't eat." She knew it was a lie, but she was denied access to you.

When was that?

Not last night, but the night before.

Yes, yes.
Your dream was the most complete of the three.
And you saw that the attack was averted.

Yes, Mother, it went away because we were chanting Sri Aurobindo's name. [Sujata sings:] OM Namo Bhagavate Sri Arabindaye....

Yes, exactly. Exactly. But it's true, mon petit!... That was good.

Were we attacked?

---

1. He was running in a sort of mobile darkness shot with pale milky-white streaks of light, through which he was escaping.

Not physically, of course.

It's good—very good. It's true. It was the night before last. Personally, I repeated the mantra all night long.

It's good, mon petit.

January 30, 1972

(Message from Mother:)

Sri Aurobindo came upon earth to announce the manifestation of the supramental world. Not only did he announce this manifestation, but he also partially incarnated the supramental force and gave us the example of what we must do to prepare ourselves for this manifestation. The best way for us is to study everything he told us, strive to follow his example and prepare ourselves for the new manifestation. This gives life its true meaning and will help us to overcome all obstacles.

Let us live for the new creation and we will become stronger and stronger, while remaining young and progressive.

February

February 1, 1972

(Notes from Mother)

Auroville is intended to hasten the advent of the supramental reality upon earth.

The help of all those who find that the world is not what it ought to be is welcome.

Each one must know if he wants to associate himself with an old world on the verge of death, or to work for a new and better world ready to be born.

*
* *

The first thing the physical consciousness must realize is that all the difficulties we encounter in life arise from the fact that we do not rely exclusively on the Divine to find the help we need.

The Divine alone can liberate us from the mechanism of universal Nature. And this liberation is indispensable for the birth and development of the new race.

Only if we give ourselves entirely to the Divine with total trust and gratitude will the difficulties be surmounted.

February 2, 1972

(Mother listens to the English translation of "Notes on the Way" of December 18, 1971, which causes a good deal of confusion between R., the American translator, and Nolini: "a muddle." Mother stops in particular at the following sentence:)

". . . Everything was simply taken away from me—the mind is completely gone. If you like, in appearance, I had

> become an idiot. I didn't know anything. And it's
> the physical mind that developed little by little,
> little by little...."

(Mother comments in English)

One shouldn't repeat "little by little." It is not little by little. It was rapid because it took place suddenly. It came like this—one night I understood.... It came ... truly it was miraculous (but I didn't want to say anything); suddenly the vision of the world and then the vision I had ... were removed and this [new] knowledge was simply put like that *(Mother gestures as if she had been suddenly crowned by or immersed into that knowledge).* But that I did not want to say.

(Mother speaks French again)

One shouldn't repeat "little by little." The correct phrase is: little by little, through successive revelations. That's how it was.[1]

(Mother stops at another sentence)

> "This [radical change] could be accomplished
> because I was very conscious of my psychic ... it
> remained and enabled me to deal with people, with
> no difference—thanks to that psychic presence...."

It is the psychic that deals with people. It was ALWAYS the psychic that dealt with people, and it continues. This [radical change] didn't make any difference.

(then another sentence)

> "I understand and hear people only when they
> think clearly what they say. And I see only what
> expresses the inner life."

Well, some people come to see me, they come in: I see only a silhouette. Then suddenly it becomes clear-cut. Then off it goes again—DEPENDING ON THEIR THOUGHT. It's extremely interesting!

(again this passage)

---

1. Owing to the confusion in Mother's room, it seems there is also confusion between the suddenness with which Mother's mind was removed and the slow emergence of the new mind "through successive revelations."

"Surrender does not imply trust; trust is something else, it is a kind of knowledge—an *unshakable* knowledge, which nothing can disturb—that WE change into difficulties, suffering, misery what is ... perfect peace in the divine Consciousness."

This is extremely important. An extremely important discovery. It was fundamental. It is WE, the distortion within OUR consciousness that changes into pain what in the divine Consciousness is perfect peace, and even joy—an immutable joy, you know. It's fantastic. And I've experienced this CONCRETELY. But it's difficult to put into words.

*
* *

(After Nolini and R. leave)

It's becoming difficult because I am talking about new things, and words are old, old, old.... The experience is very clear, very conscious, but when you want to describe it, it comes out as nonsense.

No, something filters through at any rate. Even if words are inadequate, one can still capture something.

(Laughing) Yes, provided you want it!

Well, yes, obviously.

No, but I feel that the body itself must learn to express itself. It doesn't know how to express itself yet.
And also ... *(Mother gasps for breath)* speaking is difficult.

I think it will gradually evolve its own language, Mother.

Oh, yes, it must!

February 5, 1972

(Mother listens to the conclusion of the English translation of "Notes on the Way"; she looks weary and tired from the confusion created by the translators. After they leave, she simply hands Satprem the text of a recent note, then plunges in.)

To want what the Divine wants in all sincerity is the essential condition for peace and joy in life. Almost all human miseries come from the fact that human beings are almost always persuaded they know better than the Divine what they need and what life is supposed to bring them. The majority of human beings want other human beings to behave according to their own expectations and life circumstances to follow their own desires, hence they suffer and are unhappy.

Only by giving oneself in all sincerity to the Divine Will does one gain the peace and calm joy that arises from the abolition of desires.

The psychic being knows this definitely. Thus, by uniting with our psychic being, we can know it, too. But the first condition is not to be the slave of personal desires and mistake them for the truth of one's being.

February 4

February 7, 1972

(A note from Mother)

In the depths of our being, in the silence of contemplation, a luminous force permeates our consciousness with a vast and luminous peace

which prevails over all petty reactions and pre-
pares us for union with the Divine, the meaning of
individual existence.

Thus, the purpose and goal of life is not suffering and struggle but an all-powerful and happy
realization.

All the rest is but a painful illusion.

February 8, 1972

(A message from Mother to some Aurovilians)

From a spiritual point of view, India is the
foremost country in the world. Its mission is to
give the example of spirituality. Sri Aurobindo
came on earth to teach this to the world.

This fact is so obvious, that even a simple,
ignorant farmer here is in his heart closer to the
Divine than all the intellectuals of Europe.

All those who want to become Aurovilians must
know that and behave accordingly, otherwise they
are unworthy of being Aurovilians.

*
* *

(Another note)

In the beginnings of humanity, the ego was the unifying
element. It is around the ego that the various states of
being were formed. But now that a superhumanity is
about to be born, the ego must disappear and leave
place for the psychic being which has slowly developed
through divine agency to manifest the Divine in man.

The Divine manifests in man under the psychic influence, and that is how the coming of superhumanity is
prepared.

The psychic being is immortal, so through it immortality can manifest on earth.

Hence, the important thing now is to find one's psychic being, unite with it, and allow it to replace the ego, which will be forced either to convert itself or disappear.

February 9, 1972

Good morning, Mother.

I have nothing, mon petit, you're going to get skinny!

No!

(Mother gives some flowers,
then her latest note)

The first thing one learns on the way is that giving brings much greater joy than taking.

Then, gradually, one learns that selflessness is the source of an immutable peace. Later, in this selflessness one finds the Divine, and that is the source of an unending bliss....

One day Sri Aurobindo told me that if people knew that and were convinced of it they would all want to do yoga.

(silence)

We need a message for the 21st.... Do you have something?

There are several probable texts, but perhaps you have something of your own?

Texts from where?

From Sri Aurobindo.

That would be nice.

But for the 21st, it would be nice to have something from you also, no?

Not necessarily.... Do you think this *(Mother hands Satprem a scrap of paper)* would do?

> The complete unification of the whole being
> around the psychic centre is the essential
> condition to realise a perfect sincerity.[1]

I have noticed that people are insincere simply because one part of their being says one thing and another part says something else. That's what causes insincerity. It came very clearly: a vision, you know, an inner vision. So I tried to put it down on paper; I don't know if it's clear.

But it's very difficult to remain in a permanent state of consciousness, to have always the same consciousness prevailing at all times.

But that's when you're not unified, mon petit. It's been a-l-w-a-y-s like this for me *(Mother draws a straight line in front of her)* for years and years. It comes from here, the psychic consciousness, and it's CONSTANT.

Recently, for a few moments, I had the experience [of the non-unified consciousness]; I hadn't known that in years—many years, at least thirty years.[2] From the moment the psychic being became the master and ruler of the being, it was OVER—it is over—and now it's like this *(same straight gesture)*. That is the sure sign. Constantly like that, constantly the same. And all the time: "What You will, what You will." Not a "You" up there, at the back of beyond, whom one doesn't know; He is everywhere, He is in everything, He is constantly there, He is in the very being—and one clings to that. It's the only solution.

Do you think that note makes sense?

Certainly, it makes sense!

---

1. Original English.
2. Sixty.

Read it again.

(Satprem reads the message again)

Is it understandable?

Well, I for one, understand!

What do you think?... Because it's something I discovered recently. I saw why people are insincere (even when they make an effort): because now it's one part, now the other, now yet another part of them that asserts itself; each part is quite sincere in its own assertion, but is in disaccord with the others.

But that means the psychic consciousness must penetrate the PHYSICAL consciousness.

Yes.

Because that's the only place where there is permanence.

Yes....

The psychic consciousness must penetrate the ordinary physical consciousness.

Yes.

That's what is difficult!

But, mon petit, I tell you, that's what happened to me at least thirty years ago.

The psychic consciousness has always been there, controlling and guiding the being. All the impressions, everything was referred to it, like this *(gesture of placing something before a spotlight),* so it would give the true direction. And the physical, for its part, is sort of constantly attentive to the Divine Command.

And that was constant, constant—even BEFORE coming here. It was so when I arrived here (long, long ago). And it has remained unchanged. Only recently did I have the experience [of the non-unified consciousness], for a few hours one night, two or three hours—it was horrible, really, it seemed like hell. It was to make me touch, to make me grasp the condition people live in. Imagine when the psychic is no longer there....

But it's in the BODY—in the body: the body is listening, listening, constantly listening *(gesture above or within)*—listening. But the Divine Command is not expressed in words, it comes as a will asserting itself *(a straight and imperturbable descending gesture)*.

Should I add something to make it clearer?

You said, "The complete unification of the whole being."

So that means the physical, too.
People never understand anything. But it's perfectly clear.

Oh, yes!

So you think it's all right?

Yes, Mother, certainly!

I think it's important, because it came as an experience, precisely to make me grasp its importance.
We must put: "Message for the 21st."

Yes, Mother. We need another one for the 29th, too.

February 29th, what's that?

It's the fourth anniversary of the supramental descent, in '56.

Oh! It was the 29th....

The 29th, in 1956 ... sixteen years ago.

> *(Mother smiles and remains
> absorbed awhile)*

Could we say:

> It is only when the supramental
> manifests in the physical mind
> that its presence can be permanent.

Do you think it will do?

Yes, Mother!

We should say "in the body-mind."

Well, we could add "and body-mind": in the physical mind and body-mind...?

Yes, but then it seems as if there were two of them—there aren't two.[1]

So simply "body-mind."

Is it enough, then?

Yes, Mother, we have both messages now.

So they're expecting me to go out on the balcony. I am going out on the balcony only for the 21st.... What have you heard? What are people expecting?

They're expecting to see as much of you as possible! [Laughter]

I don't know. The 29th is just one week later.... It's a big strain —not a strain, but a difficulty.

What if everyone passed in front of you, would that be more difficult?

Ohh ... two flights of stairs to climb! It used to be possible down in the garden, but two flights of stairs....

But people can move along more easily now, they've built new stairways. It's really up to you: wouldn't it be more tiring to sit there while so many people file past?

Yes, I think it would be too much.

Yes, Mother, it would be too long for you.

And it isn't very practical here: they would have to leave through the same door they come in. There should be another exit, then people could make a circle.

---

1. Meaning, we guess, that for Mother there are NO LONGER two.

But will you give a meditation on the 29th?

All right, I don't mind. Let's have a meditation at 10 a.m., then.

You wouldn't want to go out on the balcony a second time by any chance? [Laughter]

That would be a bit too much.

The body is no longer quite on this side, you see, and not yet on the other, so it lives in a kind of precarious balance, and the slightest thing upsets it—I can't swallow anymore or even breathe anymore.... The feeling of a life which is about to depend on different conditions than the usual ones. But those other conditions aren't there yet, nor is the body familiar with them, and so the transition from one state to the other is a perpetual source of problems. When I am very quiet—very quiet—everything is fine, but if there's the slightest effort, everything goes awry.

(Mother gasps for breath)

You see how it is.

(silence)

I think . . . I have the feeling that if all goes well, in a few years I'll be able to do many things . . . but not yet. If all goes well, at one hundred—I feel at one hundred years I will be strong. The body itself has a conviction that if it lasts till one hundred, then at one hundred it will have a new strength and a new life. But . . . these are just the difficult years.

The years of transition . . . *(Mother puts her head in her hands)*.

(brief silence)

It's interesting. When I am quiet, I hear a kind of great chant—almost a collective chant, I could say: OM Namo Bhagavateh.... As if all of Nature went *(rising gesture):* OM Namo Bhagavateh . . .

(Mother goes into contemplation)

February 10, 1972

(A note from Mother)

Human consciousness is so corrupt that people prefer the misery and ignorance of the ego to the luminous joy that comes from sincere surrender to the Divine. Their blindness is so great that they refuse even to attempt the experience and prefer to be subjected to the misery of their ego rather than make the necessary effort to free themselves from it.

Their blindness is so total that they would not hesitate to make the Divine a slave to their ego, if such a thing were possible, just to avoid giving themselves to the Divine.

February 11, 1972

(A note from Mother)

Supreme Lord, teach us to be silent, that in this silence we may receive Your force and understand Your will.

February 12, 1972

I have a letter from P.L. [the friend in the Vatican]. Here's what he says:

"... Thanks to Mother's Protection, things around me had calmed down a little, when suddenly the storm broke out again. To the former intrigues have now been added slander and ... a threat of expulsion (which in itself I would not mind, but they should not triumph!). This threat is in fact meant to upset me and force me to change my attitude. I feel the need to go back and see Mother—the sooner the better. But practically I cannot do it; furthermore, I am being watched; I am afraid that if they find out I am going to Pondicherry, they will try to set the Bishop against the Ashram, for, as you know, if he is now quiet, it is because of a certain intervention, which was very discreet but effective. Naturally, the others know nothing of my intercession with T.[1] ..."

I have been preoccupied with him.
One day, I was very much preoccupied with him.

(silence)

Would you like us to go into silence?

(meditation)

---

1. Tisserant, the Cardinal of France, had written to the Pondicherry "Mission" to quiet them down.

February 16, 1972

How are you?

Don't know.

> *(Mother laughs and goes on looking at Satprem)*

You don't have anything, no letter?

Yes, I received a letter from A., conveying a message from my publisher B.C. (you know, the one who published "The Adventure of Consciousness"). B.C. wrote a letter [Satprem reads it to Mother] saying he's reading "The Ideal of Human Unity," but would like to publish "The Synthesis of Yoga." So A. replied to him [Satprem reads the reply to Mother] that he is sending his letter to Pondicherry "for instructions," but that in his opinion "it would be better to publish first the 'Ideal,' which may be accessible to a larger Western audience than the 'Synthesis' and might be more suitable for Sri Aurobindo's centenary year."

That's not my opinion at all! I think it would be far better to publish "The Synthesis of Yoga" than "The Ideal."

"The Synthesis" first?

Yes. There's a difference of level between the two.

Yes, of course. But what A. means is that "The Ideal of Human Unity" is a theme with a universal appeal.

Yes, but that's just the point, it doesn't take them out of what they know! While "The Synthesis" (they won't understand much of it, but . . .) may pull them out of their routine.

Right, Mother, understood.

Perhaps only two or three people will understand, but that's better than the other one and having people say, "Oh, how nice! How very, very nice!"—but it won't jolt them out of their routine.

A question of principle remains: do we give these books to B.C. and thus encourage him to publish the bulk of Sri Aurobindo's works? After all, he's the first publisher who seems to be interested in Sri Aurobindo.

Yes! Why not?... Good for him! *(Mother laughs)* Everybody, including A., always sees things from the wrong end, you know, as if WE had to gain something—well, it's not so! It's THEM. It's THEIR chance....

Yes, of course! I fully agree, Mother!

The chance isn't ours!

It's a grace given to them.

Yes. In fifty years the whole world, all the receptive section of humanity (I am not saying intellectual, I am saying receptive), all the receptive section of the world will be embraced—not "embraced": ABSORBED in the power of Sri Aurobindo's thought.
Those who already are have the good fortune of being the first ones, that's all.

(silence)

It's very interesting, you know, the greater part live in the past; a good number (they are more interesting) live in the present; and just a few, an infinitesimal number, live in the future. That's true.
Whenever I look at people and things I always get the feeling of going backwards! *(gesture of turning around and looking behind)* I know (it's not even "I know," or "I feel," it's none of that), I AM— I am ahead. In consciousness, I am in the year 2000. So I know how things will be, and ... *(Mother laughs)* it's very interesting!

(long silence)

Three quarters of humanity are obsolete.

Yes! [Everyone laughs]

(silence)

That's all you have?... A. needs to take a dip here again, he's starting to ... *(gesture of going around in circles).*

Well then, I'll encourage this man to publish as many books of Sri Aurobindo as possible.

Yes, yes.

Starting with the "Synthesis."

The *Synthesis.*
Personally, of all those I have read, it's the book that has helped me the most. It comes from a very high and very universal inspiration, in the sense that it will remain new for a long time to come.

(silence)

Did you read all the "Correspondence with Nirod"?

I'm translating it as I go along, so I haven't read it entirely yet.

There are fabulous things in it. He seems to be constantly joking, .
but ... it's fabulous.[1]
How many years did I live with Sri Aurobindo? Thirty years, I think—thirty years, from 1920 to 1950. I thought I knew him well, but when I listen to that, I realize ... *(gesture as if new horizons were opening up).*

(silence)

But how wonderfully things get organized when you really and sincerely put yourself in the Divine's hands! This year, for instance, is like being bathed in Sri Aurobindo, you know.

(Mother goes into meditation)

You have nothing to ask, nothing to say?

There are some passages from Sri Aurobindo you might want to use this year, for the Centenary:

> "I have never known any will of mine for any major event in the conduct of the world affairs to fail in the end, although it may take a long time for the world-forces to fulfil it."
>
> (October 1932)
On Himself, XXVI.55

---

1. The "Correspondence" of 1935 was at the time being read to Mother.

"I have never had a strong and persistent will for anything to happen in the world—I am not speaking of personal things—which did not eventually happen even after delay, defeat or even disaster."

(October 19, 1946)
On Himself, XXVI.169

It's interesting.

Do you want to use one of them for the 15th of August?

Which is stronger?

The second, I think.

I think so too.

The former is from 1932, the latter from 1946.

Oh!...

February 19, 1972

(Mother gazes at Satprem for a long time.)

Do you see something?

*(Mother plunges in.
Half an hour goes by)*

No inclination to speak unless you put questions....[1]

Am I getting a little closer?

Oh, you're doing very well, mon petit! That....

---

1. This sentence was said in English.

*(Mother takes Satprem's hands
long silence)*

Last time, my impression was that the old man in you had awakened in order to be transformed. But only you can know....
I felt that because he was a totally different man from the one I know now. But only you can tell me if he has actually been transformed or if he has disappeared.

I don't know. I think he's trying to get transformed.

Yes, that was my impression. But now I have the feeling that that division no longer exists. When I look at you.... When I was there [in Satprem], I felt that the division no longer exists—only you can tell me if at other times it comes back.
As you are now, near me, it's very good—very good, it's *smooth.* I don't know how to put it, *smooth....* I don't sense any struggle or conflict or difficulty in you, none at all. Perhaps I don't see it or....

No, no! Of course, you see, Mother!

You see, the Presence is constantly here; when people come, they dim it, as it were, they create obstructions, but when you are here *(immutable gesture)*, there is none of that, it's quiet, it's....
In other words, He is here. Which to me is a sign that you're doing well.

(Mother plunges in)

All I see is very good—very close. Very close.
What shall I say?... How shall I put it?... You see, when there's nobody here, there's an eternal and luminous existence; when people come, they bring problems, difficulties. But, when you are here—when you are here, even when I hold your hands, like now—there's the same Quiet. A luminous peace that ... that leads to Joy, you follow?
It's good, mon petit, very good.
Don't worry. I can tell you: it's good.

(Satprem lays his forehead on Mother's knees)

What day is today?

It's Saturday.

So in two days, it's the 21st.

Yes, Mother.

So I won't see you again!

No, Mother.... Happy birthday, Mother!

February 22, 1972

A Note from Mother
(The day before was Mother's ninety-fourth birthday.)

All day long on the 21st I had a strong feeling that it was everybody's birthday, and I felt an urge to say "happy birthday" to everyone.

A very strong impression that something new was manifesting in the world, and that all those who were ready and receptive could incarnate it.

In a few days, probably, we will know what it was.

February 23, 1972

*(Mother gives Satprem some papers, most of which have been
published in this Agenda as "Notes.")*

And here is more of T.J.'s notebook—I haven't reread it, I don't
know what she put in it. You'll see if something is interesting.

*Normally, part of it is scheduled to be published in the next
Bulletin.*

No, only what's worthwhile. Certain things are.... One or two
things are revelations, but I don't know if she included them. I had
one or two important revelations; they seemed like nothing, but
they were.... But I don't know if they're included.

Do you want me to read them to you?

There's not enough time, mon petit.
Do you have something?

Nothing particular. How was the 21st?

(after a silence)

From the standpoint of the work, it was very important, but
physically.... I had trouble on the balcony. There was a formation (from whom I don't know); I had seen it already for some time
(I have a vague idea who it comes from, but I am not sure ... and
in fact I don't care): I felt I was going to die on the 21st.

!!!

But....
It was a formation. Naturally, it had no effect, except physically
when I went out on the balcony: it was difficult.

But you stayed out for a long time.

I stayed for five minutes.

70

It was a long time, much longer that usual.

Ah? . . .

Yes.

That's because I was determined to hold out.
I think that . . . (all these are big words for small things) I think that I have won a victory. But it was difficult.
Something changed afterwards.
In terms of consciousness, it's fabulous, but it would take hours to describe.

(silence)

But life isn't organized as it should be. . . . You see, the sense of time is different; sometimes I go into a certain consciousness—I think only a few minutes have elapsed, while it's been a very long time.
Inwardly, it's going very well—very well. That's all I can say. . . .
The body is learning, but learning slowly.

(silence)

I don't know about those papers I gave you. There were one or two very important things. I don't know if they're there.
What's the last one?

> Life on earth is essentially a field for progress; how short life is for all the progress we have to make!
> To waste time seeking the gratification of one's petty desires is sheer folly. True happiness can be attained only by finding the Divine.

There were others after this one. . . .[1]

(Satprem leafs through the pages
and comes across this passage:)

> . . . Almost all human miseries come from the fact that human beings are almost always persuaded

---

1. This last note is dated February 19. If there were any others between the 19th and the 23rd, they have disappeared.

they know better than the Divine what they need
and what life is supposed to bring them....

(Mother plunges in)

*

* *

(A note dated February 23)

Supreme Lord, Perfection we must become,
Perfection we must manifest.
This body lives only by You and says to You
over and over again:

"What You will
What You will"

until the day it knows it automatically because
its consciousness will be completely united
with Yours.

February 26, 1972

*(Mother hands Satprem her message for February 29, the
fourth anniversary of the "supramental descent" of
February 29, 1956.)*

It is only when the Supramental
manifests in the body-mind that its
presence can be permanent.[1]

Mother

This message comes from Sri Aurobindo—although it is made to
appear as mine. It was Sri Aurobindo who wrote it. All I said was:
Sri Aurobindo said "permanent."

---

1. Mother's translation from the French.

72

But, Mother, it's also your own experience, isn't it? . . .

Yes, evidently.

*(Mother laughs
silence)*

But wiser to let it settle in before we talk about it!
Once things are established, then. . . . For the moment, it's . . .
(oscillating gesture from one side to the other).

*This taming of the physical mind is. . . . I don't know how to
tackle it, I find it very difficult.*

Very difficult. It's very difficult.
First, one must be able to obtain silence at will—at any time at
all, to obtain silence. I think that's the starting point.

*But obtaining silence at will is no problem, Mother. You con-
centrate for a second and everything is stilled, and it lasts
perfectly as long as you remain concentrated. But the moment
you let go of the concentration, pfft! . . .*

(Mother laughs)

. . . Off it goes. It rushes off here and there. . . .

Well, mine has now lost the habit of running about. This habit
must be got rid of.

But how does one do that?

I don't know, for it's spontaneous. Except when someone talks
to me or something comes and breaks that state, but otherwise,
left to itself, the body is quite naturally like this *(immutable
gesture, turned to the above).* Perhaps this is the means *(same
gesture upwards):* a contemplation of the Divine.

(smiling silence)

This is its natural state *(same gesture).* The actual feeling is even
curious, you know . . . the body feels as if it were completely enwrapped like a baby, exactly like this *(gesture),* enfolded in the Divine.

(silence)

Two or three days ago (I don't remember when), something was pressing on my heart—and it hurt. It hurt, it was the 24th. I really had the feeling that ... the body had the feeling it was the end. But then immediately, it felt as if enfolded ... like a baby carried in the arms of the Divine. The exact sensation, you know, as if I were a baby being carried in the arms of the Divine. And after some time (a long time), when the body was exclusively in the Presence, it went away. The body didn't even ask for the pain to go; it just left. It took a little while, but it left.

I haven't told anyone. I thought ... I thought the end had come. It was just after lunch. . . .

Absolutely, but absolutely the sensation of being a baby nestling *(gesture)* in the Divine's arms. Extraordinary!

(silence)

You see, for a time it's like this: "What You will, what You will. . . ." And then this too falls silent and ... *(Mother opens her hands upwards in a gesture of offering and immobile contemplation).*

(silence)

The type of concentration itself must change, then.

Yes.

Because when you try to tame the physical mind and it rushes off here and there, it's mentally that you concentrate and restore the silence. So each time you use the mind to enforce discipline. . . .

Ah!

The trouble is, the second you relax that mental pressure, it. . . . There has to be a "descent" of something else. A takeover.

I think it's really the sensation of the helplessness of a baby, you understand? And it's not something you "think" or "want": it's totally spontaneous. And from there, you go into a state of ... *(Mother opens her hands, a blissful smile on her face).*

As long as there's the sense of a person who wants, a person who does, it's hopeless . . . *(same gesture, smiling with hands open).*

(Mother goes into contemplation)

Is the Lord taking care of us?

(Laughing) I believe so!

(Mother takes Satprem's hands)

Don't you feel Him?

Yes, Mother, yes.

Ah! . . .
And you *(to Sujata, who comes closer),* do you feel Him?

Yes, Mother.

(silence)

(Sujata:) Mother, what does it mean when the body itself feels a great need to be enwrapped?

Yes, isn't it!—like this *(gesture).*

Yes, Mother.

Yes, that's it.

To be enfolded. Enfolded.

Yes, exactly. That's exactly what my body feels all the time. You see, it is like . . . like a baby nestling. Exactly that sensation.
I think . . . I think my body has become excessively sensitive and needs to be protected from all those things coming in.[1] As if it had

---

1. The "formation of death" surrounding Mother, which she already mentioned on the occasion of the 21st of February, seems to have become more defined. In fact, both Satprem and Sujata remember being struck by a comment Mother made the previous year, on September 8, 1971: "The body has had moments of agony as never before in its whole life—in connection with death, which has never happened before." That remark had a strange ring to it. Mother had often mentioned before that there were a lot of desires for her body to die: "A considerable number of desires for it to die, everywhere—they are everywhere!" (May 10, 1969). But the threat or formation of death seems to have drawn closer, taken shape since that date. As if it had entered the physical realm.

to work inside, you know ... as in an egg. Yes, that's it. Exactly.

Yes, that's it. Exactly so. I think a whole work is being done within.

Oh, in terms of the old way, it's becoming more and more stupid, but the new way is beginning to emerge.

One would like, so much, to remain like this *(same enveloping gesture)*, to remain like this for a long, long, long time.

(Sujata:) Yes, Mother.

And not move.

As if one constantly felt like resting one's head on your breast, enfolded in your arms.

(Mother laughs tenderly) Yes.

(To Satprem:) Do you feel that way too?

Oh, yes, Mother! Yes, Mother.

Mon petit ... *(Mother takes Satprem's hands again)*. It's coming, we must be patient.

March

March 1, 1972

(After a long contemplation.)

I have a feeling I had something to tell you. Last time too—as soon as you left, I knew what it was. But then it faded again. I don't know why.

March 4, 1972

*(Mother has a cold. She remains in contemplation
for half an hour.)*

Nothing to say?

What about you, Mother, how are you?

I have a fever.
It was mad yesterday, they made me see two hundred people.

Yes, it's too much.

It's mad.

(Mother plunges in again)

Nothing?

And you, nothing to say?

(Mother shakes her head)

What time is it?

Ten to eleven, Mother.

Do you want to stay ten minutes more?

Yes, if you like, Mother, gladly!

Willingly. When I remain quiet like this, I am all right.

(Mother plunges in)

March 8, 1972

(Mother holds a "Transformation" flower in her hand.)

For whom?

*(she looks for another flower
to give Satprem and Sujata one each)*

Ten lakhs of rupees have just burned up in Auroville.

Ten lakhs![1]

Yes. A workshop with machines as well as the *godown* [store-room] next door which contained the stock of food. Brrff!

That's how it is, like an imperative Order: Don't step out of line or else everything will go wrong.

It's become terrible. Another Auroville child died (a one-and-a-half-year-old baby) because his parents didn't have the right attitude. He has just died. That's how it works. It's getting terrible. Terrible. A kind of Pressure—a frightening Pressure—which compels the necessary progress. I feel it in myself, on my body. But my body isn't afraid; it says *(Mother opens her hands)*, "Well, if I must be finished, I'll be finished."

That's how it is at every instant: the truth ... *(Mother brings down her fist)* or the end.

That's what seems to have descended—you remember, I said something had descended on the 21st (I wrote it somewhere), and

---

1. About $100,000.

one day we would know, we would know soon what it was.[1] Do you remember?

Yes, it was the 21st of February.

Well, this is it. Something like: "No half measures, no compromises, no halfways, no...." None—it's like this *(Mother brings down her fist)*.

And that's how it is for the body. Every instant is imperative: life or death. No halfways. You know, we have spent centuries being neither too uncomfortable nor too comfortable. Well, that time is over.

The body knows this is necessary for the supramental body to be formed: it must be ENTIRELY under the Influence of the Divine. No compromises, no half measures, no "It will come later." Just like this *(Mother brings down her fist):* a dreadful Will.

And that's the only way for things to go fast.

(silence)

There was probably nobody over in the workshop; it wasn't open yet. But when I was told the news, I had a feeling someone had been burned inside—I didn't say anything because.... It's only a vision, of course, but....

All the machines, all the stock of food, everything was burned to cinders.

Due to a wrong attitude over there?

Yes. Oh, they're all quarreling among themselves! And some even disobey deliberately, they refuse to recognize any authority.

(long silence)

When you begin to understand practically the need for transformation, when the understanding dawns and you try to do something about it, you notice that every time the material substance receives a blow, the message gets across: for one or

---

1. (Note of February 22) "All day long on the 21st I had a strong feeling that it was everybody's birthday, and I felt an urge to say 'happy birthday' to everyone. A very strong impression that something new was manifesting in the world and that all those who were ready and receptive could incarnate it. In a few days, probably we will know what it was."

two days it aspires for something, it searches; and then ... it slackens.

Yes, yes.

It is just incapable of keeping up a tension.

Not incapable.

What is it, then?

Unwillingness. Egoism (what we call egoism), Matter's egoism.

Matter's egoism....

... Which refuses to surrender.
I know it very well. I keep catching my body doing that all the time, in one part or another. It simply wants to putter along in the same old way.

It's like a slackening of aspiration, of tension.

Yes, exactly.

But what to do, then? Should one try each time to recapture it, or what?

Yes. Because it can't be stable unless it is POSITIVELY anchored to the Divine. When you are like this *(gesture, fists clenched in the air as if clinging to a rope),* then, automatically, all the critical moments take the right turn. The right turn. It's like a constant feeling of hovering between life and death, and the minute you take the right attitude—the minute the PART CONCERNED takes the right attitude—all is well. All is well, quite naturally and easily. Really extraordinary. But it's also terrible because it means perpetual danger. I don't know, perhaps a hundred times a day, a sensation like: life or ... dissolution (I mean a sensation in the cells). And if they become tense as is their wont, it gets awful. But they're learning to ... *(Mother opens her hands in a gesture of surrender).* Then things are fine.
It's as if the body were being practically obliged to learn eternity. It's truly interesting. And then I see external circumstances becoming DREADFUL (from an ordinary standpoint).

(Mother goes into contemplation)

What would you like to say?

Well, that was it; what I was finding difficult was to keep that stability.

Yes.

I find it very difficult. You try to catch hold of yourself once, twice, ten times, but you get the feeling that it's not the right way, that something else is needed, and ... really, if some higher Power doesn't do it FOR YOU, it's simply hopeless.

Yes, exactly. But I have had experiences—hundreds of experiences—showing that the minute you take the true attitude, it is DONE.

It is WE who prevent it from getting done. As though our personal control over things prevented the action of the Force (something of the sort). We must ... *(Mother opens her hands).*

(silence)

I think—I think it's the subconscient which is convinced that if it doesn't keep control, everything will go wrong. That's the impression I have, it's the subconscient which says, "Oh, I must watch over this, I must be careful about that...."

(Mother opens her hands
and plunges in)

March 10, 1972

(A conversation with Auroville's architect, who, after the recent "accident," asks for money for "fire protection.")

Well, there isn't enough money here, and there's even less there.... Because in people's minds, it's all the same thing [the

Ashram and Auroville], and so they don't know where to give anymore.

There's so much money wasted in the world—some people don't even know what to do with it!

What would be needed for Auroville's protection, how much?

(The architect:) We have to make a study, Mother. I think perhaps one or two lakhs for all of Auroville (for wells and fire hoses). That's for the time being, but there's also the future: how are we going to develop Auroville, now that it's started? At this point the main question is to know whether we shouldn't try to raise money, to ask people in the world for personal contributions in rupees, francs or dollars, so that Auroville can be built by individual people. Perhaps some action along those lines could be undertaken in various countries as well as in India? Because Auroville's financial situation is get-ting worse. It's worse than it was six months ago, and the needs are increasing, so ... I don't know, waiting may be a solution, but you should know the exact situation.

(after a long silence)

What can we do? Do you have a suggestion?

Some time back, L. [an Indian industrialist] came up with an idea which I would like to discuss further with him. The idea was to interest individuals, give them a sort of participation in Auroville. I don't exactly know what India's financial situation is, but....

India's financial situation is VERY bad. Because they used to receive a lot of money from America, but that has practically stop-ped. It's very bad—India has become poor, that's the trouble. Otherwise we could ask, but they are really in trouble.

Perhaps some other countries are ready to help.

Yes, certainly!

Germany can help, maybe the United States. But the thing is, Mother, all this should be done as a coherent policy, no longer in a haphazard way.

Yes, yes!

We should try.

If only I were given a plan. I haven't seen to these things so far, but if there were an acceptable plan, I could work on it. Right now I don't know what to do.

I'll speak to N. right away, Mother, and see what he thinks. Perhaps today we can bring you a proposal and make some decisions—leaving things as they are may be possible but dangerous.

Dangerous.
I think something should be done. But I can't say what because I don't know—I don't know what can be done practically.
For many, many years, I had merely to exert a little pressure to get money—and I got it. But that was for the Ashram. Now the Ashram doesn't have enough, and nothing comes no matter how much pressure I exert—people no longer know where to give: there's this thing and that thing, and this and that ... they are confused!
Give me a plan and I'll work on it.

There's too much dispersion, Mother.

Yes, yes!

You no longer know where you stand: there's "Sri Aurobindo Society," "Sri Aurobindo's Action," "Sri Aurobindo this and that...." The result is dispersion.

Yes, but when you tell them that—especially if you put it that way to N. [Sri Aurobindo Society], he'll say, "All right, Sri Aurobindo's Action [U.'s operation] has got to go." Each one says, "I am the one who should stay!" ... That's no solution.

The solution is that people should become one, Mother: unity.

Yes, yes, yes—yes, exactly. Exactly!
Instead of a combination where each one has his place within a harmonious unity, instead of that, everyone pulls in his own direction. The real progress to be made is a moral one.

85

You have hit the point: lack of unity is the cause of all the difficulties.

Even the Ashram has been contaminated by the disease: each department considers itself a separate entity. And since there's no more cohesion, nothing works! That's the situation.

And I can no longer go from one place to another and bring a vigorous action. I can't anymore, I am held here.

That's it, you've put your finger on it. If you could propose a specific plan of action, we could see. That's what is needed: to coordinate the efforts and create a unity with the parts.

From the beginning there has been this lack of unity, and also because of the action I no longer perform. No matter how much I tell them, "You are not here to represent your own interests. You are all one and the same"—they just don't understand! So the result is *(laughing):* N. is sick and U. doesn't feel well—there you are.

In the end it always boils down to the same thing: a SUBSTANTIAL individual progress is required—a serious and sincere progress—then everything works perfectly.

The atmosphere is dislocated; it has lost the cohesive power it had.

But if you want to collaborate, it would be wonderful, you know! I need someone, you see, someone who could get around, talk to people, see, take notes: reestablish unity on a higher level. Oh, that would be a wonderful work! Wonderful.

Once that is done, things would ease up. It's not that money is lacking, it's just being wasted, scattered.

You see, N. keeps wanting to expand and expand the Sri Aurobindo Society, he buys plots of land worth lakhs of rupees, and instead of the money being used for the general work, it is frittered away....[1] I told him, but he didn't understand. And today, the result is that he is sick.

That's the situation.

Success is certain, but on one condition—ONE condition—that we become united. Supposedly, we are preaching unity to the world—it would be only decent to do it ourselves!

Instead, we are the example of exactly the opposite.

To visitors we say, "Here we seek human unity." But WE constantly quarrel among ourselves, and we preach human unity!

---

1. This is the beginning of the fraud. N. later declared himself the "proprietor" of Auroville, because all the land was purchased in the name of "his" Society and not in Auroville's.

That's absurd. Totally absurd! We can't even be ONE in our own work.
I keep telling them, but they don't understand.
Do you want to help me?

Yes, Mother.

Good. Would you like us to work together?

Yes, Mother.

Good.

I'm ready to speak to N., Mother, if you permit me.

Yes, speak to N., it will do him some good.

I'll speak very fraternally, Mother, very sincerely, for I have a lot of things to say.

Good, good.
If he gets annoyed, tell him, "Then go talk to Mother." And....

I'll try to speak to N. first, he's the hardest. I'll speak to U. after.

U. is very bright, he'll have very good answers to offer you! *(Mother laughs)*

I've already spoken to U., Mother, I already know his answers.

But U. is beginning to change, because he is an extremely bright man, so he understood he had to change.
I am with you.

⋆
⋆ ⋆

(The architect leaves. R., an American disciple, enters.)

I could put it this way: it's either progress, or death. Each and everyone must, must absolutely progress, make the required progress, or else ... *(gesture of dissolution).*

That fire was symbolic—I suppose you know about it: there's been a terrible fire.

(R.:) Yes, yes. And I wanted to know what is the symbolic significance.

You see, we preach Unity, we say that humanity must be one, that all efforts must join together for the general progress, for the advent of the Supramental ... but everyone pulls as hard as he can in his own direction. That's the situation.

So I wanted to tell all of you, "Practice what you say, or you will cease to exist."

One has no right to preach unity to the world when one gives such an example of utter division.... That's all. It's quite simple, so simple that a child could understand—but THEY don't understand.

As for me, the power of consciousness goes on increasing; for the time being—I repeat, for the time being—the physical power is reduced to almost nought. I am forced to stay here, minding nothing, and make shift with seeing people. So I need some persons to do the practical work I used to do before and can no longer do ... *(Mother is short of breath)*. I can't speak with the same strength as before—the physical is undergoing a transformation, you know. Sri Aurobindo himself had said—and rightly so—he said (because one of us had to go, and I offered to go), "No, your body is capable of enduring it, it *has the strength* to undergo transformation." It's not easy. I can assure you, it's not easy. Yet my body is good-willed, it is really good-willed. But for the moment it is in the process of ... well, it is no longer quite on this side but not yet on the other. The transition isn't easy. So I am stuck here, like an old woman, incapable of doing any work.

If I can hold on—if only I can hold on—at one hundred things will be better. That I know. I am absolutely convinced there will be a renewal of energy. But I have to hold on.... That's all.

(silence)

So for the moment, we lack money. We lack money because money is being scattered. People no longer know where to give, so they stop giving: "Should I give here, should I give there, should I...?" They don't give anything anymore.

*(silence
then Mother speaks in English)*

I can see, I have truly the occasion to see that if I left, I have nobody here, it would be our destruction.

(R.:) Oh, complete collapse—nothing!

Then if the work must be done, if Auroville must be built, not only do I have to remain in my body but the body must become strong.

I know. I know that. All depends on what the Divine Will is—He doesn't tell me! When I ask Him, I have the impression ... (once or twice, in moments of difficulty, I have put the question regarding this body), and then *(laughing)* I seem to see a smile, you know, a smile as big as the world, but no answer.

I can still see that smile: "Don't try to know, it is not yet time."

(the clock strikes)

If we knew how to remain always in the true consciousness, there would be ... a smile. But we have a tendency to become tragic. It's our weakness.

It is our limitations that make a drama. We are too small—too small and too shortsighted. But ... the Consciousness knows—it knows.[1]

March 11, 1972

I've received a letter from P.L. This is what he says:

"... You may have already learned that Cardinal Tisserant died on the 21st [of February]. As he was in

---

1. The recording of this conversation has been kept in the Ashram, most probably never to be seen again. Satprem used to keep all the tapes of his conversations with Mother, but since this particular conversation concerned Auroville's architect and R., at the time he thought it better to entrust the tape to Mother's new attendant after transcribing it.

reality the Vice-Pope, you can imagine the pomp of the funeral ceremony, with representatives from the French government, the French Academy, the Italian government, etc.: one full week of ceremonies. Being his secretary, I had to organize everything. I am very tired.... Msgr. R. very much suffered from this loss. I think he will be coming to you in a few weeks, or a month at most: he is determined to get out. Many things have happened since his meeting with Mother....[1] While filing some papers, I came across the enclosed document which may interest you. I hope the bishopric continues to leave you in peace...."

The document is a copy of Cardinal Tisserand's letter to the Archbischop of Pondicherry:

Albano, Regina Apostolorum, 13 January 1972

To His Excellency Msgr. A.R.
Archbishop of Pondicherry

Venerable Lord,

As Your Excellency knows, I have directed the Holy Congregation for the Eastern Church for nearly twenty-five years, and one of my most cherished memories is the journey I made to your beloved country in 1953. I have always held a keen interest in your great nation, but even more so after I visited it. It was thus with a very special pleasure that I accompanied His Holiness Pope Paul VI to the International Eucharistic Congress in Bombay.

On that occasion, the Holy Father expressed the wish to come in contact with representatives of your country's main religious movements, and I know, Excellency, that he was given a biography of Sri Aurobindo.

It is in fact in connection with the Sri Aurobindo Ashram in Pondicherry that I am taking the liberty of writing Your Excellency. I am sure you are aware of the reputation it has earned beyond India's borders; I have been following its work and achievements for years. Recently, I was told of the difficulties encountered by those in charge of the Ashram in regard to

---

1. See conversation of January 29, 1972.

the proposed creation of a university—a project expressly favored by the Indian Government; some Catholic students, in conjunction with a few priests, are displaying a strong opposition to this project.

I therefore request Your Excellency kindly to use his authority to avoid any incident that, at all events, would be highly detrimental to the harmony that His Holiness Pope Paul VI so much desires, in accord with the rules laid down by the Ecumenical Council Vatican II.

With gratitude, I remain, Venerable Lord, respectfully and faithfully yours,

Signed: Eugène Card. Tisserand

It's interesting. Who has replaced him?

I don't know, nobody has been appointed yet.

But since then, they've been quiet here.

(Mother plunges in Champaklal comes up to Mother, abruptly pulling her out of her state)

I was in Italy.
Stories with cardinals. . . .

March 15, 1972

(Satprem reads Mother some parts of the conversation of March 8 for the next "Bulletin": "No compromises, no half measures, no 'It will come later' . . . it's like a constant feeling of hovering between life and death. . .".)

91

It's very true. And it keeps getting more and more acute, more and more acute. That's it. All the time, all the time like that....

Eating has become a problem. But ... at times, when the attitude is right, it's so easy!

It's good what you did.

But YOU said that, Mother, not me!

> *(Mother plunges in
> she tries to say something, then plunges again)*

March 17, 1972

(A note by Mother)

To prepare for immortality, the consciousness of the body must first become one with the Eternal Consciousness.

March 18, 1972

(No sooner has Satprem entered her room than Mother looks at him and declares categorically:)

Things are better—aren't they?

For me or for....

Yes, for you.

Well, I think so, I hope so.

Yes, but I am telling you: things ARE better—I know! *(Mother laughs)*
It's cleared up.

It was pretty tough.

> *(Mother signs the contract for the publication of the "Synthesis" in France—silence)*

Do you feel that things are also better in general, or ...

Yes.

... or is it specific?

Things are better.
A dawning of joy in the body.... It's coming, it's coming.
You remember, I told you everything was like this *(gesture on the brink of catastrophe)*, but now we are plainly—plainly on the bright side. From time to time *(a little wobbly gesture)*, but ... plainly on the bright side.
It's much better.

> *(silence)*

And your atmosphere is much clearer, MUCH clearer. There are less ... *(gesture of conflicts)*.
Have you seen this?

> *(Mother hands Satprem a paper about the restrictions on admission to the Ashram)*

Don't people ask you to come to the Ashram?

I never encourage them.

Shall we meditate?

> *(long meditation)*

You have nothing to say?

I wish everything would melt.

(Mother laughs and takes Satprem's hands)

It's very clear. Very clear.

*(Mother goes off again,
holding Satprem's hands)*

March 19, 1972

(A note by Mother)

The truth, which man has vainly sought to know, will be the privilege of the new race, the race of tomorrow, the superman.

To live according to the Truth will be his privilege.

Let us do our best to help prepare the advent of the New Being. The mind must fall silent and be replaced by the Truth-Consciousness—the consciousness of details integrated with the consciousness of the whole.

March 22, 1972

(For the last three days, Mother has been "ill": violent vomiting, etc. She gasps for breath as she speaks.)

This time it's serious.

I haven't been able to eat—I can't eat *(gesture of vomiting)*.
The body is reduced to the minimum.
We shall see. If it holds on, it will be all right.

But three nights ago, I saw a gigantic tidal wave—a tidal wave submerging everything.

Aah!

When I see that, there's usually a catastrophe the next day. But there was no catastrophe the next day—it seems to have fallen on you. I don't know ... a gigantic tidal wave.

(after a silence)

At night, I don't sleep, you know, but I go into a deep rest, and there remains only the body consciousness. Twice, last night, the body saw all sorts of images and activities showing a widespread incomprehension in people.

The body was in certain situations.... One was taking place here and the other was in Japan. I realized that the body holds certain impressions, impressions of being in a.... It wasn't in the Ashram, but the one in Japan, exactly as I was in Japan (but these are not memories, they were entirely new activities, something entirely new), showing that I was surrounded by people who don't understand. And here, too (it wasn't the Ashram, the situations were symbolic and involved people who are no longer in their bodies), I was surrounded by people and things that didn't understand. And I saw that these impressions are in the body and make things even more difficult.

They weren't actually physical things: they were the transcription of people's attitude and their way of thinking.

(silence)

I have been well aware for a long time now that there are ... I am not even sure that some people haven't been doing black magic against me.

Oh, Mother, that same night, the night I saw the tidal wave, I saw also a sudden image: you were lying down and I was holding tightly onto your feet, and by our side was a tall black being—jet-black—maybe ten feet high, who was all . . . it's not that he had black skin, but he was all dressed in black. And he was standing on a kind of black carpet.

Yes, that's it. I have the same impression.

I don't say anything (for it sounds ridiculous), but my feeling is that some people have been using black magic against me. Naturally, my only recourse is to envelop and surround myself with the Divine. But . . . that causes a lot of difficulties.

I wanted to see you to tell you that. But speaking is difficult. . . . Would you like some silence?

(meditation)

March 24, 1972

(Mother sees Sujata)

For the first time, early this morning, I saw myself: my body. I don't know whether it's the supramental body or . . . (what shall I say?) a transitional body, but I had a completely new body, in the sense that it was sexless: it was neither woman nor man.

It was very white. But that could be because I have white skin, I don't know.

It was very slender *(gesture).* Really lovely, a truly harmonious form.

That's the first time.

I hadn't the least idea, the faintest notion what it would look like, nothing, and I saw—I WAS like that, I had become like that. I thought Satprem should know, so he can note it down.

I don't know if I'll remember, that's why I am telling you. Because today is Friday and I won't see him till tomorrow. This way, I am sure I won't forget. You'll tell him, won't you?

Yes, Mother.

It's been hard.

Especially for food: it will be very different. I am BEGINNING to understand how it will work, but I don't know enough yet to describe it—I haven't had the experience, so I don't know.... Most probably, we will absorb things that don't need to be digested—there are some. But not food as such. For example, one idea these days is glucose (things of that sort). But I am not sure because I am just undergoing the experience. Once I have the vision of what to do, I'll do it.

Anyway, I wanted to tell you.[1]

Are you all right?... And Satprem?

Yes, Mother.

I'll see you tomorrow.

March 25, 1972

Did you receive the last answers to T.J. [the "Notes"]? I think there were one or two, I don't quite remember.

The last one I received is this one:

The truth, which man has vainly sought to know, will be the privilege of the new race, the race of tomorrow, the superman....

Is that all?... See if there is something you can use....

Yes, certainly there is![2]

---

1. The recording of this conversation was kept by Mother's new attendant. Something strange was beginning to happen in that room, but neither Satprem nor Sujata understood what it meant.
2. This "Note" is the last one Satprem ever received from the disciple to whom Mother was sending her answers. A strange wind seemed to be blowing over those who were connected with the work Mother was doing with Satprem; though not acting in collusion, they all seemed bent on obstructing that work, as will become apparent later. Perhaps this was the beginning of the "tidal wave" Satprem had seen in his dream.

(silence)

Sujata told me about the experience you had the other day, that vision you had of your body, the transitional body.

Yes, I WAS like that. It was me; I didn't look at myself in a mirror, I saw myself like this *(Mother bends her head to look at her body)*, I was . . . I just was like that.

That's the first time. It was around four in the morning, I think. And perfectly natural—I mean, I didn't look in a mirror, it felt perfectly natural. I only remember what I saw *(gesture from the chest to the waist)*. I was covered only with veils, so I only saw. . . . What was very different was the torso, from the chest to the waist: it was neither male nor female.

But it was lovely, my form was extremely svelte and slim—slim but not thin. And the skin was very white, just like my skin. A lovely form. And no sex—you couldn't tell: neither male nor female. The sex had disappeared.

The same here *(Mother points to her chest)*, all that was flat. I don't know how to explain it. There was an outline reminiscent of what is now, but with no forms *(Mother touches her chest)*, not even as much as a man's. A very white skin, very smooth. Practically no abdomen to speak of. And no stomach. All that was slim.

I didn't pay any special attention, you see, because I was that: it felt perfectly natural to me. That's the first time it happened, it was the night before last; but last night I didn't see anything. That was the first and the last time so far.

But this form is in the subtle physical, isn't it?

It must be already like that in the subtle physical.

But how will it pass into the physical?

That's the question I don't know. . . . I don't know. I don't know.

Also, clearly there was none of the complex digestion we have now, or the kind of elimination we have now. It didn't work that way.

But how? . . . Food is already obviously very different and becoming more and more so—glucose, for instance, or substances that don't require an elaborate digestion. But how will the body itself change? . . . That I don't know. I don't know.

You see, I didn't look to see how it worked, for it was completely natural to me, so I can't describe it in detail. Simply, it was neither a woman's body nor a man's—that much is certain. And *the outline* was fairly similar to that of a very young person. There was a faint suggestion of a human form *(Mother draws a form in the air):* with a shoulder and a waist. Just a hint of it.

I see it but. . . . I saw it exactly as you see yourself, I didn't even look at myself in the mirror. And I had a sort of veil, which I wore to cover myself.

It was my way of being (there was nothing surprising in it), my natural way of being.

That must be how it is in the subtle physical.

But what's mysterious is the transition from one to the other.

Yes—how?

But it's the same mystery as the transition from chimpanzee to man.

Oh, no, Mother! It's more colossal than that! It's more colossal for, after all, there isn't that much difference between a chimpanzee and a man.

But there wasn't such a difference in the appearance either *(Mother draws a form in the air):* there were shoulders, arms, legs, a body, a waist. Similar to ours. There was only. . . .

Yes, but I mean the way a chimpanzee functions and the way a man functions are the same.

They are the same.

Well, yes! They digest the same, breathe the same. . . . Whereas here. . . .

No, but here too there must have been breathing. The shoulders were strikingly broad *(gesture)*, in contrast. That's important. But the chest was neither feminine nor even masculine: only reminiscent of it. And all that—stomach, abdomen and the rest—was simply an *outline*, a very slender and harmonious form, which certainly wasn't used for the purpose we now use our bodies.

The two different things—totally different—were procreation,

99

which was no longer possible, and food. Though even our present food is manifestly not the same as that of chimpanzees or even the first humans; it's quite different. So now, it seems we have to find a food that doesn't require all this digesting.... Not exactly liquid, but not solid either. And there's also the question of the mouth—I don't know about that—and the teeth? Naturally, chewing should no longer be necessary, and therefore teeth wouldn't be either.... But there has to be something to replace them. I haven't the slightest idea what the face looked like. But it didn't seem too, too unlike what it is now.

What will change a great deal, of course—it had acquired a prominent role—is breathing. That being depended much on it.

Yes, he probably absorbs energies directly.

Yes. There will probably be intermediary beings who won't last, you see, just as there were intermediary beings between the chimpanzee and man.

But I don't know, something has to happen that has never before happened.

Yes.

(silence)

Sometimes I have a sort of feeling that the time of realization is very close.

Yes, but how?

Yes, how—we don't know.

Is this (Mother points to her body) going to change? It either has to change or else follow the old, ordinary pattern of coming undone and then being redone again.... I don't know. True, life can be greatly prolonged, there have been examples, but.... I don't know. I don't know.

Several times I felt that instead of a transformation, there will be a concretization of the other body.

Ahh!... But how?

We don't know the process either. But instead of this body

*becoming the other, the other body will take the place of this
one.*

Yes, but how?

How, I don't know.

> *(after a silence)*

Yes, understandably, if the body I had two nights ago were to
materialize.... But how?
Do you want to meditate?

> *(Mother goes into contemplation)*

We know nothing!
It's amazing how we know NOTHING.

> *(Satprem prepares to leave,
> Sujata draws near to Mother)*

*(Sujata:) You know, Mother, in his poem "Transformation,"
Sri Aurobindo's opening lines are:*

> My breath runs in a subtle rhythmic stream
> It fills my members with a might divine . . . [1]

Breathing, yes, that's important. "A might"?

"Might," yes, Mother.

> *(Mother caresses Sujata's cheeks)*

---

1. *Collected Poems*, V.161.

March 29, 1972

I received a letter from Y.L. You remember, last year she came to ask you Malraux's question about Bangladesh—Malraux wanted to participate in the struggle for Bangladesh. You told her to tell him he would have the answer when he came to India ...

(Mother nods)

... He never came to India. He dropped his project after meeting Indira Gandhi [in Paris].

Oh?

Yes, since India was officially going to war in Bangladesh, he didn't think there was any more reason for him to get killed ... on the official side. So instead of going to Bangladesh, he went to the United States to meet Nixon.

(Mother frowns)

Well, anyway, Y.L.'s idea is to get Malraux to participate in Sri Aurobindo's Centenary. You know that for years I've been trying to interest Malraux in Sri Aurobindo's thought, I wrote him the first time ten or fifteen years ago. And here's what Y.L. writes to me:

> *"... Malraux again and again! In your last letter, at the end of December, you wrote, 'He could be the herald of the new world.' Invited by Nixon, he obeyed the outward call. Now remains the return journey via India and Bangladesh. This morning I received a copy of your speech on the Delhi radio. I immediately sent it to Malraux...."*

*She means my article "Sri Aurobindo and the Earth's Future."
Then, a few days later, I received a second letter from Y.L., in which she says:*

*"This morning I received the enclosed reply. Please read
it to Mother. I leave it to you to decide what should be
done now. I have not informed A. ['Sri Aurobindo Study
Center' in Paris]. Your article on 'Sri Aurobindo and the
Earth's Future' is what has won his support...."*

*Malraux agrees to be a member of the Centenary Committee.
His secretary sent the following reply to Y.L.:*

> *Verrières-le-Buisson*
> *March 13, 1972*
>
> *... Monsieur André Malraux is traveling abroad
> and is not expected back before April 15, but he has
> asked me to request you to tell the Mother that he
> is at her entire disposal for anything concerning
> the Committee, and that he considers it an honor.*
>
> *Signed: S.R.*

Oh, that's good!
We will have to speak with A.
It's good. Very good.[1]

*
* *

ADDENDUM

Satprem's letter to André Malraux, seventeen years earlier.

*(In an interview in a Swedish magazine, Malraux had said,
"For the last fifty years, psychology has been reinstating the
demons in man. Such is the real result of psychoanalysis. Faced
as we are with the most frightening threat humanity has ever*

---

1. Unfortunately, nothing came of it. The narrow-mindedness of the Paris "Study Center" discouraged Malraux once and for all. The bridge that Y.L. and Satprem had so painstakingly built since 1955 with Satprem's first letter to Malraux was instantly shattered. Strange how on all sides Mother was surrounded by such a global incomprehension of the deep significance of *the* History, as if all this were merely a parochial story, or even an "ashram" story. For the record, we publish in the *Addendum* Satprem's first letter to Malraux in 1955, along with Malraux's reply.

known, I believe that the task of the next century will be to
reinstate the gods in man.")

August 2, 1955

Dear Mr. Malraux,

Your reply to the questions of a Swedish magazine regarding "whether religions have in fact promoted the conditions of tolerance and understanding among men" happened to fall into my hands just as I have started giving a series of lectures on your works at the "International University Center" of Sri Aurobindo Ashram. This coincidence, along with a long-standing familiarity with your books, prompt me to write you a few words about another testimony, that of Sri Aurobindo, which I am sure you are aware of, but whose work, still incompletely translated in French, remains poorly known in Europe.

I seem to find in Sri Aurobindo's work an answer that meets yours and develops it—for the question is indeed to "reinstate the gods IN man" after having reinstated the demons, as you rightly stated in the Swedish article—but I also find there an answer to the agonizing question constantly raised by your characters from *The Royal Way* to *The Walnut Trees of Altenburg*. Indeed, all of them seek a "deeper notion in man" that will deliver them from death and solitude—this is THE question of the West, to which Sri Aurobindo brings a solution at once dynamic and illuminating. Hence, I am taking the liberty of sending by surface mail one of Sri Aurobindo's books in the original English entitled *The Human Cycle*. I hope it will interest you.

I call on you rather than any other contemporary writer because I think your works embody the very anguish of the West, an anguish I have bitterly experienced all the way to the German concentration camps at the age of twenty, and then in a long and uneasy wandering around the world. Insofar as I have always turned to you, daring and searching with each of your characters what "surpasses" man, I am again turning to you because I have a feeling that, more than anyone else, you can understand Sri Aurobindo's message and perhaps draw a new impetus from it. I am also thinking of a whole generation of young people who expect much from you: more than an ideal of pure heroism, which only opens the doors (as does all self-offering) on another realm of man we have yet to explore, and more than a fascination with death, which also is only a means and not an end, although its brutal nakedness can sometimes open a luminous breach in the bodily prison—where we seem to have been immured alive—and we emerge into a new dimension of our being. For we tend too often to forget that it is "for living" that your heroes think so constantly of death; also I think that the young people I mentioned want the truth of Tchen and Katow, the truth of Hernandez, Perken and Moreno [characters in Malraux's novels] beyond their death.

It may seem strange to speak of you in an Indian Ashram that one would consider far removed from the world and the agonizing problems and struggles of the "Human Condition," but as a matter of fact Sri Aurobindo's Ashram is concerned with this earthly life; it wants to transform it instead of fleeing it as all traditional Indian and Western religions do, forever proclaiming that "His kingdom is not of this world." Knowing that there exists a fundamental reality beyond man, religions have focussed on that other realm to find the key to man just as your heroes focus on their death to discover the fundamental reality that will be able to "stand" in the face of death. But religion has not justified this life, except as a transition toward a Beyond which is supposedly the supreme goal; and your heroes—though so close to life's throbbing heart that at times it seems to explode and reveal its poignant secret—finally plunge into death, as if to free themselves from an Absolute they cannot live in the flesh.

The young Indian students with whom I discuss your books understand perhaps better than Westerners the reason for all those bloody and apparently useless sacrifices—the torments conflicts and revolts of your heroes condemned to death, the great Hunger that drives them beyond themselves—for they know that these are like the contractions of childbirth, and that the thick shell of egoism, routine, conformism, intellectual and sentimental habits must be broken for the inner Divine to transpierce the surface of this life—for the Divine is indeed WITHIN man, and life harbors its own hidden justification. Echoing the Upanishad, Sri Aurobindo tells us that "The earth is His foothold." He also wrote, "God is not only in the still small voice, but in the fire and the whirlwind."

I think I am correctly interpreting the feeling of my young Indian friends when I say that they see the heroes of your novels as "raw mystics," to use Claudel's description of Rimbaud. This may seem a surprising attribute, considering your heroes' atheism, but that is because we have too often confused mysticism

105

or spirituality with religion, as Sri Aurobindo stresses. One need not believe in a personal, extracosmic God to be a mystic. (That is certainly why religion has from time to time taken upon itself to burn alive all the "non-regular" mystics.) Here we touch upon a huge confusion rooted in religions. Through their monks, sannyasins and ascetics, religions have shown us a purely contemplative, austere and lifeless side of mysticism—indeed those mystics, like the religions they practice, live in a negation of life; they go through this "vale of tears" with their eyes exclusively fixed on the Beyond. But true mysticism is not so limited as that, it seeks to transform life, to reveal the Absolute hidden in it; it seeks to establish "the kingdom of God in man," as Sri Aurobindo wrote, "and not the kingdom of a Pope, clergy or sacerdotal class." If the modern world lives in conflict and anguish, if it is torn between "being" and "doing," it is because religion has driven away God from this world, severed him from his creation and flung him back to some distant heaven or empty nirvana, thus denying any possibility of human perfection on this earth and digging an unbridgeable gulf between being and doing, between mystics sunk in their dreams and this world abandoned to the forces of evil, to Satan and all those who consent to "get their hands dirty."

That contradiction is powerfully expressed in your books, it is striking to my Indian students. And they are surprised, for the urge to "do" something at all costs—"to do anything at all, as long as we do something," as one often hears in Europe—without this action being based on a "being" which it expresses and of which it is but the material translation, appears to them a strange attitude. Neither the despair, the silence or the revolt, nor the absurd pointlessness that sometimes surrounds the death of many of your heroes escape them. They feel that your heroes flee from themselves rather than express themselves. This torment between "being" and "doing" can be found in each one of them. They have apparently renounced to "be" something in order to "do" something, as one character stresses in *Hope*, but are they not desperately seeking to "be" through their actions, a "being" that they will capture only as time is abolished, in death? The same obsession seems to run through each of them: from Perken, who wants to "leave his scar on the map," to "outlive himself through twenty tribes," who fights against time as one fights against cancer, to Tchen, who shuts himself in the world of terrorism: "an eternal world where time does not exist," and to Katow, who whispers to himself, "O prisons, where time stops." In that respect, these characters clearly symbolize the impotence of a religion that has not been able to give the earth its meaning and plenitude.

To the question raised by the Swedish magazine and to the one many characters in your books ask themselves, I believe that Sri Aurobindo and his vast synthesis bring the key to a reconciliation and long-sought answer, a reconciliation between being and doing, which religion is incapable of supplying. "Through our Yoga," Sri Aurobindo wrote, "we propose nothing less than to break totally the past and present formations which make up the ordinary mental and material man and create a new centre of vision, a new universe of activities in ourselves, which will form a divine humanity or a superhuman nature." This is not an "idea" but an experience *to be lived*, which Sri Aurobindo has minutely described in his extensive body of works. It is what some thousand men and women from all over the world are trying to do at the Pondicherry Ashram.

In your reply to the Swedish magazine, you emphasize, "The major obstacle to tolerance is not agnosticism but Manichaeism." That is also why religions will never be able to unite humanity, because they have remained Manichaean in their principle, because they are founded on morality, on a sense of good and evil, necessarily varying from one country to the next. Religions will not reconcile men with one another any more than they have reconciled men with themselves, or reconciled their aspiration to "be" with their need for action—and for the same reasons, for in both cases they have dug an abyss between an ideal good, a "being" they have relegated to heaven, and an evil, a "becoming," which reigns supreme in a world where "all is vanity." I would like to quote here a passage from Sri Aurobindo's *Essays on the Gita* which throws a clear light on the problem: "To put away the responsibility for all that seems to us evil or terrible on the shoulders of a semi-omnipotent Devil, or to put it aside as part of Nature, making an unbridgeable opposition between world-nature and God-Nature, as if Nature were independent of God, or to throw the responsibility on man and his sins, as if he had a preponderant voice in the making of this world or could create anything against the will of God, are clumsily comfortable devices in which the religious thought of India has never taken refuge. We have to look courageously in the face of the reality and see that it is God and none else who has made this world in his being and that so he has made it. We have to see that Nature devouring her children, Time eating up the lives of creatures, Death universal and ineluctable and the violence of the Rudra forces in man and Nature are also the supreme Godhead in one of his cosmic figures. We have to see that God the bountiful and prodigal creator, God the helpful, strong and benignant preserver is also God the devourer and destroyer. The torment of the couch of pain and evil on which we are racked is his touch as much as happiness and sweetness and pleasure. It is only when we see with the eye of the complete union and feel this truth in the depths of our being that we can entirely discover behind that mask too the calm and beautiful face of the all-blissful Godhead and in this touch that tests our imperfection the touch of the friend and builder of the spirit in man. The discords of the worlds are God's discords and it is only by accepting and proceeding through them that we can arrive at the greater concords of his supreme harmony."[1] I believe that the characters of your books would not be seeking sacrifice and death so intensely if they did not feel the side of light and joy behind the mask of darkness in which they so passionately lose themselves.

Sri Aurobindo has constantly stressed that, through progressive evolutionary cycles, humanity must go beyond the purely ethical and religious stage, just as it must go beyond the infrarational and rational stage, in order to reach a new "spiritual and suprarational age"—otherwise we will simply remain doomed to the upheavals, conflicts and bloody sacrifices that shake our times, "for living according to a code of morality is always a tragedy," as one of the characters in *Hope* notes.

The tragedies we are experiencing—communism, Nazism—are not rooted, as the Swedish magazine implies, in the weakening or disappearance of religion, it is religion itself which is the source of the disequilibrium insofar as it is fossilized in dogmas, as it clings to a power it possesses in a human cycle drawing to its close, and as it refuses to open itself to a "new deeper notion in man" which would at long last reconcile heaven and earth. As a result, men go elsewhere to seek what religion is unable to provide: in communism or any other "ism," so great and persistent is their thirst for the Absolute—for *that* abides under one name or another and that very thirst is the surest sign of a fullness to come.

---

1. *Essays on the Gita*, XIII.367-368.

At this crucial juncture in human evolution, Sri Aurobindo brings a luminous message to which I hope to draw your attention through this letter and the book I am taking the liberty of sending you. I think the youth of Europe have a profound need to hear a great voice that would bring them face to face with their fundamental truths; none can, better than you, touch that youth and awaken the anguished Occident.

I deeply hope, Sir, that Sri Aurobindo's works will be a new source of inspiration for you.

With my best and most considerate regards,

Bernard E.

* *
* *

(André Malraux's reply)

August 10, 1955

Your letter keenly interested me. I am familiar—relatively of course—with the works of Sri Aurobindo (whom I met by chance a long time ago, without any exchange of words ...), but I did not know the book you are kind enough to send me, and which I look forward to receiving.

I agree—as you have seen—with your main thesis. But the text in question (the reply to a specific inquiry) was limited in its very scope.

Thank you again, and with sincere regards.

André Malraux

March 29, 1972

(That same day, after Malraux, the conversation took a completely different turn, which is why we publish it separately, although under the same date.)

I had a feeling I had something to give you....
Did they give you a *tape-recording*? ... I had said something to
R. and to Sujata.
Is it good?

*Yes, Mother, yes, it was good! We could perhaps publish it? It
was about the vision you had of your own transitional body.*

I simply wanted to make sure you had received it.[1]

*Yes, Mother, it's extremely interesting.... Did you see anything
new since that vision of the new body?*

No. It's something totally new for me—it was the first time and
it seems it's going to be the last.

(silence)

My body has asked for ... (it is in a constant state of aspiration,
you know), it has asked for.... It feels (I don't know how to explain it), it feels the complete Presence of the Divine, I mean in all
things, everywhere, all the time, as if it were at once enveloped
and permeated by it—and it asked for something even more concrete. Then, a kind of Consciousness answered me that the body
wasn't given a more complete perception because it would still
feel like ... (what shall I say?) fusing into the Divine, and then the
cells would ... *(gesture of explosion)*. So the body would lose its
form.

Oh, I see!

Something like that, you understand?
And I felt it was very true. I felt it.
For instance, eating is still a major problem—it's been ages
since I've derived any pleasure from eating, but now it's become a
real problem; well, any cellular contact with the divine Presence
magnifies those things [like refusing food]. I mean all external processes—food and so on—seem then so cumbersome! Without a
doubt the next creation will use something else, another way of
staying alive, but we don't yet know what it is. I have a feeling

---

1. Actually, Satprem was only given the recording with Sujata, not the other one.

there already exists a certain type of food—an intermediary type of food—which is no longer like the old kind but isn't yet ... [the direct absorption of energy], and which has a minimal material basis. But we don't know anything about it, we don't know, nobody knows, we are still inexperienced; we have to find it—but how?

Nobody knows about it; nobody can say do this or do that. I don't know.

The only thing we really know is glucose.

Yes.

That's what they give to people who can't eat normally.

Yes, that's what the doctor told me; he told me to take glucose. I take some, but is that enough in itself?

(silence)

How does glucose enter the bloodstream?

I think it's directly assimilated.

But what does directly mean? You have to swallow it.

Yes, of course, you have to swallow it!

And how....

It goes into the stomach and enters the bloodstream through the intestinal walls.[1]

Oh, that's how! It doesn't go through the kidneys?

Yes, Mother, automatically. After entering the blood, there's elimination through the kidneys.

Ah!

Always, I think.

----
1. Satprem claims no scientific accuracy!

But does the glucose itself change into blood?

No, I think the intestinal walls absorb it and the necessary chemical reactions take place during this absorption through the walls—I think (!)

Oh, that's how it is.

Yes, Mother, at least I think so.

Is there anything else besides glucose that works like that?

In liquid form, yes. There is glucose or very pure fruit juice —which is more or less the same thing.

That's almost all I take: glucose and fruit juice.

But many yogis—at least some—had the capacity to absorb energy directly, Mother, without eating. There are many such stories from the past.

Yes, but I don't know if they're true.

You don't know if they're true?... They are quite common, though, and often cited.

All that Sri Aurobindo told me is that people always eat too much. That was his experience. He went forty days without food, you know.[1] I myself went without food (I don't remember for how long) and felt I was receiving nourishment directly,[2] it simply passed through like this *(gesture through the pores of the skin).*

But couldn't you again use that sort of thing now, through the breathing process?

Yes, but I lost a tremendous amount of weight, you see, which

---

1. Sri Aurobindo is known to have fasted for 10 days while imprisoned at Alipore's jail in 1908-1909, and a second time for 23 days at a stretch, in 1910, soon after his arrival at Pondicherry. Of this second experiment he said later, "I very nearly solved the problem."
2. Mother even told Satprem that when she had once fasted for ten days, she had found the fragrance of flowers to be "nourishing." See *Agenda* VI, November 27, 1965.

112

means that I wasn't getting the proper nourishment, I was feeding on my body.

But I haven't lost too much weight now, have I?... I don't know, I can't see.

Since when?

Since I was supposedly ill.

No, not since then.

No?

No, I don't find you have.

I went foodless for a few days—almost without food.

No, I don't see any change. Although, of course, there is so little left of your body! [Laughter]

I am pretty thin!... I can't see, you know.
But I don't look thinner than usual, do I?

No, you don't, Mother. But getting any thinner would be difficult!

If something new comes, I'll tell you. . . . Is today Wednesday? If something comes, she [Sujata] can come in, just come in, and if there's something new I'll tell her.

Yes, Mother. As a matter of fact, Sujata has been wondering about her visits to you: she is afraid of imposing her presence, of disturbing you.

No, she doesn't disturb me! I'll give her a flower and she can leave, unless I have something to tell her. It's better that way; every day she'll know if there's something to tell you.

Yes, Mother, every day—but she was getting the feeling she was . . . intruding upon you!

No, not at all! It's not that. I am inundated with people so I had

113

to stop, but it was mostly *birthdays*, things like that. But she can come, bring me her flowers, take flowers from me, and if I have something to tell her, I'll tell her, otherwise she'll leave immediately. Is it all right like that?

(Sujata aside:
"My thought is mainly for Mother.")

Sujata says it's all right, but what about you?

For me it's fine. It doesn't tire me.

She's a little.... I don't know, she has something of a heavy heart.[1]

Why?

Well, exactly because of that.

Oh, no! Come here, mon petit! Oh, no, not at all.

(Sujata comes near Mother)

You know ... you see, the consciousness is very clear, clearer than it has ever been, but I can't speak—something has to be found. So I am unable to tell you, but I am always happy to see you. I haven't said anything these last days because "saying" means explaining.... But I am always happy to see you, I have thought of you very, very, VERY, often—you understand?... Do you understand?
You don't seem to understand.

(Sujata:) Yes, Mother, I do.

In any case, one thing you know: I tell the truth. If I say I am happy to see you, it means I am happy to see you. That you understand.

---

1. In fact, Sujata was beginning to come up against the invisible wall put up by Mother's entourage, who thought Mother was seeing too much of Sujata. What is clear through this conversation is that Mother felt the need to remain in daily contact with Satprem. The scene that follows has something so poignant about it, as if Mother already sensed that the connection was going to be severed. This is just a prelude.

Yes, Mother.

What is it, mon petit? You've been hurt, did someone hurt you?

Very hurt, Mother.

Why, mon petit? Did someone tell you something?

No, Mother, I was simply told that you see me far too often, and ... and that you didn't want to see me.[1]

But that's not true! I never said that to anybody.[2]

Well, Mother, each time, I see Sujata's name just crossed off [the list of visitors], so I take it that you don't have time or don't wish to see Sujata. So Sujata simply withdraws.

Who said that?

No one: I am telling you. That's how it happens.

But it's not true!

It is, Mother, that's what happens every time.

It's not true. It's not true that not to see you makes me happy— it's not true. I don't understand. I am not the source of that.

Well, practically, that's what happens. The slightest thing, and Sujata's name is crossed off. So I take it that you don't have time or don't wish or don't like to....

---

1. These were the exact words of the attendant, whose name will come up again. Mother would often ask, "Where is Sujata? Where is Sujata?" and the unvarying reply was, "She's not here." Actually, we understand it now, Mother would have liked Sujata to become her personal assistant after Vasudha, but she knew the importance of Sujata's work with Satprem, so she never asked. Had this been otherwise, the subsequent course of events would have changed.
2. As an illustration we are tempted to publish here a letter Mother wrote to Sujata's father, Prithwi Singh, way back in February 1951. Barely two months after Sri Aurobindo's passing, certain inmates of the Ashram were already showing their true colors: "My dear child," Mother wrote, "I am not aware of having said anything that could give you the slightest pain—so I advise you not to listen to what people say. Most of them take a very great pleasure in disturbing others, and when they have nothing nasty to repeat they invent."

115

But that's not true! It's not true, mon petit! These last few days, I stopped everything because I had to, but again and again I thought it would be good if you were here. Only ... you see my difficulty to speak, so....

Listen to me now—will you do as I say? Come to see me every day. Come to see me every day as before. If I have nothing to say, I'll give you flowers; if there is something I want you to convey to Satprem, I will tell you. But come, just come.

The time will be more or less the same as before. You came after who?

I used to come after R.

Well then, come after R. That's settled: you come every day after R. I even had practical things for you to do: sometimes I rearrange my cupboards and I may have things to give you and explain to you[1]; and I was thinking, "I must see her every day."

If it's all right with you, come every day after R. If I have something to say, I will tell you; if I have nothing to say, I'll give you some flowers. But never, never think that I don't want to see you, it's not true—it's a BIG lie, it's not true. It's a big lie.

You know, you must be sure of one thing: I say things exactly as they are. I may say them poorly, but I say exactly what is true. I can't speak very well nowadays, I find it difficult, but the consciousness is clear. So I am telling you: I want to see you every day. Understood?

Yes, Mother.

Good.

> *(Sujata returns to her place*
> *Satprem comes near Mother)*

That's what it is: I have difficulty speaking, I immediately ... *(Mother gasps for breath).* There's obviously something happening here *(Mother touches her chest).*

But the consciousness is clearer and stronger than EVER before. And I see that people think I am getting senile because I can't

---

1. Mother often called for Sujata for typing and filing her notes, messages, translations, etc., or else for conveying something to Satprem. Apart from typing work, Sujata also looked after Mother's toiletry and perfumery.

speak anymore. But the consciousness is clearer and stronger than ever before.

It's perceptibly stronger. It's quite perceptible.

(after a silence)

The biggest difficulty is this: if only there were someone to tell me what I should take.... Although I must say glucose is what I drink the most easily—so I'll just take more of it.

I think it's the only physical, material means; people who are hospitalized for months at a time take only glucose (usually intravenously). Well Mother, you can be fed that way indefinitely.

Good. It's all right, then.[1]

I'll see you Saturday; and if I have something, I'll tell you through Sujata.

March 30, 1972

(A conversation with R., an American disciple, then with Sujata)

(Mother speaks in English)

Since we have set aside all conventions, immediately everybody

---

1. Mother was never allowed to live her experience. A few days after she left her body, in a speech before the assembled disciples, Pranab, Mother's "bodyguard," ingenuously declared: "According to the advice of Dr. Sanyal, we were to give Her about 20 to 25 ozs. of food every day. It consisted of a little vegetable soup, milk with some protein compound, paste made of almonds, mushrooms, artichokes or things like that and some fruit juice at the end.... All those who were in the courtyard below [Mother's room] must have heard how we had to fight with Her to make Her eat a little." [Original English] This fight over food (to mention only one) created a sharp conflict in Mother's body; she was torn between their suggestions —"If you don't eat, you're going to die"—and the thrust of the Experience.

thinks, "Ah, nice place to fulfil our desires!" And they almost all come with that intention.

And because I made a maternity clinic for the children of those people that I was obliged to send away from the Ashram, so that they could have a place to have their child, people think that the maternity clinic is established for all children born in an illegal way!

I don't care for legality, I don't care for law, I don't care for convention. But what I want is a more divine life, not an animal life.

And they use the liberty for license, for the satisfaction of desires, and all these things that we truly have worked all our life to master, they indulge in—dissipation. I am absolutely disgusted.

We are here to give up all desires and to turn towards the Divine and to become conscious of the Divine.[1] To realize and manifest the Divine in our life is the way, not to become animals, living like cats and dogs.

Sujata enters.

(In French) How I would like to be able to go and tell all of them, right to their faces, that they are wrong, that this is not the way. But I think it's time to put it in writing.

Because I say I am against the old conventions, it means we can live like animals.

But, Mother, your force is extremely active right now, you know.

Yes, I know. I know: when I am like now, I always see the Force—it isn't "my" force, it is the Divine Force. I try—I only try to be like this *(gesture like a channel).* This body tries to be simply ... simply a transmitter, as transparent as possible, as impersonal as possible. So the Divine can do whatever He wants.

(silence)

---

1. Later, Mother added the following: "The Divine we seek is not far away and beyond reach: He lies at the very core of His creation and what He expects from us is to find Him and, through personal transformation, become capable of knowing Him, uniting with Him, and finally manifesting Him consciously. To this we must dedicate ourselves, it is our true raison d'être. And our first step towards this sublime realization is the manifestation of the supramental consciousness."

It has become very transparent. For as soon as something is put before you, the action is done immediately.

(silence)

Yesterday, it was fifty-eight years since I came here for the first time. For fifty-eight years I have been working FOR THAT, for the body to be as transparent and immaterial as possible, so that it doesn't obstruct the descending Force.

Now—now it's the body itself, the body wants this with all its cells. That is its only purpose in life.

To try, to try to create on earth one completely transparent, translucent element that would let the force pass through without any distortion.

(silence)

Au revoir. You'll tell Satprem. Satprem will see what he can do with all this.

April

April 2, 1972

(Sujata's vision the night of April 1)

One Thousand Years

(original English)

We enter the courtyard of a building, Satprem and I. We see sad-faced people. Head bent, solemn and silent. The Mother is dead. Everybody thinks that The Mother is dead.

A few are scattered here and there, individuals or groups of three or four. But most go out from a side door to our left. Another door is to the left at the top of a stairway which mounts from the court-yard below and ends in a sort of bridge or passage. I see one or two

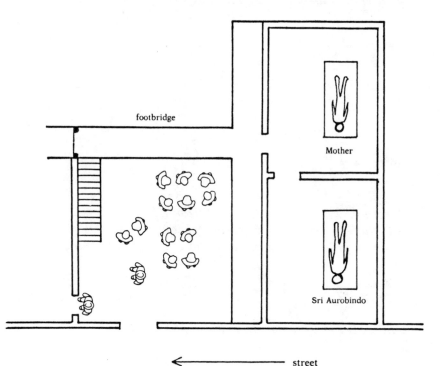

persons going out from this bridge-door. Turning to the right, this passage leads straight to the Mother's room.

We enter Mother's chamber. The Mother is lying on a bed. She is dressed in white satin or silk (the couch also). Four or five people are inside, disconsolate. Slowly they wander out. One or two pass to the adjoining chamber. Finally only Satprem and I remain. He is near the Mother's bed. The Mother sits up and starts talking to Satprem. She is explaining to him about the transformation of the body. She talks for a long time.

I am standing a little away and behind.

Suddenly Sri Aurobindo beckons me from the adjoining chamber which is His. He too is lying on a cot. I draw near Him. He puts two fingers (index and middle) on my right palm, and says, "You have to carry faith and aspiration during one thousand years."

Satprem and I come out from the Mother's chamber and take the passage leading to the left (exit) door to announce to the world that THE MOTHER IS ALIVE.

My dream ends before we have crossed the threshold.

April 2, 1972

(Meeting with Auroville's architect, N. and U.—N. is the Secretary of the Sri Aurobindo Society and U., his rival, the Secretary of Sri Aurobindo's Action. The architect gives Mother a flower.)

What is it?

I think it's "Supramental Clarity" or Vibration.

(Mother speaks in English)

I will tell you that we are preaching unity—unity of humanity—

and we are all quarreling—horrible quarrels, resentments and all sorts of urgings that we condemn in the others. We are giving a nice example, and people laugh! Voilà.

It has come to me from many quarters.

Begin with yourself, they say, and they are right.

Each one, all of you have good reasons, everybody seems to lie. Everybody has "good reasons." You know, the ego is the most clever rogue I have ever met. He takes such nice, nice appearances, and each one says: "I would, but I can't." Voilà. And I tell you, from some places far away and from near, from far and from near, from India and from other countries: Begin with yourself. That is, we are ridiculous—ridiculous. And such good reasons we have!—all the people have good reasons. It is above reason, it has nothing to do with reason, nothing to do with that, we want ... a new creation.

If the Divine had only for one hour the same feelings as men have, there would be no more world. That I can tell you. I have seen clearly—you believe me if you want—I have seen the world with the eye of the Divine. It is something so terrible, you know, so contrary to what it must be, that if the Divine said "only He," brrt! everything would go, there would be no world, there would be no men, there would be only That. Des ego pulvérisés [smashed egos].

It is difficult, it is the most difficult thing—we are here to do difficult things. We are in the period of transition. I can't tell you: be like this or be like that, because there is no example as yet. It is being done, and we are just at the time of the transition. It is very, very difficult—but very interesting.

For centuries and centuries, humanity has waited for this time. It has come. But it is difficult.

I don't simply tell you we are here upon earth to rest and enjoy ourselves, now it is not the time for that. We are here ... to prepare the way for the new creation.

The body has some difficulty, so I can't be active, alas. It is not because I am old—I am not old. I am not old, I am younger than most of you. If I am here inactive, it is because the body has given itself definitely to prepare the transformation. But the consciousness is clear and we are here to work—rest and enjoyment will come afterwards. Let us do our work here.

So I have called you to tell you that. Take what you can, do what you can, my help will be with you. All sincere efforts will be helped to the maximum.

(Here Mother starts talking in French again)

Now is the time to be heroic.

Heroism is not what people say, it is to be completely united—and the divine help will always be with those who have, in all sincerity, resolved to be heroic. Voilà.

You are here now, I mean on earth, because you once chose to be—you don't remember it, but *I* know; that's why you are here. Well, you must stand up to the task. You must make an effort, you must conquer pettiness and limitations, and above all tell the ego: your time is over. We want a race without ego, with the divine consciousness in place of the ego. That's what we want: the divine consciousness, which will enable the race to develop and the superman[1] to be born.

If you think I am here because I am bound, you are wrong. I am not bound. I am here because my body has given itself for the first attempt at transformation. Sri Aurobindo told me so, he told me, "I know of no one who can do it, except you." I said, "All right, I will do it." It's not ... I don't wish anyone to do it in my place, because ... because it's not very pleasant, but I am doing it gladly, because everybody will benefit from the results. I ask only one thing: don't listen to the ego. That's all. The time of the ego is over. We want to go beyond humanity and its ego, to leave it behind, we want a race without ego, with a divine consciousness in place of the ego. There, that's all.

Anything to say?

(silence)

If there is a sincere "yes" in your hearts, you will have satisfied me fully. I don't need words: I need your hearts' sincere adherence. That's all.

(silence)

(To the architect:) Did you follow?

Yes, Mother.

Are you in agreement?

Fully in agreement.

———

1. Mother later corrected "superman" to "supramental being."

(the other two are silent
Mother turns to them and speaks in English)

(To N. and U.:) You and you, you must agree. You are here for
that. You have come to this place at this time for that. We must
give to the world the example of what must be, not petty egoistic
movements, but an aspiration towards the manifestation of Truth.
Voilà.

(silence)

I can assure you that all sincere effort will be *pleinement*, fully
helped by the Divine. Of that I am sure. And I can assure you of
that.

(silence)

That is all I had to say.

April 3, 1972

(Meeting with the American woman disciple)

Things are going fast.

The body must learn not to think of itself. That's the only way.
As soon as it thinks of itself, its condition gets horrible.

But honestly, sincerely, it doesn't think anymore. It is here for a
certain work; the work must be done, and that's all. What will be
will be—it's true, after all, what will be will be, what does it matter to it! ... It says, "Everything is for the best." It can't stay
forever in its present precarious condition; so it must either be
transformed, or else lose its form and come undone. Well ... it
needn't worry about it, just leave it to the Lord to decide—truly
and sincerely.

If it can abdicate to the point of really becoming a transparent
instrument, so much to the good.

It's none of its business—it is incapable of knowing what has to
be done. And it is becoming increasingly incapable PURPOSELY, I

127

know it. So ... let Your will be done, Lord, that alone matters.
Nothing else.

*
* *

Sujata enters

*(What has happened between April 2nd and 3rd that Mother
should suddenly speak in the following terms?)*

Good morning, Mother.

Good morning, mon petit.
Everything's all right? ... Really?

Yes, Mother.

(silence)

I want to tell you something.... I had already explained to
Satprem that if the time for transformation comes, if my body
grows cold, they should not rush to put it in a hole in the ground.
Because it could be ... it could be only temporary. You understand? It could be momentary. They should arrange to keep it
here until it shows signs of complete ... of the beginning of
decomposition. I am telling you this because I want to make sure
it's understood; it would be stupid to put it in a hole and have all
the work stop because of that.
You understand? Do you understand what I mean?

Yes, Mother, your instructions are noted.

You see, make absolutely sure that I have left my body.
I don't know.... I know an attempt is being made to transform
it—it knows it and is very willing—but I don't know if it will be
able to do it.... Do you follow? So for some time it may give the
impression that it's over, although it would be only temporary. It
would start again—it might start again. But then I would be ... I
may be incapable of speaking at that time, of saying this.
So I am saying it to you—Satprem knows. One other person
should also know.

I believe Pranab also knows it.

128

I don't know, I have never said anything to him.

Because we had noted it down, and your instructions are here in the drawer. They've been kept here as "instructions."[1]

I don't know, I have never said anything to him.

(Mother's attendant, speaking in Bengali to Sujata:) He knows.

It seems silly to make a fuss. Better say nothing. It's enough if just a few people know.

It doesn't really preoccupy me, but.... This body is truly very willing, it wants to do its best.... Will it be capable?... Ultimately, if the Lord has decided this one will be transformed, it will be transformed, that's all!

(Laughing) For the time being, it feels very much alive! That much it can say.

And I have nice children to look after me![2]

April 4, 1972

(Meeting with S.S., the third member of the trio of rivals. He reports to Mother that some Aurovilians are rumoured to be "American spies.")

(Mother speaks in English)

Some people say that they are spies and are kept by the American Government, some others (some Americans) tell me that the Americans would never take such incapable spies! So myself I don't see the.... To tell the truth, I don't appreciate them very much, but I have nothing very positive against them. That's all. It's all like that.

---

1. On January 14, 1967, for the first time, Mother had spoken of this possibility of cataleptic trance—five years earlier.
2. This last sentence was intended for those who were all ears and were not supposed to be listening.

I tried my best to push them out, that is to say, that they would
WANT to go. But they ... it didn't happen, they really willed to
remain. If we could have evident proof that they are spies, then it
would be very easy. I would tell them to go. But for so many years
they have been here. It must be proved, it can't be a feeling or an
idea or something like that, there must be a concrete proof. Voilà.

I would like that the Divine's will should manifest very clearly,
in a very positive way. Because human appreciation is worth
nothing. He alone knows the Truth, and it is He who has to decide.
Like that. I don't know if you understand and follow; what I say
may not be clear. But I—you see, to tell the truth, I have no
respect for human appreciation and outlook, and I am absolutely
convinced that only the Divine can see the truth. What I do is to
tell, to show clearly His way so that we will do only what He says,
what He sees. We are not capable of seeing. We will go by the
Divine.

(silence)

Que Ta volonté soit faite [let Your will be done]—WHATEVER it
is. Voilà. That's my position.

(Auroville's architect enters)

*(The architect:) There has been a chain of events which makes
it necessary for me to ask you a question. I have read this question to S.S., because we have spoken together at length, insofar
as we feel that certain decisions must be made to try and
improve the situation in Auroville. But we keep running up
against the same problem, which I have summarized in this
letter:*

> *"Auroville is burdened by a small group of people who
> are contaminating its life and spirit and jeopardizing its
> progress. They thwart any effort to implement safety
> and hygiene measures, working decisions, and they
> behave in contradiction to Auroville's ideal. One solu-
> tion would be to send some of these people back home
> and, for a certain period, to limit newcomers to those
> elements directly useful to the building of Auroville.
> "We see that, in practice, this possibility has not been
> endorsed by you. Is the presence of these elements—*

130

which according to us are undesirable—necessary to Auroville for reasons known to the Divine Consciousness? Are we supposed to build Auroville amidst the difficulties they represent? And are they useful to Auroville's development?"

(*Mother speaks in French*)

In a general and absolute way, difficulties are ALWAYS graces. And due to ... (how can I put it?) human weakness they fail to be helpful. Difficulties are ALWAYS graces. I have been on earth for quite a while this time and always—always, always, always, without a single exception—I have seen in the end that difficulties are nothing but graces. I can neither feel nor see things otherwise because it has been my experience all my life. I might be upset at first and say, "How come, I am full of goodwill, yet difficulties keep piling up...." But afterwards, I could have simply given myself a slap: "Silly you! It's just to bring more perfection to your character and the work!" There.

(*silence*)

Some persons have been driven out of the Ashram into Auroville. Those, I admit, are difficult elements who make things difficult. I wish they would be naturally driven out of Auroville to ... somewhere else. This wouldn't be very nice for the rest of the world—but never mind! Although in a free environment, they may be tolerable. Practically, one would have to speak to each one individually.

Now go on, tell me what you wanted to say.

(The architect:) Well, Mother, I simply wanted to know if we are supposed to accept the presence of these seemingly undesirable people as a necessity for Auroville's growth, and if so, we'll just have to act accordingly and face the difficulties they represent; or should we take definite measures to solve the problems of safety, the problems of hygiene....

What problems of hygiene? What problems of safety?

For example, Mother, it's absolutely useless to give them fire extinguishers, hoses and water if they don't make any effort to

131

learn how to use the fire extinguisher and keep the water hose in proper condition.

Yes, that's plain.

The same for hygiene.

Is there no one who could be given the responsibility for those things?

Yes, Mother, we'll have to manage with what we have.

Yes. Something could be organized with the people we can trust, and if the others are dissatisfied, they can leave. Do you understand what I mean? Instead of taking an active position of "Go away" (which for many reasons is very difficult), if we put them under an authority they don't accept, they will be forced to leave. They will protest at first, but we must remain firm: "This is how it is."
We must find the people capable of doing this, with the required strength of character, and once we find them, they can be given the authority, and if the others don't like it, they'll have to leave! And that's that. But we can't dismiss people who are already there as long as we don't have the person or persons capable of actively assuming that position.

Yes, Mother, it's clear. But there's also the problem of admissions to Auroville.

Oh—well?

For instance, certain elements seem absolutely undesirable to us from the start. And yet these people are sometimes accepted. Is there a reason for this?

On trial. Only on a trial basis, never otherwise.

But, Mother, once they're here on trial, nobody can ever send them away!

Ah, no! If they are not satisfactory, they can be sent away. I was only speaking of those (this is in fact what I was saying to S.S.)

whom I was forced to remove from the Ashram because they were totally undesirable in the Ashram,[1] and they went to Auroville; these people should either go, or else feel ... as I said, feel that they have no place here. But the newcomers, those who are accepted on a trial basis and who turn out to be undesirable, can be sent away. I meant the old-timers, those who have been here for years and years. But the newcomers, all those who have been taken on trial and are not satisfactory, they can leave—they MUST leave. I give you full authority to send them away.

You see, some people come to me—I don't know their names, I don't know what they do, I know nothing about them; the new requests for admission should come to me through one of you two (because you know the practical situation and the people). Unfortunately, many people write to me, and I don't know, you see, I never remember names; I only remember when I know who they are, what they do and so on. But if you know these people's worth and can tell me, "This one is like this or that," I trust what you say; and if you tell me, "That person is undesirable," well, he must go. But I have to be informed beforehand, because people usually go through one person, then another to get their request to me, and I don't keep track, I don't know. Do you see the picture? I give a general answer, and they take it as ... because I think it's somebody else. I don't remember, I forget names—the next minute I have forgotten. My head is full of ... something far vaster than all that, you know. There should be one person—one or two (two is very good)—to present the admissions to me, the new admissions to Auroville, and I fully agree to send back those you find undesirable.

Do you understand?

Yes, Mother. But at present all the requests are presented by S.S. No one else presents requests from newcomers. So things should be simple?

Are you sure about that?

For instance, the other day (I use this example, Mother, because for me it was a real problem), there was a girl who

---

1. In particular one of N.'s nephews. This undesirable person did not hesitate later to lodge a false complaint with the Supreme Court of India to have the recalcitrant Aurovilians expelled from Auroville and his uncle installed as Auroville's legal proprietor.

was on drugs and who had been expelled from Auroville; she asked S.S. to be allowed to come back. And we ...

A girl?

Yes, Mother. S.S. and I were against it, but you said, "She must be given one more chance."

Yes—yes, for one month?[1]

(S.S.:) They have been there for a week now, on trial.

You must give them at least one month. At least one month. But if they show the slightest insincerity, you understand, if they say, "I don't do this, I do that, I won't do this, etc ...", just tell them, "You can leave." You don't even need to ask me, you can just send them away. Simply inform me: such and such person has been found unsatisfactory. I give you the authority to do it. I won't protest. But I must be informed because plenty of people come to me and ... they're very cunning, you see: they find another person to channel their request.

(The architect:) The question in our minds, Mother, was to know whether you saw these people as being useful in providing Auroville with a certain type of difficulty.

No! Certainly not! No, no, I don't favor deliberately adding difficulties! I know they come for.... But they shouldn't be invited—on the contrary. They shouldn't. Things should be made as easy as possible. Only, we shouldn't be ruffled by difficulty, that's the point. I am not at all saying that difficulties should be accepted—don't invite them at all, at all, at all; life is difficult enough as it is! But when a difficulty comes, you must take heart and face it courageously.

We must strive for Order, Harmony, Beauty and ... collective aspiration—all the things which for the moment are not there. We must ... you see, being the organizers, our task is to set the example of what we want others to do. We must rise above personal reactions, be exclusively attuned to the divine Will and be the docile instruments of the divine Will—we must be impersonal, without any personal reaction.

----

1. Mother's memory is not that bad, after all!

We must "be" in all sincerity. What the Divine wants—let it be. That's all. If we can be that, then we are as we ought to be, and THAT is what we must become. For the rest . . . for all the rest, we do the best we can.

I know it's not easy, but we are not here to do easy things; the whole world is there for those who like an easy life. I would like people to feel that coming to Auroville does not mean coming to an easy life—it means coming to a gigantic effort for progress. And those who don't want to keep up with it should leave. That's how things stand. I wish It were so strong—the need for progress, for the divinization of the being, so intense—that those who are unable (unable or unwilling) to adjust to it would leave by themselves: "Oh, this is not what I expected." As it is now, all those who want an easy life and to do what they please as they please, say, "Let's go to Auroville!" It should be just the opposite. People should know that coming to Auroville means an almost superhuman effort for progress.

It is the sincerity of our attitude and effort which makes a difference. People should feel that insincerity and falsehood have no place here—they just don't work, you can't fool people who have devoted their entire life to go beyond humanity.

There is only one way to be convincing—it is to BE that.

Then we'll stand strong, we'll have all the divine force on our side.

We are here to prepare a superhumanity, not to fall back into desires and easy life—no. ,

People must feel it; it should be so strong that the sheer force of our sincerity would drive them out—that's what they have to feel. At that point, we will be what we should be. The power of the realization—of the sincerity of the realization—is such that it's UNBEARABLE to those who are insincere.

(silence)

That's all.

Yes, Mother.

(silence)

If in all sincerity we are on the side of the Divine, we ARE all we should be.

That's what Sri Aurobindo always said. If men only knew this: if in all sincerity—in all sincerity—they give themselves to the Divine and side with the Divine, they become all they should be.

It may take time, there may be turmoil and difficulty—you must be ... inflexible: "I am for the Divine and the divine manifestation, in spite of everything and anything." Voilà. Then it is omnipotence —EVEN OVER DEATH.

I am not saying tomorrow, I am not saying immediately, but ... it's a certainty.

April 5, 1972

(The first part of this conversation concerns the translators of "Notes on the Way." One of them wants to give up the work.)

It's the ego demanding that things be done without forgetting its due respect—*(laughing)* Mister Ego wants to continue enjoying all due respect!... It complains shrilly before departing.

Oh, I have seen such fascinating things, mon petit! For hours I was a spectator—the consciousness witnessed an encounter between the Ego and the superman's consciousness ... *(laughing)* it was like a duel! The ego was arguing so glibly! It seemed to be saying, "See, if you send me off, the world will become hellish!" And it was showing the most frightful scenes: "If I withdraw from this one," it said, "this is what he will do; if I withdraw from that, this is what will happen...." *(Mother laughs)* Horrible things, you know, the most staggering catastrophes!... It went on for hours.

At night I don't sleep, you know; I remain very still, and I am then a spectator of all those scenes.

Told in detail, they would be very interesting.... Later, perhaps?

The Characters in the Play

The following conversation makes it necessary to explain the physical conditions Mother was living in. Alas, at the time I was still half-blind to these conditions, for Mother had wrapped me in such a cocoon of light that I could not really see what was happening—she knew my impetuous nature, she knew I would never have tolerated the situation in her room nor people's petty intrigues had I known what was really happening there. But gradually I did become aware of certain things.

Unknowingly, I was a witness to a tragedy.

But "tragedy" is afterwards, when it's too late. At the time, there are only people coming and going, with their everyday gestures, their empty words and simmering little desires, no worse or better than anybody else, and who don't really know what they are doing or where they are going. And yet the tragedy is already sealed in this little gesture, that careless action, those few fleeting words. Was the Trojan War not taking place "every day"? Did Alexander not die on "one fine day"? Destiny seizes upon a few beings and abruptly crystallizes a great moment in History, but the players are neither "cruel" nor "gentle"—they are much like everyday people, but with only a tiny distinction in their hearts. Each player plays his part, in black or white, for an unfathomable goal where everything is reconciled.

But in the meantime....

Mother's immediate entourage was then composed of: Pranab, her "bodyguard," a former boxer, a violent and arrogant man whose flagrant flaws were the reverse side of a Love he never accepted, because it would have meant surrendering himself. "A for-mi-dable pride," Mother once told me.[1] He trusted nothing except his biceps and was frustrated in his dreams of "superman" without any tangible physiological realization. In his own way, he was perfectly devoted, as a sportsman who knows he has lost the game he had hoped to win but sportingly plays on till the end. He treated Mother like a brute and talked to her like a brute, but he served her brutishly, sparing no pains, although with a growing impatience. He served Mother for more than twenty-five years. Pranab had an instinctive aversion toward me, as he had toward

---

1. See *Agenda VIII*, August 2, 1967.

*Pavitra (whom he badly mistreated), and in general toward any-
thing that exceeded his primitive intellect—Pranab could only love
what he was able to dominate. He was also openly xenophobic: the
"sahibs," as he would say, forgetting, or maybe not, that Mother,
too, was a "foreigner." There were never any exchanges between
Pranab and myself, we lived in completely different worlds and the
work of one did not infringe upon that of the other. He only showed
his annoyance and contempt for me when, entering Mother's room
ponderously, he would find her in contemplation, holding my
hands—perhaps he was eager for a Love that eluded him. I never
spoke a word to him. He never said anything to me.*

*The second person in Mother's entourage was her physician, Dr.
Sanyal. A completely devoted, clear and uncalculating man but
with a total lack of faith, except in his medicine and medical
methods. He lived for some twenty years with Mother with
no understanding of what she was doing, sowing her body-
consciousness with his doubts and medical impossibilities. Mother
has referred to him on several occasions in this Agenda.*

*The third person was Mother's helper, Champaklal, who had also
been Sri Aurobindo's attendant. A pure-hearted man, simple and
utterly devoted. There is nothing to say about him, except my
respect. He had come from his Gujarati village straight to the
Ashram, some fifty years earlier, at the age of eighteen. There was
nothing between his village and Sri Aurobindo. He understood
nothing of what was happening—he simply served and did as he
was bidden.*

*The fourth and last person was Mother's new attendant. She is
going to appear in the following conversation. I was particularly
blind about her because she was young and affectionate—but she
was completely under Pranab's thumb and ruled by her passions. I
had, of course, noticed that she was listening in on my conversations with Mother, thus subtly clouding the atmosphere, invisibly
breaking in upon Mother's free expression; for, needless to say,
Mother sensed all that went on in the atmosphere. How many times
did she stop in the middle of a sentence, invisibly interrupted: "I
can't speak"—that was not just because she was short of breath.
Hence, the atmosphere of our conversations was no longer what it
had been for the last fifteen years, until 1970. But in addition, we
were responsible for a new and sad turn of events. We knew that
Mother frequently spoke about Auroville, or with one disciple or
another, and we regretted the loss of those words—to us each of
her words seemed to have so much importance for the world, even*

if we were not yet fully able to understand all that she was saying. So with her approval, we managed to obtain a small, easy-to-operate cassette recorder. It had been agreed with Mother that her attendant would record all the important conversations in Mother's room, then pass them on to me to be added to the Agenda. At first, I noticed that the attendant was keeping the tapes, but an innate shyness kept me from saying anything lest I appear to "monopolize" things or seem pushing, and also I didn't know exactly whose instructions she was obeying. Then, gradually, the attendant stopped giving me the recordings altogether, even those of Mother with Sujata. At that point, the situation in Mother's room was so fragile that I didn't want to say anything, for fear of sparking an outburst that would have ultimately bounced on Mother. I was already feeling also the invisible barrier against Sujata, whose name was systematically crossed off the list of visitors under one pretext or another, along with those of the few young women who were the Ashram's positive—and silent—elements. And how could we possibly argue when Sujata was told, "Mother cannot see you ... Mother is sick ..."? Once, Sujata mentioned it to Mother, but when the same incident occurred three, four, ten times, there was nothing to be said. Without knowing why, I too was feeling my own meetings with Mother threatened and precarious. In fact, we were alone, facing an obscure league of opposition. Why the opposition? There is no answer—except human pettiness, which does not understand and hates everything that exceeds it. Even Mother's own son was jealous of my place near her, not to mention the others, the "liars" pure and simple, as Mother used to call them, who were, and still are, directing the Ashram. Finally, much later, I discovered that the notorious cassette recorder, whose recordings I was no longer even receiving, was clandestinely used to record my own conversations with Mother—on whose behalf?

That was the end. The atmosphere had become so rotten that, obviously, it could not last much longer—Mother was suffocating there. I later discovered in my own body and from direct experience that all bad thoughts are agonizing to the body, they create a sort of oppression as if you were short of air. Yet, even when they closed Mother's door on me, a year and a month later almost to the day, on May 19, 1973, I COULD NOT believe it was the end. I was convinced that this was the last stage, that Mother was finally going to shake off the old slavery to food: the last tie to the old physiology. But, as we now know, her "bodyguard" would not let her. In his speech on December 4, 1973, he declared, "In the beginning [from May 20], She refused to take any food or drink, but somehow we persuaded Her to take them."[1] She did fight as much as she could, and then.... At times, I seemed to hear her faltering little voice up there: "Where is Satprem? Where is Satprem?..." and then silence. Had I attempted to force the barrier, this Agenda would never have seen the light of day. In a way, the following conversation is therefore prophetic.

Such was Mother's immediate entourage: a devoted but uncomprehending helper, a doctor with no faith, a violent and despotic bodyguard, and a blind and blinded little being controlled by her passions and by Pranab.

Henceforth, we will let the facts speak for themselves.

*
* *

(After a silence, Mother resumes the conversation.)

The body has been weakened by the transformation, the doctor says it is showing signs of weakness.

What is true is that it feels a kind of tension whenever it has to exert too great an effort. But I think that will pass. I am convinced—as I have already told you—that if I reach one hundred, at one hundred I will be strong.

But what about the other day, Mother, when you told Sujata again about the possibility of your body becoming apparently lifeless, "dead," as they say ...

Yes.

... as part of the process of transformation. And if this were to occur, we should make sure not to put you into the hole....

Yes.

But why?... Did the thought occur again that you may have to....

---

1. We would like to know how they "persuaded" her. I cannot help thinking of the vision I had eleven years earlier (*Agenda II*, February 11, 1961), in which Mother had "died" because she had eaten "a grain of rice."

Yes.... I don't know. At any rate, I would like someone to prevent such a stupid thing, because then all the work would be ruined.

Yes, of course. But people like K. will be there [Satprem turns toward the bathroom door and gestures to Mother's attendant to come closer].

Yes.

People like K. will be near you.

Yes, mon petit, but K. is a young girl, she does not have any authority.

Of course, she does, Mother! [K. laughs]

(Sujata:) As a matter of fact, Mother, we don't have any authority either.

People with some authority should be there and say *(Mother speaks forcefully):* YOU MUST NOT DO THIS—Mother DOES NOT WANT.

(Satprem:) Yes, Mother, but I see only K. or Sujata near you who could say that—I mean, what can the others possibly say?

Yes, and what about you?

Me? What say do I have? Who will listen to me? They'll say I'm crazy—they won't even let me enter your room!¹

(Mother laughs with a sort of surprise)

It's true, they won't allow me to enter your room. But people who are here, like K. or Sujata, WITH THEIR FAITH, they can do something—or Pranab. But Pranab, only you can....

But Pranab ... Pranab will think I am dead!

Yes, that's so.

---

1. On May 19, 1973, six months before Mother left, Pranab closed Mother's door on Satprem, and on everyone else as well, including Sujata.

Exactly.

Yes.... Yes, Pranab doesn't believe, he doesn't have faith.

(Mother nods)

Personally, I think that only the faith of people like—well, yes, "little girls" like K. or Sujata can have authority with their faith. That's all I can think of. They will have to be there.

(Mother nods approvingly,
Sujata remains silent till the end)

Possible, but not certain it will happen [the deep trance]. Sometimes, when I see all these things, I am.... My difficulty of speech is caused by that weakness, you see; I have trouble expressing myself; all of a sudden, I feel ... I feel a sort of ... I don't know, I can't say fatigue or exhaustion but ... as though life were literally drained out of me—and yet the consciousness is more ALIVE, stronger than ever!

Suddenly, the body doesn't know if it will be able to go through it—that's what happens.

So, for this reason, appearances may be very deceptive.

(Satprem, aside to K.:) But couldn't someone like Champaklal understand that?

(K.:) I don't think so.

The big difficulty is the government, you see: a bunch of dimwits who know nothing outside of their rules and regulations.

(Satprem:) No, no, Mother, I can assure you that....

(K:) No, no!

(Satprem:) In any event, as long as we're alive, we will do everything we can to safeguard you....

Yes.

For sure.

Mon petit. . . .

(silence)

No, I really don't think anything will happen, Mother.

(K:) I don't either.

(Satprem:) I don't think anything will happen. If you must remain for a given number of days in a state of apparent samadhi, well, you will be protected and everything will be all right, that's all.

(Mother nods approvingly)

All that's needed is ONE person with real faith.

Yes, YES, exactly. Exactly so. Yes.

Well, there are at least three of them right here with real faith!

(Mother laughs) Yes.

Even four! [Vasudha, Mother's former assistant, has just entered the room.¹]

(The clock chimes
Mother takes Satprem's hands
she looks reassured
long silence)

So, K. has recorded a lot of things—did she give them to you?

This morning?

---

1. Stricken with cancer, Vasudha could no longer serve Mother actively but came and saw her every day for a few moments. Her exit was a real tragedy. Had she been there, nothing would have happened—she knew and she understood. For so many years she had discreetly kept watch not only over Mother but also over the privacy and secrecy of our conversations with Mother, making sure that no one disturbed us and above all encroached on the time Mother gave us. I can never express enough gratitude to her—and my infinite regret. There was *someone* in that pack who understood and that someone was taken away from Mother—why?

(K.:) Not today—yesterday.

(Satprem:) Yesterday, yes, Mother. I haven't yet looked at them.

I no longer speak with the force I used to have, because speaking is difficult. What I say doesn't have the power it used to have.

But there's power behind it!

Yes, the consciousness is stronger than it has ever been.

Exactly!... No, I really find that the power is still there, behind.... True, you don't speak like an orator!...

That's right! Far from it!
Well, my children, there. We'll do what we can, we'll do as best as we can.

Yes, and we'll look after you well and ... WE WON'T LET YOU DOWN.

Good. Well, all right, then! *(Mother laughs)*
Au revoir, mon petit.

(to Sujata, very tenderly)

Mon petit....

*
* *

Postscript

"We won't let you down...." How these words still ring with an agonizing question mark, eight years later! What could we possibly do? A scandal? Useless—it would only have unleashed the pack before we had time to get this Agenda to safety. Here are the facts, as reported in English by Pranab himself in a public speech, on December 4, 1973:

"I arrived at about five past seven [in Mother's room, the evening of November 17] and saw that Dr. Sanyal was already there examining

144

Her. Dyumanbhai [the disciple who brought Mother her meals] also had come. I went and felt the Mother's pulse. It was still there, beating at long intervals. There was still some respiration. But slowly everything stopped. The doctor gave an external heart massage to Her. It had no effect. Then he declared that the Mother had left Her body. This was at 7:25 p.m. Then, being present and feeling my responsibility, I thought what I should do. At that time there were present André [Mother's son], Champaklalji [the helper], Dr. Sanyal, Dyumanbhai, Kumud [the attendant] and myself. I talked with André and told him that I wanted to wait for some time and then take the Mother's body down, place it in the Meditation Hall for people to see. We would keep the body in such a way that it was not disturbed, then we would decide what to do. André agreed to my proposal. He wanted to remain with us but as he was not well I suggested that he should go home and take rest and come the next day. He left. We remained there and discussed what to do.

Now we thought that if people immediately came to know about the Mother's passing there would be a big rush, and the crowd would all clamor to see Her. There would be noise and shouts and a tremendous confusion. So we thought of keeping the event secret for some time. Also Dr. Sanyal said that we must not disturb the body in any way for several hours. So the Mother was left as She was and after 11 o'clock, when the gate of the Ashram was closed, we cleaned Her body with eau de cologne, put a nice dress on Her, arranged everything and then Dyumanbhai and I went down and called Nolinida. Nolinida came up, saw everything, and asked what we were going to do. I mentioned my plans to him. He said the Mother had once told him that if it looked to us that She had left her body we should not be in a hurry, but see that Her body was properly kept, and then wait. I said, "We are just about to do the same. We have cleaned Her, otherwise ants and insects would have come. We have put on Her a new dress and we shall carry Her quietly, carefully downstairs and lay Her in the Meditation Hall. After some time we shall call people." He agreed to our proposal.... At about 2 o'clock [in the morning] we brought the Mother's body down, placed Her on the bed, arranged everything. Then I went out, called Mona, told him to come and see me with four other boys, five of my lieutenants, so to say. When they came I explained to them what to do: to call the photographers first, then to call the [Ashram] trustees, then all those who were very close to Her.... From 3 o'clock the people who had been called started coming. While we were upstairs, we prepared some kind of statement that could go to the Press and to All India Radio so that no wrong information might go out.... Our draft of the statement we got corrected by Nirodda and gave it to Udar to circulate. At 4:15 in the morning we opened the gate of the Ashram for people to come in and have a last Darshan...."

Thus, SIX HOURS AND THIRTY-FIVE MINUTES after Mother's so-called death, they brought her downstairs, they removed her body from the peace and protection of her atmosphere . . . and then they threw her to thousands of avidly curious visitors amidst glaring neon lights and droning fans, just EIGHT HOURS AND FIFTY MINUTES after her heartbeat stopped.

What universal complicity bound all these people together, who ALL fully knew that Mother's body was to be left in peace in her room, who ALL were fully aware of Mother's "instructions"?

Had they wanted to get rid of her, they could not have rushed any faster.

Pranab himself brazenly declared in his speech:

"One thing She repeated to me often quite some time back, and to some other persons also. She said that all the work She was doing on Her body could be spoilt in two ways—one, this force She was pulling down on Her could be so strong, so great, that the body would not be able to tolerate it and the body might fail.[1] That was a possibility. The second thing was that if ever She went into a deep trance and it looked to us that She had left Her body, then if by mistake we put Her in the Samadhi [tomb], that would absolutely spoil Her work. And She gave instructions that we should give the body the necessary protection, we should watch, and only when we would be absolutely sure that She had left Her body we should put Her in the Samadhi. I think we have done as She had wanted."

True, they did all that was necessary "to be absolutely sure." Removing her from her room was in effect condemning her to a sure death.

Naturally, no one ever informed us of anything. We were not among those "close" to Mother. It is Sujata's brother, Abhay Singh —himself alerted by the public rumor, who sent word to us. We arrived at the Ashram around six in the morning, stunned, to find thousands of people in line, waiting their turn—it had been six months since we had last seen Mother. Less than five minutes later, Nolini called me to translate the press release into French as well as his own "message"—they all had a "message" ready. He handed me a piece of paper. I could not believe my eyes. I read like an automaton:

---

1. Which was not the case, since in Pranab's own words, "It [Mother's passing] looked to me as if a candle was slowly extinguishing."

"The Mother's body belonged to the old creation. It was not meant to be the New Body.[1] It was meant to be the pedestal of the New Body. It served its purpose well. The New Body will come.... The revival of the body would have meant revival of the old troubles in the body. The body troubles were eliminated so far as could be done being in the body—farther was not possible. For a new mutation, new procedure was needed. 'Death' was the first stage in that process."

I read once again, in speechless outrage: "The Mother's body belonged to the old creation. It was not meant to be the New Body...." I looked at all those people staring at me in Nolini's room. A terrible silence fell. And then I said NO. "I will NOT translate that." They looked at me as if I had gone mad. I left.

The battery of droning fans, the huge crowd, the glaring lights reflected on the zinc ceiling. Her little white figure, which seemed to be absorbed in a powerful, almost fierce concentration. Scream? Scream what? To WHOM? Could my screams bring her back to her room? Were they going to cancel their messages and prepared statements? There was no one to listen. They had arranged every-thing to perfection. There was not a single dissenting voice. The collusion was total.

April 6, 1972

(Mother sees Sujata)

I don't want to speak anymore.
Yesterday, I told Satprem what I had to say.

(silence)

---

1. This last sentence ("It was not meant to be the New Body") was later deleted for the official version of the message, probably in part because of Satprem's reaction.

Some people come and deluge me with their problems; others come and say nothing; in both cases, I am silent. I don't care what they say, even that I've become stupid, I don't care in the least.

Oh, no!... People who can say such things are only showing their own colors.

Yes. That's their own business, I have nothing to do with it.
Up above, in the consciousness, *I am with those who are there.*
And that's that.

> *(Mother clasps Sujata's hands and sits gazing)*

Yes, this is good, this is good.
You know I am with you! Do you know that?
Tell Satprem too I am ALWAYS with him.
There, mon petit.

(Then Sujata relates the dream she had on Sunday in which she and Satprem saw Sri Aurobindo and Mother in a room at the end of a footbridge. The dream had to do with the physical transformation of Sri Aurobindo and Mother. While Mother was talking to Satprem, Sri Aurobindo called Sujata and, placing two fingers in the palm of her right hand, said, "You will have to carry faith and aspiration during one thousand years." After listening to Sujata, Mother remains silent. Sujata tries to comment on her dream:)

The thousand years are over.... And now the transformation is accomplished.

Yes, that's it, mon petit. Good, mon petit. Good. Now there remains only to transform ourselves! *(Laughter)*

April 8, 1972

Perhaps you remember that in January, Msgr. R. wrote to you, and you concentrated on him for a long time; then you asked me to write him and ask "if he had been conscious of something."[1] I have received his reply: one letter addressed to me and another to you. Here's what he writes to me (his answer was delayed because of Cardinal Tisserant's death):

"My brother,
  ... Actually, on the 29th of January (between five and six o'clock), Mother paid me a visit. An inner visit, but to me it was beyond a shadow of doubt. She told me so many things ... in so short a time.

I think I am now ready to break with an entire past that has brought me nothing but deception, illusion and trickery...."

And this is what he writes to you:

"Since that unforgettable 29th of January (between five and six o'clock), I have been constantly living with you. I have never felt your presence so strongly. Not a bodily presence next to mine, but a spiritual presence made of affection and love.

I have heard and understood your message.

Yes, I know, I must change the direction of my life. The time has come. Soon nothing will keep me from doing it ... not even pseudo-duty to this one or that one.

I would like, I want to work with you to pursue an ideal—an ideal that fills my whole being with enthusiasm.

Everything I have so painstakingly created is collapsing.... I am left with a feeling of having worked and suffered in vain and for nothing.

And so I turn to you in total trust.

The death of Cardinal Tisserant, who for twenty-one years was a peerless father to me, has plunged me into

---

1. See conversation of January 29.

*total disarray.... I feel like an orphan.... It is thus
with all my earnestness that I say to you: Mother, help
me to live again."*

*(Mother remains concentrated for a
very long time)*

It's a beautiful letter.

(silence)

Is he French?

Yes, Mother.

What day is it today? And what time is it there?

*Today is Saturday. It's about five o'clock in the morning
there.... Do you have a message for him?*

Tell him (words are so restrictive) that when I heard his letter, I
saw—I saw and felt—the marvelous action of the divine Grace.
There was a sort of ... flood of Grace concentrated on him, and it
stayed there, on him—it is there, concentrated on him *(embracing
gesture).*
It is very concrete—very concrete and very powerful: a concen-
tration.
As if the Grace were concentrated on an instrument of the
Divine, of the divine Power—an instrument.
For me, you see, there was constantly: May Your Will be done,
Lord, may Your Will be done, Lord.... As if he were chosen as an
instrument, as one of the instruments. May Your Will be done,
Lord ... with a great force of concentration.

(Mother plunges in)

*
* *

*(Mother then listens to several texts from Sri Aurobindo for
the message of April 24. Sujata suggests the following passage
from Savitri, which Mother immediately accepts:)*

He comes unseen into our darker parts
And, curtained by the darkness, does his work,
A subtle and all-knowing guest and guide,

Till they too feel the need and will to change.
All here must learn to obey a higher law,
Our body's cells must hold the Immortal's flame.

Savitri, I.III.35

That's excellent.

April 12, 1972

*(Mother shows Satprem a card with her photo and the following
text in English printed on it:)*

No human will can finally prevail against the
Divine's will.

Let us put ourselves deliberately and
exclusively on the side of the Divine
and the victory is ultimately certain.

The Mother

Strange how human nature resists that. Ordinary human nature
is such that it prefers defeat on its own terms to victory in another
way. I am making amazing discoveries these days—just amazing.
Human stupidity is abysmal. Abysmal.

It's as if the Force I mentioned before[1] wanted to go like this
(gesture like a power drill), deeper and deeper into the subconscient.

There are incredible things in the subconscient—incredible. I
spend entire nights watching them. And it goes down and down
and down . . . IMPERATIVELY.

So the human subconscient cries out, "Oh, not yet, please, not

---

1. The descent of February 21 (the "frightening pressure to compel the necessary
progress"). See conversation of March 8.

yet—not so fast!" And that's what you are up against. A general subconscient.

Naturally, the resistance brings about catastrophes, and then people say, "See! See your beneficient action, it is only causing catastrophes." Unbelievable, they are unbelievably stupid.

I see it in myself; never have I felt the resistance of the lower nature in such a....

Yes, oh yes! It has increased tremendously.

Yes, tremendously. One wonders how it will end, and at times one gets really worried.

No, you shouldn't. You simply ... keep clinging to the Divine. For, of course, the resistance has such wonderful reasoning! "You see," it says, "You see where all this is leading you, you see...." Oh, it's ... it's more than a resistance; it is PERVERSE.

Yes.

A perversity.

Yes, Mother, quite so. I can see that. I clearly see that it really is a perversity.

Yes, a perversity.

But I don't know what to do. Nothing seems able to subdue it. I don't know what to do.

Well, the only way is.... If you can avoid listening, it's better, but if you do listen, the only reply is: "I don't care what you say, I don't care"—constantly. "You'll become stupid"—I don't care. "You'll spoil all your work"—I don't care.... To all those perverse arguments the same reply: I don't care.

If you can experience that it's the Divine that does everything, then with an unshakable faith, you say, "All your arguments are worthless; the joy of being with the Divine, conscious of the Divine, surpasses everything"—it surpasses the creation, surpasses life, surpasses happiness and success, it surpasses everything *(Mother raises one finger):* THAT.

152

That's all. Then all is well. And it's over.

It's as if That drove all the worst things in nature out into bright daylight, out into the open, into contact with that Force ...

Yes!

... so as to have done with them.

Besides, it seems to attack what was good-willed in us.

After some time it becomes absolutely wonderful, but one goes through some difficult moments.

Yes. Yes, there are times when you wonder if everything isn't going to be swept away.

(Mother laughs) That's absurd! Absurd. What's going to be swept away is the resistance.

But. . . .

(Mother plunges in, smiles)

More and more I feel there's but one way.... (Laughing) It makes an amusing picture: to sit on the mind—just sit on the mind: shut up. That's the only way.

You sit on the mind (Mother gives a little slap): shut up.

(silence)

The subconscient contains the memory of all the *previous* "pralayas,"[1] and this memory is what always gives us the impression that everything is going to dissolve, to collapse.

But if you look at things in the true light, there can only be a more beautiful manifestation! Théon had told me this was the seventh and last one. Sri Aurobindo (I had told him what Théon said), Sri Aurobindo concurred, for he said, "This one will see the transformation towards the Supermind." But to reach the Supermind, the mind must SHUT UP! And I always get the impression (laughing) of a child sitting on the mind's head (gesture like a child kicking its feet), playing on the mind's head! If I could still draw, it would make something really funny. The mind—that huge terrestrial mind (Mother puffs out her cheeks)—which thinks itself so

---

1. *Pralaya:* the end of a world, apocalypse.

important and indispensable, and then a child sitting on its head and playing! It's so funny.

Ah, mon petit, we don't have faith! The moment one has faith....

We say, "We want a divine life"—but we're afraid of it! The second the fear disappears and we are sincere ... really, everything changes.

We say, "We want nothing more of this life," but ... *(laughing)* something in us clings to it!

Yes!

It's so ridiculous.

We cling to our old ideas, our old ... to this old world bound for extinction—we're afraid!

While the divine child sitting on the mind's head plays! ... I wish I could draw that picture, it's so wonderful.

We are so silly we even say *(Mother puts on an air of offended dignity)*: the Divine is wrong, "You shouldn't handle things that way!" It's comical, mon petit.

(silence)

The best remedy (I mean the easiest) for me, is: what You will —what You will, in all sincerity. In all sincerity. And then—then understanding comes. Then you understand. But you don't understand mentally, not here *(Mother touches her head)*.

What You will.

(silence)

So I can see the resistance in people, I see (they don't say anything, but they think it; I see it in the mental atmosphere like this—*gesture all around)*: the twaddle of an old woman!

That's the situation.

Oh! ...

154

April 13, 1972

(Conversation with Sujata. From now on, none of the recordings made in Mother's room by her attendant will be communicated to Satprem. What follows was noted down from memory by Sujata. She first reads to Mother a letter from one of the schoolchildren; Sujata was trying to build a bridge between Mother and the mass of anonymous people who truly loved her but had no access to her.)

Sweet Mother,

It seems that you no longer see everyone on their birthdays. Is it because of a lack of time or for some occult reason? People say that seeing too many people every day tires you, but if such is the reason, twenty people coming to receive your Blessings on their birthdays take perhaps less time together than one person who sees you every day! Besides, it is the only day—once a year—when we can see you to receive your Blessings and be near you. Of course, no one wants to disturb you, and I certainly don't.

But I was curious to know the reason for this new arrangement. I hope I am not being impertinent to write this way to you.

Signed: V.

(Sujata:) ... They need to see you, they need your help, it's a difficult period for everyone.

My help is there for all those who need it—it's the ego that prevents people from receiving it. Does V. understand the difference between the ego and the psychic being? ... Ego is the obstruction. Ego was necessary to shape humanity, but we are now preparing the way for a superhumanity, a supra-humanity. The job of the ego is over—it did its job well, now it must disappear. And it is the psychic being, the Divine's representative in man, that will stay on and pass into the next species. So we must learn to gather all our being around the psychic. Those who wish to pass to the supra-humanity must get rid of the ego and concentrate themselves around the psychic being.

But does he know the difference between the ego and the psychic? Because the ego is very artful—a rogue!...

April 15, 1972

(Mother had some cardiac trouble the day before.)

So?... Do you have something?

What about you? [Laughter]

Me ... *(laughing)* it's all right. It's one difficult thing after another. Yesterday was what I call the "change of government" for the heart, so ... it's a difficult moment. But now it's all right.

The other day, when I saw that little child playing (I still see it), on top of a HUGE mental head, kicking it—it's the supramental. But what are we going to call that being?... We mustn't call it "superman," it isn't the superman: it's the supramental. Because, you see, the transition from animal to man is clear to us; the transition from man to supramental being is accomplished (or isn't) through the superman—there may be a few supermen (there are) who will actually make that transition, but that's not actually how it works. First, that supramental being has to be born.[1]

Now it's becoming plainer and plainer. The other day, I saw that little being (symbolically a child) sitting on a big mental head: it was the supramental being sitting, to symbolize its "independence," I could say, over the mind.

Things are becoming clearer. But we are just in the transitional period, the most difficult time.

Will some reach a similar state—at least similar or at any rate precursor to the supramental?... Such seems to be the present attempt, what is taking place now. And so you are no longer on

---

1. By mistake, Mother said "overmental being," which is probably what prompted Satprem to ask the next question.

this side, not yet on the other—you are ... *(gesture in suspense)*. Rather a precarious condition.

Evidently, all those who are born now and are here now have asked to participate in this, they have prepared for it in previous lives. From the standpoint of global knowledge, it would be interesting to know what's happening and how it's happening. But from the individual standpoint, it's not exactly pleasant (!), the period is difficult: you are no longer on this side, not yet on the other—just in between. There we stand.

Indeed, for passing into the supramental being it isn't necessary to pass though the overmind.

I don't understand.

I mean that for contacting or reaching this SUPRA-mental consciousness or being, it is not necessary to pass through the overmental being.

What do you call "overmental being"?

What Sri Aurobindo calls "overmind."

Oh, no! No.

I see. Not necessary.

What Sri Aurobindo called overmind is the realm of the gods.

So it isn't necessary to pass through that.

Oh, no, the realm of the gods ... stands apart. I don't think it has much to do with the earth's problems. Only sometimes those gods enjoy meddling in earthly affairs. But they don't have much in common with the great Movement of transformation.

Yes, quite so.

They are immortal, aren't they, they are free (to a large extent, they are free and immortal). They have taken part in the earth's development only out of curiosity, as a sort of pastime!

Yes.

They may have helped humanity to understand that there is something beyond earth-life.

That was their usefulness.

At one time *(laughing)*, I was very close to all these beings, they used to manifest in me, they would—well, they enjoyed it! And I enjoyed it, too! I was interested; but I never considered it as something essential.

So, in other words, the new being you saw is the supramental baby!

(Laughing) Yes! But I think this "baby" is a baby only symbolically.... I don't know if he will come as a child and then grow up—I have no idea. There are still some things that I don't know—plenty!

But what happened the day before yesterday is that, in the middle of the night, the heart passed from the old government of Nature to the divine government, so at one point there was ... it was difficult. But accompanied by a ... strange sensation, a sort of feeling that ... the closest thing is the psychic consciousness. It has been governing the being for a long, long time—that's why the mind and the vital could be removed, because the psychic being had taken up the reins long, long ago.

As a matter of fact, I wanted to tell you (I don't know if I did[1]): the first time I went to Tlemcen (I don't remember the year), the first day I arrived at Tlemcen, Théon came to meet me and said ... (I didn't understand then, but now I do!), he said, "You are now alone with me, aren't you afraid?" And I replied (I was absolutely conscious and calm).... I remember we were walking in his huge estate, we were walking up towards the house, and I told him *(Mother raises her index finger)*, "My psychic being governs me—I am afraid of nothing." Well ... *(gesture of Théon starting as if he had been burned).*

I acquired that psychic consciousness just before leaving for Tlemcen. And it grew stronger there.

I don't know if this has been noted down somewhere....

Yes, you did tell me once.[2]

---

1. A few days earlier, apropos a biographical datum, Satprem had asked Mother in exactly which year she had experienced the full government by the psychic being. Mother had replied: in 1907, at Tlemcen. Mother's first visit to Tlemcen actually took place in July 1906.
2. See *Agenda II*, February 4, 1961.

Oh, I told you about that conversation?

Yes, Mother, you told me about it.

It struck me, I never forgot it. All at once, my psychic being was there: "I am conscious of my psychic being, it protects me, I fear nothing...." Those may not have been the exact words, I don't know, but that was the general reply.

(long silence)

You have something?

I sense a change in me.

Ah! What?

I don't know. Last time you spoke of the "resistance" [of the subconscient] and that very evening I felt something like "a light of grace."

Yes.

And then I felt lighter.

Aah! Yes....

And now I have the feeling—I don't know if it's an illusion, but I really have the impression that something has changed, as if ... the Grace came and untied a knot in me.

Yes.

I feel something has changed.

It's true. It is true, but I wasn't sure you were fully conscious of it.

Oh, I was! I felt ... but I'm always afraid of deluding myself, you know.

No—no, that's the mind in you, mon petit, give it a tap on the head!

159

I tangibly felt that . . . the Grace had DONE *it.*

Yes, that's right. Only the Grace can do that.

Yes, Mother, yes!

This is exactly the meaning of my vision: the transition won't take place according to mind's ways, it's a baby sitting on the mind and playing. I can still see it.

Yes, I experienced strongly how it's really the Grace that accomplishes everything.

Yes, yes.

All we can do is . . . call the grace, and that's all.

Yes, call, be receptive—eager for an answer.

I felt that very strongly, yesterday. I was going through a difficult moment—pain in the body, with irregular heartbeat (alternately starting and stopping), painful—when, just at that instant, the being simply . . . *(Mother opens her hands):* "What You will, Lord, what You will." Within a few hours everything was back in order. How was it done? I don't know. Only this *(Mother opens her hands).*

And for everything, everything, all problems, do like this *(Mother opens her hands):* what You will, Lord, what You will. . . .

I know—I say "will," but it's neither a vision nor the will of the Divine, it's . . . His way of being. A particular way of being—successive ways of being. We always think of a "conscious will," but it isn't like that: it's His way of being. The way of being of His consciousness. He has projected His consciousness into a creation: it's His way of being. And it's His way of being that changes.

Then, one understands that the mind isn't necessary—it's the way of being that changes. You follow?

(meditation)

April 19, 1972

And what about your "change" [of government]?

It's going on!

(silence)

The conscious will seems to want to assume a larger role. It makes life ... much more efficient, obviously, but also more difficult.

More difficult in what way?

Well, usually we passively leave it up to Nature to set things right when something goes wrong—that's totally disappearing. Now it is a process of consciousness, and no longer.... You see, the mind *(laughing:* it's going on—the supramental is still sitting on it!), the mind has been worked upon for years, so that it doesn't meddle when it's none of its business and lets Nature take care of all the damage; but now Nature is being told, "Keep quiet, a higher Consciousness will settle things." But that means the consciousness must be CONSTANTLY alert.
Constantly alert.
The consciousness' own attitude towards the Divine is to be as if nestling in the Divine—I could even say engulfed in the Divine: what You will, what You will, what You will, what You will.... As a "basic" attitude it's very good, I could say. But when suddenly, something in the body goes wrong, and you don't know why (oh, most of the time it's due to an outside cause, like a disorder coming from outside), so then you don't know what to do—there is no longer a mind to decide what to do; while the consciousness remains like this *(hands open upwards).* But then you don't know what to do, so you do nothing.
There is certainly something to be learned.

But if the consciousness is turned upward, doesn't the Intervention or the Action take place automatically?

Probably.

It must.

That's my constant experience. But....
How are things for you?

I don't know. Better, I think.

Yes. Do you want me to see?

> *(Mother holds Satprem's hands,*
> *and closes her eyes)*

Much better.

> *(Mother plunges in until the end,*
> *smiling and holding Satprem's hands)*

April 22, 1972

(Mother silently hands some flowers to Satprem. Then she looks ... at what? She seems quite tired. Satprem informs her that he is moving to his new house at "Nandanam," on the outskirts of Pondicherry. Mother goes off ... somewhere, for forty minutes.)

April 26, 1972

> *(Mother hands Satprem a letter:)*

This is what I sent to Indira. You can read it to me, I don't even remember what I put.

"India shall take her true place in the world
only when she will become integrally
the messenger of the Divine Life."[1]

What was the occasion?

She wrote me a very nice letter to express her gratitude, and she asked if I had something to tell her, so that's what I replied.

It seems she speaks in earnest about India's spiritual mission.

She's worried about America. She wants to send people to America to try to create a harmonious atmosphere.

We shall see.

But isn't the danger rather from the Chinese side?

I don't think so.

I have always seen material help coming from the United States —always. But that President,[2] who is a brute, stands in the way. There won't be a new President until November. Something should be done in the country to block him (because he's a candidate), so that he doesn't get reelected.

He's virtually the favorite.

Over there people don't like him.

Yes, but he has the backing of Big Business.

Yes, quite so.

He MUSTN'T be reelected, and there's no point in seeing him either [Indira's overtures]. He mustn't. It MUST NOT happen.[3]

The consciousness must support, help, enlighten and strengthen all those who don't want him.

(silence)

And how are things for you?

---

1. Original English.
2. Nixon.
3. Watergate began two months later, on June 17. But Nixon was triumphantly reelected in November.

... What shall I say? Physically it is still difficult, but the body has understood, I think *(Mother opens her hands)*. The body has understood, but there are still some old habits, some semiconscious reactions. That's what pulls. To me, you see, if the body had truly understood, it should become younger—not "younger" but conscious. Instead of founding its base in the subconscient as everybody else, it should found it in the consciousness—it is beginning to do it. It wants to; it wants, it strives. But there are still some ... sort of habits. All in all, it's the subconscient that should be transformed.

Almost no spontaneous reactions remain of the kind that come from the subconscient—almost none, but still a few ... still far too many.

How was the balcony?[1] Where were you?

I didn't come.

Oh, you didn't come.

No, Mother, I didn't come. Sujata was there.

(Sujata:) It was very good, Mother.

I wasn't too stooped?

No, Mother, you looked better than the last few times.

Ah! It was better.

Yes, Mother, better.

I tried.

You also walked much more, and you stayed for a long time.

Where were you?

As usual, Mother, in my house, downstairs.

Ah, there; yes, I went that side [with inner eyes].

Yes, Mother!

---

1. During the Darshan of April 24.

The body is more conscious—the consciousness is penetrating. But....

I have a strong feeling (I mean the body), the body has a strong feeling that if I can last until one hundred it will become younger. Not younger, but ... more capable of manifesting the Force. I don't feel weak, but some things still drag.

The subconscient is full of stupid fears, of lack of trust and ill suggestions (although I am not so sure it's the body's fault, I have the feeling that some people—at least one person, I don't know who—are sending catastrophic suggestions[1]). The body fights all it can to accept only the suggestions from the Divine, but there's still a pull.

Whenever I protest or complain, I am "told" (that's how it comes), I am told that things come to me from here or there ... *(gesture to the four corners)* for me to act upon them, for That to act upon the world—it has nothing to do with thought, it isn't a thought, this *(the head)* is very silent; it's here *(gesture above)*, and then like this *(gesture rising from the bottom to be offered)*, from the subconscient. And all the work that is being done is not just for this body; the body is doing it for all those who are receptive. In which case I have nothing to say, everything is perfectly all right. If such is the case.... Because *(Mother turns her head toward the bathroom door)* the body lives in particularly good conditions. It is very well taken care of.

(silence)

How is it over there?[2]

(Satprem:) I have to get used to it.... I find it very difficult to reconcile the inner consciousness with material life. Material life is a dreadful burden to me: all material things are so heavy, so leaden.... I find it very difficult. I can't seem to reconcile the two.

Oh! ... Did you go to the performance of *The Gold Washer*?[3]

Yes, Mother.

---

1. This is the second or third time this year that Mother mentions this to Satprem (see conversation of February 23: the "formation of death").
2. The new house at "Nandanam."
3. Some Aurovilians (who have since left Auroville) had staged parts of Satprem's novel.

Was it good?

Hmm ... sort of. They did it with a lot of love and—with lots of love. But their interpretation of it was.... I don't know, it seemed a bit sinister.

Sinister?

Yes. I don't know, they showed me an aspect I didn't recognize.

(Mother laughs) Well, well! That's funny.

You see, in that book, I was trying to create light out of pain; and, well, there's only pain in what they staged, not too much light.[1] They made it into something very melodramatic, you know.

Oh! ...

Nevertheless, the atmosphere is good, a surprisingly good atmosphere. But strange: something I didn't recognize.

(Mother remains silent, gazing)

Strange. I liked the book very much when I read it, but the only image that remains now is a primeval forest with a huge tree and you struggling to blaze your way through the tree—that's what I see all the time *(Mother looks again)*. Why? ... That's it, that's what stayed in the consciousness. I can still see you with an axe, hacking off huge branches to open up a passage. Strange. Is it symbolic? Do you mention that scene in your book?

Not exactly, but I lived something like that[2]—it's both true and symbolic at the same time.

---

1. I must admit I left in the middle, I couldn't stay till the end.
2. Strangely enough, although I did not mention the scene in the book, it had remained deeply etched in me, and that's what Mother remembered: she remembered my own memories! One day, I had found myself in the midst of a huge tangle of fallen trees (when a giant tree falls, it uproots dozens of trees all around it), within a kind of green cataclysm redolent of torn earth and destruction, and in a silence of the end of the world.

166

Strange, when I think of that book, that's the image I see. I also remember ... you described the death of your friend?

Yes.

That struck me very much. That and the huge tree. But the tree is larger than life, it's symbolic; and with a big axe you are hacking off branches—huge branches, as big as trees—to open up a passage. Strange.

Well, I guess I'm still hacking away at branches!

(Mother laughs) Yes, exactly! That's right.

Material life is.... I don't know why, perhaps it comes from past lives, but I find it unbearable.

Oh! ... In what way is it unbearable? Do you have particular difficulties?

No, nothing, small difficulties, nothing to speak of, but everything is a burden. I can't seem to infuse any consciousness into this material life, you know; there's a sort of gulf between the two. I feel well only when I stop everything and sit. Then everything is fine.

Ahh!

But as soon as I touch material things ... it's awful. There's no bridge between the inner life and Matter—none AT ALL, a complete chasm.

(after a silence)

From what Nirod is now reading me from his correspondence with Sri Aurobindo, it seems to have been the same with Sri Aurobindo. From what he writes (you'll see when you read it), everything is always done by me. He says, "Mother says, Mother does, Mother...." I mean, for anything involving the Ashram organization—contact with people and so on—it seems to be done quite naturally and all the time through me.

But what a humor! Oh, you know, I've never read anything so marvelous! ... He had such a way of looking at things ... it's extraordinary. Extraordinary. But it would seem that the external world was something . . . absurd to him, you know.

Yes, exactly.

Absurd.

Absurd. Yes. I've reached the point where the only material life I could tolerate would be that of a sannyasin in a hut—and even then, a naked sannyasin, because even clothes are a nuisance!

Ohh!

You see, everything seems dreadfully. . . . I just can't infuse any consciousness there.

(*Mother continues smiling*)

Oh, it's so interesting. So interesting. Since childhood, I have always endeavored, as it were, to attain total indifference—nothing is annoying, nothing is pleasant. Since childhood, I recall a consciousness striving for . . . (that's what Sri Aurobindo meant) for indifference. Interesting! It makes me understand why he said that it was I who could attempt the transition between human consciousness and supramental consciousness. He said that. He said it to me and he says it here (it's written among Nirod's things). Now I understand why. . . .
Ah, I understand!

(*silence*)

Yes, I understand.
Well?

The farther I go, the worse I feel I'm getting.

Oh, no! Not at all!

But I feel I'm downright awful!

(*Mother laughs cheerfully*) That, mon petit, may be my. . . . My body is exactly in that condition! (*Laughing*) Maybe that's why!

168

What's more, it feels awful and ridiculous. Ridiculous and awful. It's the first effect of the consciousness of what has to be, it exerts a pressure. Even higher humanity is an awful and ridiculous thing for the overmind *(Mother corrects herself)*, for the supramental ("supramental" is a word I don't like too much; I understand why Sri Aurobindo used it, he didn't want "superman"—it's not superman at all). There is a far greater difference between a supramental being and a human being than between a human being and a chimpanzee.

Oh, yes!

But the difference is not so much external: it's a difference of consciousness. I can sense it, I sense it so vividly, and so close! When I am very still, it comes, from over there, and even the highest and most intellectual human consciousness is ridiculous in comparison.

Yes.

Awful.

Yes, Mother. I don't know if I am in contact with "that," but when I remain still I sense something so full, so strong....

Yes, yes, that's it.

I am at ease.

Yes.

You feel that's IT. But then when you leave it to go back into Matter, it's terrible....

(Mother laughs)

Because "that" doesn't permeate here....

It does permeate, but.... To be exact, we can say that it permeates with difficulty, but it does permeate. That's what causes the impression that life is awful. Personally, I feel that life is downright ridiculous—grotesque. Grotesque.

(silence)

169

One must be thoroughly convinced of it before one can expect to receive that Consciousness. You know what I would say? It's a good sign—it's not pleasant, but it's a good sign.

But, of course, at best—at the very best—we are transitional beings. And well, transitional beings.... But the consciousness of the inner being ultimately gets stronger, you follow? Stronger even than the consciousness of the material being. So the material being can be dissolved, but the inner consciousness remains stronger. It is of that consciousness that we can say, "This is me."

Yes.

There you are. THAT is the important thing.

The important thing.

As for me, the purpose of this body is now simply: the Command and the Will of the Lord, so I can do as much groundwork as possible. But it isn't the Goal at all. You see, we don't know, we don't have the slightest knowledge of what the supramental life is. Therefore we don't know if this *(Mother pinches the skin of her hand)* can change enough to adapt or not—and to tell the truth, I am not worried about it, it's not a problem that preoccupies me too much; the problem I am preoccupied with is building that supramental consciousness so IT becomes the being. It's that consciousness which must become the being. That's what's important. As for the rest, we'll see (it's the same as worrying over a change of clothing). But it must truly be IT, you see. And in order to do that, all the consciousness contained in these cells must aggregate, form and organize itself into an independent conscious entity— the consciousness in the cells must aggregate and form into a conscious entity capable of being conscious of Matter as well as conscious of the Supramental. That's the thing. That's what is being done. How far will we be able to go? I don't know.

You understand?

Yes, Mother, I understand very well.

How far we'll go, I don't know. I feel that if I last up to my hundredth birthday, that is, another six years, much will be accomplished—much. Something significant and decisive will be accomplished. I am not saying that the body will be able to get transformed ... I have no such signs, but the consciousness—the physical, material consciousness becoming ... "supramentalized."

That's it, that's the work now in progress. And that's what's important. You too, you must be able, you must be destined to do that also, hence your disgust. But instead of dwelling on the disgust, you should dwell on the identification with the consciousness you are in when you are sitting still. You follow? That's the important part.

That's the important part.

*(Satprem rests his forehead on
Mother's knees. Sujata approaches)*

I am beginning to understand why Sri Aurobindo always said it was woman *(Mother caresses Sujata's cheek with her finger)* that could build a bridge between the two. I am beginning to understand. One day, I'll explain. I am beginning to understand. Sri Aurobindo used to say: it is woman that can build a bridge between the old world and the supramental world. Now I understand.

(Satprem:) Yes, I understand too.

Then it's all right. We must have patience.

*(Mother presses her index finger against
Sujata's chest:)*

Will you remember what I said?

April 29, 1972

How are you?

I don't know, so-so.

Nothing particular?

No, Mother, nothing particular. And you?

(silence
Mother sits gazing)

You are more conscious of what has to be demolished than of what is being built.

Yes, it's true—yes, I am very conscious of that.

Yes, of what must be demolished, but it's more interesting to be conscious of what's being built.

But, Mother, when at every step you're made to face all sorts of things that aren't very ... that you want to get rid of.

But that's down there *(gesture to the ground).* You must look above.

(silence)

But is it getting built in spite of all the resistance?

Fortunately! Fortunately—because those who ought to be helping aren't helping. Thank God it's happening in spite of everything!

(silence)

It's like asking me whether the divine Consciousness is stronger than the obscure little consciousness of humans.

(Mother plunges in)

May

May 4, 1972

(Mother sees Sujata)

Strange feeling.... Since last night, a strange impression that the Divine has become ... (how to formulate it?) like a golden Force pressing down like this *(gesture of pressure on the earth).* They alone, who by their aspiration are able to pass through to the Divine Origin, will escape catastrophes.

There was a catastrophe in Madras: one of our best cars was in a very serious accident.

Only those who have an aspiration, a sincere and *unconditional* aspiration towards the Divine, only they will escape—they will stand in a golden glory.

Extremely interesting.[1]

May 6, 1972

(Mother sits "looking")

What do you see?

(silence)

I think I already told you, there's a kind of golden Force pressing down *(gesture);* it has no material substantiality, and yet it feels terribly heavy....

Yes, yes.

... It presses down on Matter, to force it, to compel it to turn INWARDLY to the Divine—not an external flight *(pointing above)*

---

1. Noted from memory.

but inwardly turning to the Divine. And the apparent outcome seems to be inevitable catastrophes. But along with this sense of inevitable catastrophe, there come solutions to situations or events that look simply miraculous.

As if both extremes were becoming more extreme: the good getting better and the bad worse. Like that. And a stupendous Power PRESSING down on the world. Such is my impression.

Yes, it's very perceptible.

Yes, it's as tangible as this *(Mother feels the air between her fingers).* And even in life circumstances, many things otherwise indifferent are becoming suddenly acute—acute situations, acute differences, acute ill wills—and at the same time, singular miracles. Singular. People on the verge of death are saved, inextricable situations are suddenly untangled.

And the same for individuals too.

Those who know how to turn to ... (how shall I put it?) who SINCERELY call upon the Divine, who feel it's the only salvation, the only way out, and who sincerely offer themselves, then ... *(gesture of bursting open)* within a few minutes, it becomes a wonder—for the least little thing: there's no big or small, important or unimportant, it's all the same.

The whole scale of values changes.

The vision of the world is as though changed.

(silence)

This gives an idea of the change brought about in the world by the supramental Descent. Things that were insignificant are becoming quite categorical: a small mistake becomes categorical in its consequences while a little sincerity, a true little aspiration becomes miraculous in its results. The values are intensified in people. Even materially, the least little error has huge consequences, while the slightest sincerity of aspiration has extraordinary results.

The values are intensified, they stand out more.

Mother, you speak of mistake, of error—I don't know, maybe it's a fallacy, but I have a stronger and stronger notion that mistakes, errors are unreal. It doesn't work that way. They're only a means, as it were. Yes, a means of broadening the scope of our aspiration.

Yes, that's perfectly correct.

They cause pain—mistakes, errors are basically pain, which is the means of awakening some aspiration in the deeper recesses of our being.

Yes, quite true. The overall perception is that everything is ... everything is meant to lead to the conscious ascent of the world. It is consciousness evolving towards divinity. And perfectly true at that: what we perceive as mistakes stems entirely from an ordinary human conception—wholly and entirely.

The only mistake—if it exists at all—is in not wanting something else. But when you start wanting something else....

Well, that's not a mistake, it's plain stupid!

Yes, exactly, stupid. But it seems to me, the moment you want something else, each error or mistake—everything—serves a purpose.

Yes, yes. Perfectly so. Really, it's very simple: the whole creation must want nothing but the Divine, want nothing but to manifest the Divine; all its actions (including its so-called mistakes) are a means to make it inevitable for the whole creation to manifest the Divine—but not a "Divine" as man usually conceives of, with all kinds of limitations and restrictions: a TOTALITY of tremendous power and light.

Truly the Power is IN the world, a new and stupendous Power which has come into the world to manifest the divine Almightiness and make it "manifestable," so to say.

Through careful observation and attention, I have come to this conclusion: I have seen that what we call the "Supramental," for lack of a better word, is actually making the creation more susceptive to the higher Power, which we call "divine" because we ... (it is divine compared to what we are, but ...). It's something *(gesture of descent and pressure)* that will make Matter more susceptive and *responsive* to the Force. How can I explain it? ... At present, whatever is invisible or imperceptible is unreal to us (I mean to human beings in general); we say that some things are "concrete" and others are not. But this Power, this Might, which is NOT MATERIAL, is becoming more concretely effective on earth than earthly material things. That's it.

177

And that is how the supramental beings will protect and defend themselves. In its appearance it won't be material but OVER MATTER its power will be greater than material things. Day by day, hour by hour this is getting truer and truer. The feeling that when this Force is guided by what we call the "Divine," it has POWER, a real power—the power to move Matter, you understand; it can cause a MATERIAL accident, or save you from a wholly material accident, it can cancel the consequences of an absolutely material event—it is stronger than Matter. This is the totally new and incomprehensible fact. But it ... *(fluttering gesture in the atmosphere)*, it creates a sort of panic in the ordinary human consciousness.

That's it. It seems that ... things are no longer what they were. There's really something new—things are NO LONGER what they were.

All our common sense, our human logic, our practical sense— collapsed, finished! No longer effective. No longer realistic. They are no longer relevant.

A new world, really.

(silence)

And in the body, whatever has trouble adjusting to this new Power creates difficulties, disorders and illnesses. Yet in a flash you sense that if you were totally receptive, you would become formidable. That's the sensation. That's more and more my sensation: that if the entire consciousness, the entire most material consciousness—the most material—were receptive to this new Power ... one would become for-mi-dable.

(Mother closes her eyes)

But there is one essential condition: the ego's reign must come to an end. The ego is now the obstacle. The ego must be replaced by the divine consciousness—what personally I call divine consciousness. Sri Aurobindo called it "supramental," so we can call it supramental to avoid confusion, because as soon as you say "Divine," people start thinking of a "God," and that spoils everything. It isn't like that. Not like that, it is the descent of the supramental world *(Mother slowly lowers her fists)*, which is not mere imagination *(pointing above)*: it is an ABSOLUTELY material Power. But *(smilingly)* with no need for any material means.

A world is trying to be born into this world.

(silence)

On several occasions, my body felt a sort of new discomfort, an anxiety; and something, not exactly a voice but it became words in my consciousness, said, "Why are you afraid? This is the new consciousness." It happened several times. Then I understood.

(silence)

You see, what in terms of human common sense says, "This is impossible, it's never been before," that's what is finished. This idiocy is over. It's become a stupidity. Now we could say: it's possible BECAUSE it has never been before. This is the new world and this is the new consciousness and this is the new Power; it is possible, and it is, and will be more and more manifest BECAUSE it is the new world, because it has never been before.

It will be because it has never been before.

(silence)

It's lovely: it will be because it has never been before—BECAUSE it has never been.

(Mother looks up as if about to say something, then goes into meditation)

It is active—in you too.
Not material and yet more concrete than Matter!

Yes, almost crushing.

Crushing, yes, just so.... Oh, it's....
Whatever isn't receptive feels crushed, but all that is receptive on the contrary feels a sort of ... extraordinary expansion.

Yes. But that's what's so odd, there's both!

Yes, both together.

You feel so expanded, as if everything in you would blow up, but at the same time there's a sensation of being crushed.

Yes, but what feels crushed is what resists, what is unreceptive. One has only to open oneself. Then it becomes like a ... a for-mi-dable thing. Fabulous! It's our centuries-old habits that

179

resist and give us that feeling, you know, but whatever can open up.... You feel as if you were becoming larger and larger and larger.... Magnificent. Oh, that's it!...

May 7, 1972

(Mother sees Sujata)

The Force I spoke of yesterday is more and more active *(gesture pressing down)*.
The Action is becoming imperative.
Crushing.

May 13, 1972

(The subject here is the conversation of last April 2 with Auroville's architect, N. and U., when Mother was trying to bring some harmony among the three. The recording of the conversation, which was never returned to Satprem, started circulating in the Ashram in all kinds of distorted transcriptions. Satprem's initiative in giving the tape, which was intended to preserve the authenticity of Mother's words, was diverted for a typical Ashram purpose: gossip and one-upmanship, each party using Mother's words to outdo the other. Nor do we know what happened to all the other similar recordings....)

Did they give you that text?... It was corrected a little. Did you see it? Is it all right?

Yes, Mother, certainly! Is it for the "Auroville Gazette"?

There's a complete confusion.... Don't ask me *(Mother turns towards the bathroom).*

Yes, yes, Mother.

But I thought of one thing that would be good for the *Bulletin.*

Oh, yes, Mother, that's something else. We kept it, and it will be published in the next Bulletin. Yes, it's done.

What was it? I don't remember.

It's when you say, "You are here now on earth because you once chose to—you don't remember it, but I know; that is why you are here...."

Yes, I feel such people are found EVERYWHERE on earth. That was the idea: that some people reading this suddenly feel it's their destiny.

(silence)

Nothing to ask?

The other day you spoke of that golden Pressure becoming stronger and stronger ...

Yes, yes.

... perhaps bringing a possibility of catastrophes, you said. Are you thinking of a collective danger?

America is doing horrible things. They have mined Haiphong.[1] Nobody had ever dared do that so far.

Yes, there's a strong impression that that whole abscess should burst open—that nest of wickedness should burst.

---

1. Mother actually said Hong Kong, but she was certainly talking of Haiphong and the resumption of American bombings over North Vietnam, followed by the blockade ordered by President Nixon.

(after a silence)

But how to put it into words?... There are also things that were miraculous in the past and will no longer be so—both possibilities. Both are there together.

I don't know if it's just because of this transition period, or if the Supramental will in fact bring about very categorical effects....

The same for the body: the least thing seems to produce consequences completely out of proportion—in either good or bad. The customary "neutrality" of life is disappearing.

(silence)

For the individual being *(Mother)*, it's peculiar how both extremes coexist: the individual feels like a complete cipher ... a thing with no strength, no force, no power of decision of any kind, but at the same time *(Mother slowly lowers her fist)*, through that individuality such a TREMENDOUS Action is taking place! And totally unexpected, you know. Both collective and individual actions, which seem absolutely miraculous because they are like this *(same gesture)*—all-powerful. And the two extremes are there AT THE SAME TIME.

I've never had such a feeling of ... nothingness—nothingness. Nothing. I am nothing anymore. But at the same time, there's the vision, the perception of an absolutely irresistible Force *(Mother lowers her fist)*. It's as if the individual had to be nonexistent first in order to become a real instrument.

Yes, I too often have that feeling of complete void.

Yes, void. Complete void. But then, at the same time (almost the same time, sometimes even exactly at the same time), you perceive a Power acting so formidably through that void! And on a collective scale, you know: winning victories, destroying certain things —fabulous! Fabulous.

(silence)

And the same for the body. It's as if every minute the body could die, and every minute it's miraculously saved. It is ... incredible. Incredible.

And with a constant perception of world events, as if everything, but everything were *(Mother intertwines the fingers of her hands)* ... as if interlinked—a link.... One could say: one single Will manifesting in innumerable actions.

(Mother plunges in,
palms open)

May 17, 1972

How are you?

How about you? You haven't been well lately?

It's strange, luckily—luckily—one thing happens after another, one after another, but every single bodily function is changing ... (what's the right word?), I have it, "changing government." Functions that worked naturally—that is, in accord with the laws of Nature—all of a sudden, brrm, finished! They stop. Then ... something ... which I call the Divine—perhaps Sri Aurobindo called it the Supramental, I don't know; it's something like that, something that is plainly concerned with Matter, with this Manifestation, and which is tomorrow's realization (I don't know how to name it); so when everything is thoroughly upset and I feel really awful, then "That" consents to intervene.
The transition isn't pleasant. That's all.

(Mother gives some flowers to Sujata)

Here, mon petit.
Along with sharp pains, and ... impossible to take any food, etc. etc.
Evidently someone had to do it. When Sri Aurobindo left, he told me that I alone could do it. I said all right.... So, I don't do it out of ambition—I just accepted, that's all.
Possibly it's due to the stupidity of my body that I suffer the way I do. If it were more receptive and more ... *(Mother opens*

183

her hands), yes, more receptive, there would be less friction. I can see, I see clearly that pain, conflict, incapacity are all a product of our own stupidity. There's no doubt about it. We have only ourselves to blame. Every time—EVERY single time and in whatever circumstances—every time we take the right attitude, that is, when we are like this *(Mother opens her hands)*: let Your Will be done—honestly, sincerely, integrally—everything is fine.

Therefore it's entirely our fault, we can only blame ourselves. And our complaints are childish—oh, personally I don't complain but . . . abruptly I can't do anything anymore.

There.

And what about you, what do you have to say?

Nothing, Mother.

Nothing happened to you? . . . I was hoping it would have helped you at least a little!

Nothing happened?

No.

Well, never mind.

Still too mental.

(silence)

So if you like, we can go into silence. Don't you have anything to ask? No news?

You said "still too mental," do you mean . . .?

It means that instead of receiving directly, you see, without thinking, thoughts come in and disturb the process—they limit the receptivity and disturb. That's the point. I see it in myself, you know; I've had to struggle so hard with this, in order to. . . . The need to understand things, the need to find explanations is simply a return to the old habitual movements. We must consent to be imbecile—for as long as necessary. Personally, as soon as I consent to be imbecile . . . beatitude. But the old habits return.

The foremost realization for man is understanding—understanding things. For the Supermind, realization means Power *(Mother stretches out her arms in a sovereign gesture)*, the creative willpower.

184

But naturally, it would be quite disastrous if human intellectual capacities, mental capacities, were to gain control of that power —it would be terrifying! It would cause terrible havoc. Hence the need to consent in all humility to become imbecile before being able to acquire it.

(silence)

But I must tell you that you were all the time in my consciousness —and there are only very few (Mother counts on her fingers), perhaps two or three. Otherwise, ohh, they are far, far away.... You were continually present, that's why I was hoping you would feel a change. You were all the time in my consciousness.

I saw you last night.

Ahh! You see! Then?

Then I don't know, I looked at you and.... How to put it into words? At first I was a little afraid, then I don't know, it all melted and I lost consciousness in a kind of deep sleep. And I had a feeling you were smiling.

(Mother smiles) But that's very good! What you call your consciousness is your intellectual consciousness.

Afterwards I had great difficulty coming out of that so-called sleep. I had to exert a great effort to come out of it.

But why did you want to come out of it!

I suppose it was time to wake up.

(Mother laughs) It doesn't matter.

(Mother goes into contemplation
till the end and opens her eyes
just as the clock strikes eleven)

What's the time?

Eleven o'clock, Mother.

185

So you see, when I went in, I told myself: I will come out of the meditation (not "meditation," but anyway . . .), I'll speak at eleven o'clock! *(laughter)* That's why I asked you the time. Interesting!

When you become simple, you know, like a child . . . all goes well.

But you mustn't be afraid. Neither afraid of falling ill, nor of becoming imbecile, nor even . . . of dying—you must be like this *(vast and quiet gesture, like the sea)*.

If we could only have (I have it from time to time, it comes: it's on its way) a feeling of smiling trust. But to get that the consciousness must be as vast as the creation itself. You are as vast as the creation, and totally trusting. . . . Ultimately, it always boils down to this (which can be put in a very childlike manner): He knows better than we what has to be done.

There.

He knows better than we what has to be done.

That's my own method. I find it the easiest; there may be other methods (I am sure there are), but for me it's the easiest. Whenever something is apprehensive or balks: "He knows better than you what's necessary." That's all.

(Holding Satprem's hands) If we could smile, it would be so much easier.

(Satprem rests his forehead on Mother's knees)

Au revoir, mon petit. . . . But truly (it's not mere words), I am always with you. It's a fact. The kind of fact, you know *(Mother feels the air between her fingers)*, palpable.

It has reorganized the environment in a most interesting way. Most interesting.

As much as possible, as much as it can, the body tries to be nonexistent: just letting That pass through, That pass through all the time, like this *(gesture with her hands)*. Let the body be only a point of concentration and diffusion, like this *(gesture of something flowing through Mother)*. As supple, as impersonal, as . . . (how to term it?) without any personal will. Without any personal will, just like that, like a transmitter: let That pass through—untainted.

Untainted, undiminished. . . . Just as it is.

(Satprem gets ready to leave,
Sujata approaches Mother)

You know, Mother, I had an odd dream yesterday morning....
In my dream I saw Satprem's garden. I was walking in the
street, passing by his garden, and I glimpsed an "Adoration"
tree[1] covered with adoration flowers. I was filled with such
joy. Then, a little farther on, behind this tree, I glimpsed
another plant—it was very tall and it was the "Mind"[2]....

(Mother nods her head)

Then, I really looked, and on the branch of a tree (a coconut
tree, I think, or a palm tree), I saw a bird ... it was mostly
white, a bird much like a pigeon but with a very long tail and a
kind of golden circle on its breast, I think.

Oh!

Its head was a little ... not quite orange, a little gerua[3] (you
know, like the earth), like that, and it was perched on a
branch.

(Pointing to Satprem) It was him.

(Sujata, surprised) Him, Mother!? I don't know.

Yes, I am telling you, it was him! *(laughter)* It's good.

May 19, 1972

(Coincidentally, this conversation with Sujata took place exactly
one year before Mother's last meeting with Satprem, on May 19,
1973. These last few days, transcriptions of some recordings
made in Mother's room were on display in the showcase of
SABDA, the book business. Sujata voices her surprise.)

---

1. Geiger tree.
2. Yellow oleander.
3. *Gerua:* ocher color of the sannyasins.

How can this be, Mother? For so many years we have kept all your recordings private and nobody knew anything, and now they are on public display—and in an incorrect transcription moreover.

They don't listen to me.

But, Mother, how did they get out of here?

The Ashram no longer belongs to me.

(Sujata, taken aback) I feel very distressed. The Ashram belongs to Mother....

Oh, mon petit, that ceased being true a long time ago. Ever since I stopped going out, people have been thinking that Mother is no longer looking after things, she doesn't know what's going on.... We ought to start a new Ashram with perhaps a nucleus of ten people—and even then.

May 20, 1972

Are you tired?

Me, it's continuing....

> *(Mother plunges in,*
> *has great difficulty surfacing,*
> *then plunges in again)*

May 24, 1972

You are ... *(Mother holds Satprem's hands)*. I don't know if you are aware of it, but you are associated in all this work of transformation, like this *(gesture of being carried along in the wake)* ... as if you were fastened to it.

(silence)

But the work is taking place in a region beyond words.

Yes.... For some time now I've been very much feeling your presence.

Ahh! ... As for me, I always feel you're there, as though you were clinging to me, so each time something is accomplished, it is naturally passed on to you.
(Laughing) Clinging like a child.

Yes, I really feel it's the only solution.

(long smiling silence
while holding Satprem's hands)

All depends ABSOLUTELY—absolutely and uniquely—on the divine Will. If He has decided we will be transformed, we will be transformed. I myself am powerless—there is no "I," it doesn't exist as this! *(indicating her body)* For those who cling to me, it's the same as clinging to the Divine, because ... *(Mother smiles exquisitely)*. Ultimately, what happens is His will.

(Mother goes into
contemplation for forty minutes,
while holding Satprem's hands.
That day there was realization.)

Mon petit....

(Mother opens her eyes wide)

May 26, 1972

(The following text is read aloud to Mother:)

"Each cellular nucleus holds in its chromosomes the plan of the entire organism.... The chromosomic apparatus of any one cell represents both the "totality" of the individual and the "local" organ it belongs to. This organization could best be compared to that of an ideal human community in which each member would be conscious of the whole community and at the same time of his own intelligent personal function within the community."

(Werner Schupbach)

May 27, 1972

(Mother is late)

There's a concrete proof (not always convenient) that supramental time is not the same as physical time.... Sometimes, a few seconds seem, oh, endless, while at other times several hours go by in an instant. And concretely so. The result: I am late, I am always late.

But what can I do? I don't know.

(silence)

The consciousness is really changing—not the deeper consciousness (which is becoming clearer and clearer), but the consciousness we might call "practical" is in the process of changing in quite a striking way.

I'll be eating, and suddenly everything present vanishes, and long afterwards, I realize I am like this *(gesture, one hand suspended in midair)*, with a spoon in my hand!... Not very practical! *(Laughter)*

But during that time, when you suddenly go off . . .

Oh, it's quite interesting! But I don't "go off," you see. . . . I am not at all in a trance, not at all: I am wide awake and FULLY active. I see things, I do things, I hear people, I . . . the whole time. But I forget—I simply forget about material life. Then someone comes and abruptly calls me back.

I don't go out of material life, but . . . it appears different.

(silence)

Nothing to ask?

No, Mother.

Or to say?

No, Mother, not really. . . . I am in the course of revising the "Sannyasin," the book I wrote a few years ago, and I must say that all those experiences from above just seem so pale now. . . .

Ahh!

Almost like a dream . . .

Yes.

. . . compared to what there is now.

So true!

I really think the physical world is changing. People will probably notice it only in a few hundred years, because it takes a long time for it to become visible to the ordinary consciousness. But the touch *(Mother feels the air between her fingers)*, feels . . . as if a different texture.

From time to time, something tells me, "Don't talk, don't talk!" I have to keep quiet otherwise people around me would think I am becoming deranged.

!!!

(long silence)

191

You say it isn't the way you see the physical world that's changing but the very quality of matter?

Yes, yes, it's not at all my own way of seeing—not at all.... I don't know.... But it's odd.

You see, I have at the same time (to speak in the old way), at the same time the CONCRETE experience of a tre-men-dous Power and of total impotence.

The old methods, the methods that even yesterday were effective and powerful, all seem nonexistent. Yet, side by side, when that Force comes, I concretely feel (and I have proof, a factual proof) that a simple expression of will, or even a simple vision of something is ... *(Mother lowers her hands)* all-powerful. Materially so. Some people on their deathbeds are returned to life; some healthy people, brrt, suddenly pass away—to that extent, you know. Circumstances that seemed inextricable find marvelous solutions —people themselves say it's miraculous. It's not miraculous to me, it's very simple: just like this *(Mother lowers a finger)*. But it's INDISPUTABLE. Indisputable and new in the world. No longer the old method, no longer a mental concentration or a mental vision, none of that *(Mother lowers a finger)*: a fact.

A fact.

I am myself still too much tied to ... [people's thoughts]. Thank God *(Mother sweeps her hand across her forehead)*, the mind is gone! Ah, you know, I am ... what an extraordinary blessing it is! But from the ordinary external standpoint, I seem to have become an utter imbecile.

!!!

It's good that I have someone like you near me who knows there's something else [than what they think].

Oh, indeed! [laughing] Indeed, there's "something else"!

And I feel such a force, you know.... When I rest, I don't sleep, I consciously enter that supramental activity, and.... Oh, mon petit!... I see myself doing things with such a fabulous power! And there's no longer any ... you see, when I speak, I am forced to use "I," but it corresponds to nothing, it's ... it's the Consciousness, it's a consciousness. A consciousness that knows and has power. Yes, a CONSCIOUSNESS; not a person but a consciousness—

a consciousness that knows and acts. And which uses this *(Mother points to her body)* to keep a contact with people.

Yes, that's it, it's not a person anymore—sometimes, you know *(laughing)*, I feel like a puppet *(gesture of dangling at the end of a string)* whose purpose is to enable contact with people. But the physical strength is like this *(wobbly gesture)....* I feel very strong—very strong, and almost nonexistent. Both extremes together, you understand.... I must really look stupid.

But there *(Mother stretches her arms upwards, then slowly extends them as if to embrace the universe)*, it's luminous, it's clear, it's strong, it's wide.... Physically, too. It is PHYSICAL, that's what is amazing! Before, I used to withdraw into an inner state of being (I know them all, I've experienced them, I've had a conscious life), but all that, all that is ... finished. Completely finished.... *(Smiling)* As if the physical world were becoming double.[1]

Naturally, to the ordinary eye, I am still an old woman sitting in a chair and unable to move freely. Although at times, I suddenly feel that if I stood up, I could walk perfectly well.... But something tells me, "Patience, patience, patience...." So I wait.

And there's a persistent idea *(hammering gesture)* that if I can reach, if my body can reach one hundred, it will become young again. It's very persistent, but doesn't come from me, it's like this *(hammering gesture from above)*, so that I remain patient (although I am not impatient). Patience.

From now to one hundred is six years?

Yes, six years, Mother, it's not much.

But the body's capacities will change BEFORE its appearance changes—the appearance changes LAST; and I don't know, that never enters the picture.

What really matters is how the Consciousness can use this. It's not that I will become young again, it's not "young," it's another type of capacity that will emerge and use this body. Will it transform it? Or will it use it for another purpose? That I don't know.... I don't know. Strangely enough, only when you are here do I speak or think about these things, as if it were necessary for someone to know—otherwise, I never think about these things *(gesture of hands open)*.

Sometimes I spend hours in contemplation doing a very, very

---

1. "He discovered the two worlds, eternal and in one nest." *(Rig Veda, I.62.7)*

active work. Sometimes there are a few minutes . . . a few minutes
of silence and contemplation . . . that last hours. And they seem
like a few minutes. That's how it is.

(silence)

And you?

I'm all right, Mother.

Oh, mon petit . . . *(Mother takes Satprem's hands).*

You overwhelm me.

Something . . . *(Mother leans towards Satprem)* something in me
takes you in my arms and embraces you very, very tenderly.

(contemplation)

May 29, 1972

*(Mother sees Sujata. On this day, thirty-four years before,
Sujata decided to stay with Mother. She was twelve and a half
years old, the youngest disciple in the Ashram. She had made
her first visit to Pondicherry when she was nine.
She gives Mother a spray of "Service" flowers.
This will be the last May 29th.)*

It's from your tree.

*(Mother holds the flowers for a long time,
then gives them back to Sujata)*

I've put something there. For you and Satprem.

May 31, 1972

(Mother remains absorbed a long time. She often asked Satprem if he had any "questions," but truly speaking Satprem didn't come to see Mother to "ask questions." Rather he wanted to efface himself all he could and let her experience flow out if she liked to give it expression, or remain silent if so she preferred. He did not want his mind to grind thoughts, with its thousand questions, lest it should cloud the atmosphere and bring pressure upon Mother. Questions seemed pointless to him unless they arose on the spur of the moment, springing from within, because then they responded to something IN Mother. Indeed, Satprem wanted to be simply a sort of catalyst for what was happening in her. And then, too, seeing her gasping for breath very much affected him.)

So what do you have to say?

Nothing much.

(Holding Satprem's hands) What do YOU have to say?

Really nothing much, Mother.... I wish all the last recesses of my being would open up—that's what I wish.

Why—tell me why do I keep seeing an image of you (it's strangely persistent), as I saw you the last time at the Government House.[1] I had gone to see the new governor, and you were sitting in the room ... on the verandah.... There was a bench, a sort of long bench, and you were sitting there, and when I came out I saw you sitting there, silhouetted against the sky. It was either a balcony or a verandah, I don't remember....
It keeps returning again and again and again.... Why?
Do you remember that?

No, Mother [= I don't want to remember].

Why did it strike me so? ... You weren't alone, there were other

---

1. In 1949, after the departure of Governor Baron. Mother has already mentioned that episode in the conversation of September 1, 1971, *Agenda XII.*

people with you, perhaps two or three, I don't know. I don't even remember who they were or what they looked like or anything—I saw only you. And I was....

It was actually my last visit to Government House. You were still there, but the governor had left—I mean Baron.

Why?

You don't remember your own feeling?

No, Mother.

Why does it keep coming back to me like that?

It was like a foreknowledge of the place you would occupy in my life.

Everything else was blurred, indistinct—nonexistent—but you ... I still see it as if it were yesterday. And you were sitting ... sitting on that.... You were in a rather mocking mood.[1]

I was quite stupid.

What?

At the time I was pretty stupid—now I'm a little less....

(Mother laughs)

Thanks to you.

(silence)

Mocking, I don't think so, Mother. I was never really the mocking type.

No, not mocking....

I was rather defiant, or suspicious!

Yes, yes! That's it. Yes, that's exactly it.

As if you were saying to yourself, "What on earth is this!" *(laughter)*

Ah, Mother, what a grace to have met you!...

(Mother takes Satprem's hands)

---

1. Not "mocking" at all—very angry.

I KNOW.

(after a silence)

Oh, mon petit ... both together, you know, it's so incredible: a fabulous power—you feel you just do this *(Mother closes her fist on a little bit of air)*, and it's done—and at the same time ... you know nothing, understand nothing.... My memory is gone. There's no more, no more ... *(Mother touches her head, indicating a void)*. Some decisions go through the consciousness, but as soon as they are uttered or implemented, they're gone.

I remember nothing, nothing, nothing, except like this *(Mother picks up a point in the air)*, one thing in a thousand. But why?

(silence)

Say, listen. A strange experience it is. All the daily occupations, the most ordinary things—getting up, going to bed, taking a bath, "trying" to eat (which is rather in vain)—are.... It sounds ridiculous, but they are accompanied by a feeling that they can be an occasion of death (there isn't a single thing that isn't an occasion of death, that is, to leave the body), yet at the same time—at the very same time—there's a feeling of immortality. Almost ... it's almost indescribable.... Both opposites are there—not "opposite," but ... (they are only opposite in our language).

(silence
then Mother smiles as if
she had just discovered something)

Ah! Ah! ... You see.... Oh, listen, it sounds utterly absurd, but I'll tell you. This consciousness here is as though conscious of the divine decisions; as though there isn't a single trifle that can't be an occasion to leave the body if the Divine decides that the body has to go, nor is there a single moment when one can't have the feeling of immortality if the Divine decides that one should have the feeling of immortality. The SAME thing. Do you understand what I am saying? The SAME thing.

For example, take that image I keep having of you sitting on that bench and staring at me like—yes, as if saying, "What on earth is this!" because I visited Government House (I used to come very often during Baron's time, but I stopped coming after he left), so I came and you seemed to be saying, "What on earth is this?" as ...

yes, as if you were thinking, "How quickly one forgets!" or some-thing of the sort[1]—anyway you weren't overly friendly! *(laughter)* At least that was my impression.... But why does it keep recur-ring like that?... You see, that encounter ... that occasion was the starting point—the starting point of a great action between us, together. A great action together. So why these trifling little ripples, just when destiny was being shaped?

One could almost say they were there to prove how appearances are illusions.

Yes. Yes.

ALL appearances are illusions—there's something ... something which for me is becoming increasingly concrete and tremendously powerful: the Lord's Will. This conscious will is not like ours, it's something like this *(Mother lowers her outstretched arms)*. Inex-pressible. It's unlike anything we know. And it is a formidable will —formidable, you understand, in the sense that all appearances, all contradictions, all human wills are zero: THAT alone *(same, powerful gesture of lowering both arms)*. That's it, THAT is what I feel going through me, as if I bathed in it. Exactly like that.

There isn't any ... there's nothing here *(Mother touches her forehead)*, it's empty, empty, completely empty—hollow. Hollow. I don't think. There isn't any "I," or any.... It's almost like an empty shell, yet with that formidable Force ... *(vast, powerful gesture, arms outstretched)*.

(long silence)

The supramental consciousness must be trying to take posses-sion of it.... This *(the body)* is just like a shell.

A shell.... Will it be able to change? I don't know.

(silence)

A constant feeling of ... *(vast, powerful gesture, arms outstretched)*.

(silence)

---

1. What a fabulous memory Mother has!... Twenty-three years before, she had passed in front of me a few seconds, and she even remembers what was never ex-pressed. The whole scene has remained vivid: I was furious with Mother because I thought she was "betraying" Baron by paying a visit to his successor (who had used the worst intrigues to oust Baron).

(Smiling) It's profoundly interesting.

(silence)

As if a superhuman Power were trying to manifest through millenniums of impotence.... That's it. This *(the body)* is made of millenniums of impotence. And a superhuman Power is trying to ... is exerting a pressure to manifest. That's what it is. What will be the outcome? I don't know.

(silence)

And the famous day when I saw you there, sitting against the sky ... it's as though the place you were going to occupy in this creation were decided AT THAT PRECISE MOMENT. Truly ... it's truly, miraculously interesting.

And the same goes for everything—everything, absolutely everything. There are MOMENTS when things are decided.

(meditation
the clock strikes the hour)

Time does not exist anymore....

(Mother nods her head)

As if another time had entered this one.

June

June 3, 1972

Constantly, but constantly, I have things I would like you to know, but I don't have a chance to tell them. The ordinary memory is all gone, do you know, so if it comes, it comes; if it doesn't come . . . it's just lost.

Really . . . fantastic things.

(silence)

As if I were walking on a very thin and narrow line: on one side, imbecility, and on the other genius! That's how I progress *(gesture of standing on a ridge)*.

What does it depend on? I have no idea.

All the old methods are obsolete, but the new ones aren't yet established. Although sometimes, they come all of a sudden: for a few minutes, there's a dazzling flood of light . . . something marvelous, the feeling of a power over the entire world. And the next minute, all gone.

Night and day, like that.

Sometimes, for no apparent reason, I am in such a horrible discomfort, I feel it must lead to death, but then . . . something says, *"Don't mind,"* as though Sri Aurobindo were watching over me—*don't mind, don't mind.* . . . So I . . . *(Mother opens her hands)*. And after a little while: gone, it's inexplicably gone.

(silence)

I can't eat anymore—oh, it's so difficult! So difficult. Eating is really the most difficult of all. . . . I am not really disgusted by food, nothing of the sort, but I just can't put it in my mouth. I can still drink . . . for the moment.

There's nothing there, nothing *(pointing to her forehead)*, it's empty, empty, thoroughly empty. . . . And when I remain like this. . . .

(Mother goes into contemplation)

June 4, 1972

(Mother sees Sujata)

... People are so corrupt, you know, that were the Grace to withdraw but one hour, everything would go ... brrm! *(gesture of violent explosion).*

June 7, 1972

What do you bring?... And how do you feel?

Well, I think I can feel your presence better.

Ahh!

In fact, I feel that alone can straighten things out.

It's the Lord's presence passing through me—through what people call "me." An aggregate of cells which ... *(laughing)* took this form pretty long ago!

Yes, but this form is very....

This form is.... It's most peculiar, you know: that [cellular] consciousness gives an impression of something trying to become fluid. Something is obviously trying to make it manifest a ... an otherness.
Be an otherness. But how?...

(silence)

The body is comfortable only when it is conscious of the divine Force acting *(gesture of descent through the body),* but otherwise it's....

Any concentration on the body itself causes a kind of strange discomfort, a discomfort which stops only when it is conscious of the Force—of the Force working *(same gesture of descent through Mother)*, the Force working, when "That" comes and flows through it. Then the . . . I can't say "the old method" is gone, it's not at all that, it's . . . something.

(Smiling) There's a phrase that comes to me in English: *the joy of nothingness.*

(silence)

But don't you have any questions?

Personally, for example, before, my tendency was to turn to Sri Aurobindo or to a Force . . . to THE Force—to That, to the Lord, I don't know. Well, but the effect has not at all been the same since I really started to turn to you as a person.

Ahh!

But since I really turned to you as a person, I have felt a more decisive action taking place in me.

Quite possible. Only, the person is. . . . It's not a human person.

No, of course not!

It's a supramental person. Something the cells don't quite understand yet, but they know, they sense. They feel as if they were thrust forcibly into a new world.

That's what is now pressing all the time like this *(gesture of pressure and descent)*. In spite of an apparent weakness (which is purely illusory), there's a . . . tremendous Force here.

Yes, certainly.

Mind you, it's a Force seemingly too strong for the body; but when the body stays VERY quiet, like this . . . *(gesture, hands open)*, and as nonexistent as possible, then all goes well.

Then, you feel . . . *(gesture of something flowing through Mother)*. But that Force is . . . *stupendous!*

Oh, yes! Yes, indeed, the few drops one can taste seem . . . seem just overwhelming.

205

Overwhelming.

And instantly effective.

> *(Mother goes into contemplation for forty minutes
> holding Satprem's hands)*

June 10, 1972

> *(Mother unwinds a garland of "Patience" from her wrist to
> give to Sujata.)*

Do you want patience?

(Sujata:) Very useful, Mother!

(To Satprem:) What did you feel?

When, Mother?

All the time, mon petit!

*Well, I feel you are more and more present, close to me—your
help, I mean.*

Ah! Yes, that's true.
But....
The Help is getting more and more accurate, more and more
conscious, but ... I must say it's VERY difficult.

Yes.

But it doesn't matter. Since we have agreed to do it, let's do
it. There's no point in complaining. But the Power—the Power is
stu-pen-dous, only ... *(Mother points to her body)*, this is like a
mockery: the slightest thing gets inordinately magnified! Even

physically. Physically, it's so strange, I've got insect bites on a spot that's completely covered *(Mother touches her leg);* for a mosquito to reach it is impossible. And, I don't know . . . I am told there are no fleas or bugs here!

There are ants, Mother!

Do ants bite?

Yes, Mother, certain kinds of ants do.

Aaah! So that's it: there ARE ants here. Oh, some ants bite!

Yes, yes, Mother! I learned that here, I didn't know myself.

Well, neither did I! *(laughter)* Ah, that's what it is! Well, thank you! *(laughter)*

(silence)

But I would be interested to hear your observations.

I may not be conscious enough. It's very general. I have a feeling you are very much present, and as soon as I call a little, you are right there, the Help is there.

That, yes, definitely.

When I remember how it was just one or two years ago, naturally I can see, I can realize what a tremendous Power there is now.

Yes, there's a difference.

Yes, tremendous. It's tangible.... And, I must add, at times it falls upon me without my even calling it.

Yes, yes.

It really falls upon me like ... I don't know, like a flood of power.

Yes, yes. One must be, one absolutely must be ... passively

receptive. The slightest activity brings back the old way, I don't know. For me, now, it's *(gesture, hands open).*

When I am like that, time flies by. Time doesn't exist anymore.[1] When the old way comes back, a few minutes seem in-ter-mi-na-ble.

Something is really happening . . . a new way of time.

The other day, you said that when you go within, it isn't like before when you withdrew into an inner state to work—you said you don't go into trance, you are just. . . .

Interiorized.

Interiorized. And you added, "As if the physical were becoming double."

> *(Mother remains engrossed for a long time then comes out with a smile)*

I remember (I don't know when it was, whether at night or . . . but it was at a moment when I was quiet, when I was alone), I remember telling you, "You see, THIS is the Supramental." "This is IT, I know, THIS is the Supramental." I said that to you.

But when I tried to recall it so as to keep it in the ordinary consciousness (not the "ordinary" consciousness: the intermediary consciousness, like this—*gesture of a bridge*—the one I have all the time), it . . . it sort of evaporated. When I am not active, when I am like now, it's crystal clear: that's IT.

> *(Mother plunges in)*

---

1. That same morning, Mother sat for forty minutes with a glass of fruit juice in her hand. This conversation started one hour late.

June 14, 1972

(This concerns a serious and devoted person who works at the Louvre in Paris, restoring old paintings. She writes to Satprem referring to a letter he received from André Gide in 1946, when he was traveling in Egypt on his way to India: "I persuade myself that God does not yet exist and that we must obtain him." And she adds, "Thus, from partial truths to partial truths, we progress towards the Truth, before which the whole being can only surrender entirely. Only at that point does True Life begin, for we have at last found what the heart, deep down, was unknowingly always seeking." And she asks Mother, "Wouldn't it be better to live in the Ashram to help the Work more effectively?")

I really think she should stay in France.
Coming here is difficult.
Did you read what Sri Aurobindo said about the Ashram? He said that the Ashram symbolized all the difficulties to be resolved, so after a while people coming from the outside are beset with difficulties instead of finding help. It's much better for her to stay where she is.
But you can assure her that I FEEL her very well, and that I am with her, my help is very consciously with her.

June 17, 1972

(Mother gives Sujata and Satprem a garland of "Patience")

One needs a lot, a lot, a whole lot of it.

Yes!

The signs are increasingly clear, but what PATIENCE one needs!

209

The slightest wrong movement immediately provokes a dreadful discomfort. The merest trifle.

Life is tolerable only like this *(Mother opens her hands upwards)*.

The body—the body itself—feels like a little baby cradled in the arms of the Lord. But if it leaves this attitude only for a few seconds, it feels it's like death—instant dissolution. That's how it is.

The shortest hours are at night, from 8:30 at night till 6 in the morning—I don't sleep, but ... *(immense, silent gesture)*.

Then it's fine.

(silence)

What about you, what do you say?

I wish all the recesses of my being would open up.

Mon petit, it's patience, patience, patience, patience.

(Mother plunges in,
holding Satprem's hands)

Can you feel?

Yes, Mother.

Once I go into that consciousness, it's very difficult for me to come out.

*
* *

(As Satprem is about to leave, Mother hands him a note she
has just written in English:)

Sri Aurobindo is an emanation of the Supreme
who came on earth to announce the manifestation
of a new race and the new world, the Supramental.
Let us prepare for it in all sincerity and eagerness.

June 18, 1972

*(Mother sees Sujata, who has just lost her eldest brother, and
she comforts her. This fragment of conversation
has been noted from memory.)*

What has to be done for each one is done.

Our consciousness is limited *(microscopic gesture)*, it sees only a
little part. The divine Consciousness is . . . *(gesture):* it sees.

What has to be done for each one is done.

If someone has given himself to the Divine and trusts the Divine,
the Divine looks after him. And . . . (how to explain?) for instance,
all that has to be done for you is being done every minute; and if
you in turn ask the Divine to look after someone, that too is done.
And done for the best. But this best is as the Divine sees it.

You must be in peace. The peace of absolute trust.

Peace has the power to annul the obstacles.

June 21, 1972

*(Satprem reads to Mother a few fragments of "Notes on the
Way" for the next Bulletin. Towards the end of the second
fragment, Mother seems to be elsewhere. Suddenly, she moans
and hides her face in her hands. We pray.)*

June 23, 1972

(Mother gives Sujata the manuscript of a note she wrote for Auroville:)

"Jesus is one of the many forms the Divine has assumed to come in contact with the earth. But there are and will be many others. Auroville's children must replace the exclusivism of one religion by the vast faith of Knowledge."

June 24, 1972

(Mother has not been well lately. She listens to Satprem read the conversation of May 6, 1972 for the next Bulletin: "A golden force pressing down on the earth.... An absolutely material Power, but with no need for any material means.... A world is trying to be born into this world.")

What you've written is very good, it's far better than what I said!

(Satprem, somewhat flabbergasted:) But it's the exact transcription of what you said, Mother!!

*(Mother laughs,
unconvinced)*

This way it's turned out very good.

But it's exactly what you said! I just added a few commas and colons, that's all [laughter], and the paragraphs. But that's all!

And that's what I experience more and more clearly and precisely.

(silence
Satprem offers a flower to Mother,
"Supramental Light in the Subconscient."
Mother keeps it by her side)

Do you want to ask something?

I think Sujata has something to ask you.

Good.

(Sujata:) Mother, the other day you told me that for those who have sincerely given themselves to the Divine, for such persons what has to be done is done.

Yes, yes.

And you went on to say, "If such a person asks something for somebody else, that too is done."

Yes, but not so completely.
What is unreceptive in that person distorts the Action.
Take for example someone who is ill and BELIEVES in the reality of his illness; the effect of the Action is lessened in proportion to his wrong belief.
It's hard to explain.
But what did you want to ask?

(With a little mischievous smile:) I wanted to know, Mother, if I, for example, pray to Sri Aurobindo that "Mother be well," does it help you?

But Mother IS well!
Yesterday afternoon, for instance, I vomited—I wasn't sick. I don't know how to explain it.... The way to take food had to change. I mean, this happened to make me understand the attitude I had to have in taking food. But I wasn't sick: it was AS IF I were sick. It was just meant to make me understand the attitude with which to eat. It was like an object lesson—I understood. If I hadn't vomited, I wouldn't have paid any attention.
It's very complicated, mon petit!
So the people around me should have a certain bearing towards

213

me, take certain precautions; and in order to do so they must think and believe certain things, otherwise they won't do it. And that's how things happen quite naturally. *(Turning to Satprem)* I don't know if you follow?

Yes, I do.

Everything is organized down to the minutest detail, but it's not preplanned as we do with our ordinary consciousness: the Force simply PRESSES down and produces the required result. I could almost say: by any means whatsoever—any necessary means. It's a Force that is PRESSING down upon the earth and making people do the most improbable things, those who seem the worst as well as the best, just to ... to obtain the necessary result.

More and more it is so.

All our notions of good and evil are....

We have to keep reacting to things, precisely the reactions based on "good" and "evil," the human conception of good and evil (it isn't exactly a human "conception," but an approximation of the Harmony)....

> *(Mother plunges in*
> *and comes back moving her hand,*
> *as if waves were going through her fingertips)*

Vibrations ... vibrations transmitting the Divine without distortion. That's it. That's what is needed. And depending on circumstances or people, it takes one form or another—you understand?

Yes, Mother, I understand.

Everything we say is said using old ways of speaking.

> *(silence)*

The Action is evident.... And it is the ego's authority which is disappearing—increasingly disappearing. With total acceptance, you know, one that doesn't even need to understand. We always want to understand in the old mental way—there's NO NEED to understand. An acceptance like this *(gesture, hands open)*.

Under that Pressure, the old remnants of authority, the remnants of the ego's authority should disappear and be replaced by this *(same gesture, hands open)*: a receptivity and obedience (not "obedience," because there is no need to understand): to be impelled exclusively by the Divine. This in place of the ego. The last traces of the ego getting erased, and . . . *(gesture, hands open)* being replaced by . . . *(same gesture)*.

I continually have the feeling (fifty times a day, perhaps) of being a little baby *(gesture, kicking hands and legs)*, completely wrapped in and tossed about by the divine forces! *(laughter)* Exactly like that.

There are still. . . . It isn't completely transparent, naturally, there still remain some old things, the ego's old rule over the body, which causes grating and friction, but otherwise . . . otherwise just like a baby!

Like a baby.

June 28, 1972

(Mother first listens to some letters from Sri Aurobindo to Nirod, and in particular the following ones, which catch her attention and amuse her.)

> *Why not write something about the Super-mind which these people find so difficult to understand?*

> What's the use? How much would anybody understand? Besides the present business is to bring down and establish the Supermind, not to explain it. If it establishes itself, it will explain itself—if it does not, there is no use in explaining it. I have said some things about it in past writings, but without success in enlightening anybody. So why repeat the endeavour?

October 8, 1935
On Himself, XXVI.164

*
* *

What disciples we are of what a Master! I wish you had chosen or called some better stuff.

As to the disciples, I agree!—Yes, but would the better stuff, supposing it to exist, be typical of humanity? To deal with a few exceptional types would hardly solve the problem. And would they consent to follow my path—that is another question? And if they were put to the test, would not the common humanity suddenly reveal itself—that is still another question.

August 3, 1935
On Himself, XXVI.178-179

*
* *

Strange, it comes in gusts. A sudden gust comes in which everything is clear—the supermind is evident. And the body sees, it even sees what it is expected to do. The next minute, poof! *(gesture of curtaining)* it's veiled again.

These are like two different ways of being in relationship with the Divine—both are relationships with the Divine: one is the old way and the other the new way. Formerly, you see, whenever I had a difficulty, I would immediately curl up in my relationship with the Divine, and it would go away. But now it's no longer the same. The relationship with the Divine is itself on a different footing.

So really . . . *(Mother gestures to indicate that she does not know).*

My shelter, my lifelong shelter, which helped me get through everything, seems to be gone. Now . . . it's no longer the same. Now, that, too, has to be surpassed. *(Mother shakes her head and raises her arms as if to say: but how?)*

(Mother plunges in)

July

July 1, 1972

Do you like patience?

(Mother hands Satprem her garland of "Patience")

Yes, one needs it, it seems.

What would you like to tell me?

Have you found the new attitude?

I don't know.
I am no longer the same person, I don't know.
All, absolutely all the reactions are new. But I don't find the....
My only impression is that of CLINGING to the Divine every minute
of the day. It's the only way out.
That's how the body functions.
The body's experience is that without the Divine, it would ...
crumble.
That's all.
It has in fact a growing sense of nonexistence—of the absence of
a separate individuality *(Mother touches the skin of her hands)*.
But it is well aware that this is only a transitional consciousness
—what will be the ultimate consciousness? I don't know.

(silence)

For example, the body asks the Divine, "Give me consciousness."
And there's a kind of answer (a wordless answer): "Not yet, you
would no longer want to live separated." Like that. If the body
enjoyed the complete consciousness of the divine Presence, it
would no longer want, no longer want the separate consciousness.
Obviously, there's still a lot of progress to be made.

(silence)

Nothing to ask?
I don't like to speak.

Yes, Mother.

219

What's left of the personal consciousness feels so stupid!...
But when I am like this *(gesture, immobile in the Lord)* ... then,
it's nice.

(Mother plunges in)

July 5, 1972

I barely eat anymore. I don't know ... I can't swallow.

But isn't energy penetrating the body?

I don't know.
I don't feel weak.
But I don't "feel" energy penetrating the body.

(silence)

I don't know....
You don't have anything to ask?

*If only one could open EVERY SINGLE part of the being to your
Light—is it possible?*

Of course it's possible!

(Mother plunges in)

July 8, 1972

Any questions?

I always wonder what you do when you plunge in, like now?

(after a silence)

It's not always the same.

(silence)

The body tries to be entirely under the Divine's Influence.
That's its all-consuming preoccupation.
The most external form is the mantra: the body spontaneously repeats the mantra, but that's only the most external form.
It tries. It tries to ... *(gesture, hands open)*.
It aspires and tries to receive nothing but the divine Force.
Food is still the big stumbling block. The body knows it must still eat, but it isn't hungry; food just seems.... It eats out of habit and necessity.
It takes very little, though.

(Mother plunges in)

July 12, 1972

I am always late!... I think we should fix ten-thirty [instead of ten o'clock].

Well, if you say ten-thirty, it'll mean eleven! [laughter]

Yes, yes! *(Mother gives Satprem a little tap on the shoulder.)* What do you say?

Well, I say that Mother doesn't talk much!

221

(silence)

Before, you ... you talked more readily.

Yes.

(long silence)

I have a feeling I am becoming another person.

No, not just that: I am entering ANOTHER world, another way of being ... which might be called a dangerous way of being (in terms of the ordinary consciousness). As if....

Dangerous, but wonderful—how to express it?

First, the [body's] subconscient is in the process of changing, and that is long, arduous and painful ... but marvelous as well. The feeling of ... *(gesture as if standing on a ridge).*

More and more, the body's sensation is that faith alone can save —knowledge is not yet possible, so only faith can save.

But "faith can save" still sounds like an old manner of speaking.... How to phrase it?... The feeling that the relation between what we call "life" and what we call "death" is becoming more and more different—yes, different *(Mother nods her head)*, completely different.

Not that death disappears, mind you (death as we see it, as we know it and in relation to life as we know it): that's not it, not it at all. BOTH are changing ... into something we don't yet know, which seems at once extremely dangerous and absolutely marvelous. Dangerous: the least mistake has catastrophic consequences. And marvelous.

It is the consciousness, the true consciousness of immortality —not "immortality" as we understand it, something else. Something else.

Our natural tendency is to want certain things to be true (those we deem favorable) and other things to disappear—but that's not it! It isn't like that. EVERYTHING is different.

Different.

From time to time, for a moment (a brief moment): a marvel. But the very next minute: the feeling of ... a dangerous unknown. There you are. That's how I spend my time.

(silence)

The subconscient is full of, oh, full of fears, of anxieties, of....

That place is disgusting *(gesture rising from below).*

(silence)

The body doesn't even have faith in its own faith! That's right: it feels its faith isn't the real thing, it doesn't have faith in its own faith.

Life . . . life used to be simpler with that faith that predominated over all else, but now . . . *(gesture of a complete collapse).*

(Mother plunges in)

July 15, 1972

Do you have something?

No, nothing in particular, except that it's difficult.

No questions?

It's difficult.

(silence)

I had some things for you *(Mother feels the objects on the table near her),* it was in an envelope.

> "One must not confuse a religious teaching and a spiritual teaching. Religious teaching belongs to the past and stops all progress, spiritual teaching is the teaching of the future. It enlightens the consciousness and prepares it for the future realization.
>
> A spiritual teaching is above religions and strives towards a total truth. It teaches us to come into direct contact with the Divine."

It's for a lady who came from I don't know where and wanted to teach in a parochial school. So I replied with that.

223

There's also the message you gave All India Radio for August 15:

The message from Sri Aurobindo is a sunshine
radiating over the future."[1]

And for the darshan here [of August 15], do you have a message?

(after a silence)

I could say:

Sri Aurobindo's message radiates over the future
like an immortal sun.[1]

(silence)

You have nothing?

*Last time, you spoke of the difference between life and death.
In other words, life is no longer the way it was, but death
neither ...*

Yes.

*(with a gesture
Mother dismisses the question)*

I'd like to LIVE like that.... I don't know.

*(Mother plunges in a long time
then comes back)*

Sri Aurobindo's message is an immortal sunlight
radiating over the future.[1]

That's right. That's much better.

*(Mother plunges in again
till the end)*

---

1. Original English.

224

July 19, 1972

How are you?

Not so well.

Why?

I don't know.

What's wrong? . . . The head or the body?

No, it's rather within.

Ohh! That HAS to be all right. Within, we're the masters—we want to be well, we are well. It's only this *(Mother points to her body)* that doesn't quite obey.

(long silence
Mother holds Satprem's hand)

The subconscient is a mass of defeatism. That's what keeps rising to the surface. As we ABSOLUTELY need to change that, the subconscient must be clarified so that the new race can come. We must clarify the subconscient. It's a mire. It's full of defeatism —defeatism, the first reaction is always defeatist. It's absolutely disgusting, mon petit, I've seen it, I am working there . . . a disgusting place. We absolutely must . . . we must be categorical and vigorous—fearless, you know. Change it MUST.
It's nasty.
And it keeps rising to the surface . . . *(gesture from below).*

(silence)

A fantastic energy is *checked* by that, by that foul thing.

(Mother gives flowers to Sujata)

Here. Do you want a garland?

225

We must.... *(To Satprem)* YOU have the capacity to ... *(Mother drives her fist down into Matter)*. Defeatism belongs to the sub-conscient—it MUST change, it must. Defeatism is anti-divine.

(silence)

There's but one way: to want what the Supreme Consciousness wants—whatever the consequences in terms of our silly little conception.
Like this *(Mother opens her hands):* to want what You want.

Do I have a relationship with that Supreme Consciousness?

Oh, mon petit! That goes without saying!
You do have a relationship—and even a conscious one; not only do you have a relationship, but you have a conscious relationship.

(silence)

I have gone through all sorts of terrible things in my life....

Yes, so does everyone.

Yes, but I think I've had a ... special share.

Don't you think I've had my share too?

Oh, certainly, I think so.

So?

But I had (even when I didn't know you, when I didn't know the Ashram, I mean), I had the feeling there was something behind me....

Yes.

Something that was helping me.

Of course! But of course there was! Of course there was: THAT.
Personally, I call it "Supreme Consciousness" because I don't want to say "God"....

226

Ah, no!

It's full of ... the very word is full of deception. It's not that way, it's.... We are—WE are the Divine who has forgotten Himself. And our task, the task is to reestablish the connection —call it by any name you like, it doesn't matter. It's the Perfection we must become, that's all.

The Perfection, the Power, the Knowledge we must become, that's all. Call it what you like, it doesn't matter to me. That's the aspiration we must have. We must get out of this mire, this stupidity, this unconsciousness, this disgusting defeatism that crushes us because we allow ourselves to be crushed.

And we fear. We fear for its life *(Mother touches the skin of her hands)*, for this thing, as if it were precious, because we want to stay conscious. But let's unite with the Supreme Consciousness, and we'll stay conscious forever! That's IT, that's exactly it.

I could put it this way: we unite our consciousness with what is perishable and we're afraid to perish![1] Well, I say: let's unite our consciousness with the eternal Consciousness and we will enjoy eternal consciousness.

How stupid can one be!

(silence)

But, you see, when you are here, I can express these things because your atmosphere is conducive to expressing them.

We must ... we must put this at the service of the Divine— always. Always. With faith, an absolute faith: whatever happens is what the Divine wants to see happen. The Divine—I say "Divine" because I know what I mean by that word, I mean supreme Knowledge, supreme Beauty, supreme Goodness, supreme Will— all ... all that must be manifested in order to express ... what must be expressed.

(long silence)

We are disgusted with the world as it is—and we have the POWER to change it. But we are such fools that we can't bring ourselves to abdicate our silly little personality to ... to let the Marvel unfold.

And that's all accumulated in the subconscient: everything we

---

1. Mother was in fact fighting not only with the subconscient's defeatism, but also with that "formation of death" in the atmosphere.

227

have rejected is there, and now it must be brought in contact with the transforming Force . . . so that this unconsciousness may come to an end.

(Mother plunges in for half an hour)

Mon petit. . . .

*
* *

(The following has already been the subject of several conversations the past year and will unfortunately come up again. It concerns the sales of my books abroad and a subsequent traffic in foreign currencies to which I was impudent or imprudent enough to call attention. But the real problem was that certain people were outrightly and openly robbing Mother. My books were in fact only a small part of a vaster racket that involved all of Sri Aurobindo's works. Much like Don Quixote, then, I was pitching headlong into a battle whose outcome was foreseeable. It may be recalled that the head of SABDA, the book business, is the brother of the man who tried to appropriate Auroville. In reality I was taking on a well-organized mafia. But I was still unaware of it. This anecdote is reported here only insofar as it is symbolic of a larger whole.)

You have nothing to ask?

I had a practical problem, Mother, but it's perhaps too late?

What time is it?

Ten past eleven.

No; what is it?

Oh, that problem really bothers me. It's about my books with All India Press.

Then, mon petit, you should discuss it with André.[1]

---

1. André = Mother's son. Only after Pavitra's passing away, in 1969, did Mother try to involve him. A weak man, constantly swayed by everybody. He was Mother's son but also, one forgets too often, his father's son.

*Yes, I did speak to André. I don't know what they're doing
with my books. You see, they don't give me any statements and
don't tell me anything about what they're doing. I don't know
what they're doing with my books in Europe—in Switzerland
in particular—they don't inform me of anything nor have I any
control over what's happening. I wrote a letter to M. [the director of All India Press], a nice, polite letter in which I asked him
to keep me posted up with what they're doing with my books
—he never replied. So I thought something should be written
to M. and that none but you could do it.*

It isn't M., it's . . . *(Mother tries to remember a name).*

SABDA?

Yes.

*I thought of drafting a short note, and André approves of the
note. Could I read it to you?*

What is it?

I put: "To All India Press."

No, you must put SABDA.

Good. [Satprem reads:]

> "Satprem's books will not be translated, reprinted
> or subject to any commitment without his formal
> consent. . . .

That's obvious. Self-evident!

Well, yes, "self-evident," but. . . . To continue:

> "A yearly statement of the sales must be sent to
> him at the end of each year, and meanwhile a
> statement from the beginning up to date."

*In other words: in such and such a year we sold so many
copies, in such and such a year so many—so I know how many
copies they sell.*

Very good.

I had already asked—they never replied. So the only solution is for you yourself to send them the....

Yes, you're right. But I'll send it through André.

Good. If you sign it, I'll give it to André. So should I put SABDA instead of All India Press?

Just add "SABDA" after, below the other.

I simply want to be kept informed, you know! They do all sorts of things without telling me.

(Mother remains absorbed)

July 22, 1972

I have some things for you.

*(Mother gropes for something
on the table beside her and
hands Satprem a note in English)*

Man is the creation of yesterday.
Sri Aurobindo has come to
announce the creation of tomorrow.

Is that all?
I wrote it in French and I put, "The creation of tomorrow, the advent of the supramental being." Because they are likely to call it "superman" if I don't put "supramental being." The advent of the supramental being.
We are just in between. No longer this, not yet that—the time that's the most....

(brief silence)

*
* *

(Thus, I sent to SABDA *and All India Press the note signed by Mother. As was to be expected, the reaction was swift: I was accused of being "after money." Mother well knew the hornet's nest I was about to stir up, and the day before she had written me a letter—which I did not understand—to try and tell me to move to a higher plateau, to another consciousness, instead of struggling against crooks. The following conversation is the saddest memory of my seventeen years of meetings with Mother. It was so painful to see her weariness yet have to fight to unmask that falsehood—as if she didn't know it! But we are writing History here and we are trying to give as factual an account as possible and to describe the characters just as they were.)*

What did I write you?

You wrote unjustified things.

Unjustified.

Yes.

That would surprise me.... It wasn't I who wrote. So that would surprise me. What were those unjustified things?

You said my action was distorted.

No—I certainly didn't say that.

Well, that's what I understood.... Later you wrote me [in a second letter], that you trusted me....

Yes, of course!

Well, if you trust me, you must defend me and help me.

Defend you?

And help me.

Defend you against whom?

As a matter of fact, I didn't want to come and see you this morning. I came because Sujata persuaded me to come. She said that if I leave, the worst elements will remain and they ... they won't help you. I came here out of a sense of duty.

Are you that angry?

Yes, Mother. I came here this morning out of a sense of duty, because I think that....

Don't you love me at all?

But, Mother, that's not the point. The point is a practical one.

Practical?

Yes.

Practical questions are in a total confusion.

Well, that's just the point, Mother. If you trust certain people, you must believe their word and not yield or listen to people who deceive you.

But I don't know what you mean, because ... *(Mother holds her head in her hands).* I don't understand anymore.

Yes, Mother, I do know you no longer understand these material questions. Several times I have explained the situation to you. I told you that I asked SABDA for some information....

But didn't they give it to you?

Of course not.

But I told them, I wrote them they absolutely must give it to you.

Yes; whereupon M. [the director of All India Press] writes you a letter and you reply, "I am very satisfied with your work." Result: he says to himself, "Fine, I'll just continue as before."

No, I told him he must ... didn't André tell you?

But that's precisely what André told me! André said, "Mother told M.: I am satisfied with your work." So everything is for the best!

But this breaks all bounds!

Indeed, Mother!... In the essential truth, I am with you forever, as you know, there is no doubt about it. So far so good. But when I deal with Matter, I have to fight using Matter's laws along with whatever truth I may have. As far as Matter is concerned, I saw there was falsehood; I'm fighting against that falsehood, and I'm asking your help to fight it.... Or else one simply withdraws from all action altogether.

But I know that falsehood! I told M.! And that's what baffles me, there's something I don't understand. Because not only did I tell M. that his doings were not proper, but I also told him what he had to do. So I am completely baffled.... Who has ...? There's something fishy somewhere.

Exactly, Mother, these people are very skilled at confusing everything. That's their main power: they confuse the issue.

But I don't believe M. in the least! I don't believe a word he says to me! I told him.... So they distort what I say?... No, I am really baffled. Not only did I send word to M. but also to ... what's his name?

B. [Sabda]

Yes, B. And B. said I was quite right. So where is the confusion?[1]

Yes?

(silence)

What I wrote you is....
Will you read me what I told you?... To tell the truth (I don't like to say this), but to tell the truth, it was Sri Aurobindo who

---

1. Most probably, Mother's messenger, André, was afraid of saying things straight out.

came and told me to write this to you. There must have been some
reason, mon petit.

Yes. Here's what you say:

> "An individual being, whatever his merit, is but a
> point in the universe. . . .

That's certain!

Yes, that was the point.
Next?

> ". . . He really begins to exist only when his con-
> sciousness becomes universal through union with
> the Divine. . . .

That's perfectly exact.

> "Truly we begin to exist only when we let the
> Divine act through us . . .

That's entirely true.

> ". . . without any ignorance distorting His Action."

Yes, it's quite correct.

*Yes. So when you sent me that, I understood that I distorted
His Action.*

No, mon petit!

Then what does it mean, Mother?

That's not what it means. It means. . . . Oh, it was so clear when
he told me! . . . The question was by no means that of an individual: it was a question of the whole, a vision of the whole—that
things aren't as they seem to be, behind there's . . . *(Mother holds
her head in her hands).* I don't know anymore, mon petit.
I know that when it came, it was meant on the contrary to tell

234

you not to pay attention to people's mistakes because ... things had to be seen from the standpoint of the whole, within the Whole. That was it. I felt this was the last stage, which would propel you into the Vision, the vision of the whole I mentioned. When I wrote that, I felt you were ready to have that vision of the whole and had to be told just so that you would give your external consent to it. When I was told you were unhappy [with my letter], I was puzzled —I didn't understand. How come? ... On the contrary the feeling was that the time had come for you to rise above all human conceptions and to look at the creation and all circumstances—ALL circumstances—within the Great View, the all-encompassing divine view. Such was my impression.

Yes. But what is to be done, then? Should one withdraw in that Consciousness, seek to attain it and, well, just let the material world unfold as it can with the fakers and liars, or else....

That's what I am myself brought to do now.

But is it what I should do, too? Does it mean I should simply cede the ground to that falsehood?

What falsehood? I know what I said to M. and to B.: I told them (and especially M.) that this was no way to behave, that they should not behave that way. That's what I told him. I told him that nothing concerning your books should be decided without consulting you first.... So I don't understand at all.

Yes.

There's something I don't grasp in all this. I told him quite plainly. What did André tell you? Didn't he tell you that?

No, Mother. But André is straight, André tells the truth. André isn't with those crooks, naturally! Neither André nor I are people who tell lies.

He may not have understood, then. Do you want to call André and we see it together?

Calling André is all right, Mother, but that remains in the

*realm of words. These people have been told on your behalf
—André told them on your behalf—that they had to give certain
statements, but they don't do a thing! They don't lift a finger.
They don't obey your orders.*

They didn't send you anything today?

*No, nothing. And also for Sri Aurobindo's books—that's where
they're directly deceiving you. They don't lift a finger, they
simply do nothing. They won't give the least information about
what they're doing—what are they HIDING, these people, I'd
like to know? ... As long as they're told words, it's completely
ineffective. I wonder what action will make them move? ...*

(silence)

I know in any case that the letter I wrote you was really Sri
Aurobindo insisting on the need to attain that Consciousness, and
he told me you were ready for it. He told me that.

Then should I withdraw from action, Mother?

What do you mean by "withdraw from action"?

*Well, let things follow their own course. Stop doing anything.
Really stop doing anything until the consciousness reaches
that state.*

No. . . .

Just closet myself, go to the Himalayas and stay put.

"Doing" ... there are many planes of "doing."
Maybe if ... (Mother props her head in her hands).

I am tiring you, Mother, I'm really sorry.

You see, one "does" in higher regions. Sri Aurobindo insisted,
he said you were ready to get the superman's consciousness—not
"superman": supramental, the supramental consciousness. And
that's what he wanted to give you. He wanted ... he insisted that
you should be preoccupied with THAT, concentrated on that,

because you have the capacity. In this domain the numbers are VERY small, so it's important that all those who can do it do it. That's how I saw things.

I understand.

... And how I understood them and wrote them to you....

Yes, I understand what you mean.

... That all the preoccupations stemming from the other consciousness, the old human consciousness, however enlightened it is, are to be left aside for the moment to allow the full emergence into that Consciousness. That's all. That's all I said.

Yes, that I understand.

I told those people what I knew, I told them that they were wrong and had to change their ways. What else could I do?

Yes.

(silence)

What did you ask them?

Listen, Mother, if I should stop involving myself in these questions (which greatly disturb me), do you want Sujata to follow them and be present tomorrow when M. comes to see you? Sujata will be present and you can give your instructions to M. in front of her, and she will do the follow-up. And I won't be troubled anymore.

You see, the trouble is, I don't give [M.] my instructions in person, I give them through André. Perhaps he didn't understand?

But if M. comes before you tomorrow, and Sujata is here, and you give him your instructions, Sujata will follow up. Unless you prefer all three to come, André, Sujata and M.?...

(Mother puts her head in her hands)

I'm sorry, Mother, I am forced to do a dirty job. But it must be settled once and for all—and not only for me, but for Sri Aurobindo's works as well.... Because André doesn't say anything, but he's like me, he's upset. He is upset with this situation. For he sees these people deceiving and distorting with impunity.

So André didn't say anything?

But, Mother, "saying" isn't enough! If they come before you—André, M. and, say, Sujata, all three—and you spell out your instructions, then he will be forced to do as you say. And it will be all over.[1]

But what instructions, regarding what?

Regarding the accounts they should give you about what they're doing with Sri Aurobindo's books and Satprem's books.

They're not giving any accounts?

But I am not talking of financial accounts! I mean what they're DOING, how many copies they sell....

Ohhh!

I am not at all asking about money but how many copies they sell in India and abroad. Nothing else.

Ohh!

I am not asking for money,[2] but for the means of knowing exactly, of controlling what they're doing. In other words, they should tell you: we have sold so many copies of Sri Aurobindo in Switzerland, so many in Germany.

That, I know, they haven't done.

So!... But that's just the way of controlling what they're doing.

---

1. What an illusion!...
2. So much so that the Ashram is still today pocketing my royalties from India and a few other countries—not without having first expelled me from the Ashram, of course!

238

Ahh!

And that's what I want for my books—not money!

Oh, then there's a confusion, because from what André told me, I understood it was money.

But who cares about money, Mother! Nobody cares about that—except them.

Ohh!... Then André himself didn't understand. Or I didn't understand what he said.

> *(at this point, the attendant*
> *comes out of the bathroom to defend M.,*
> *saying that he gives all his money to Mother;*
> *the Mafia extended to every floor)*

This is not at all a question of money, not at all—as if André or I were interested in money! We don't care a jackstraw. But what we do care about is to know what they're DOING.

But of course! At least to me, they should give an accurate report.

Exactly! But they'd rather be caught dead than do that.

I can see that—ahh, I understand! Now I get it.

And that's why they reacted so violently against me when I asked for the information, because they felt somebody was beginning to uncover their scheme.

Ohh!... But, you know, I have such difficulty speaking....

Yes, Mother, I know, and I hate to draw you into this.

... Because if I can't speak when M. is here, it will look stupid.

(silence)

Listen, will you do me a favor?

Certainly, Mother, I only want Truth to triumph!

Go find André and bring him here.

(Satprem goes out to fetch André. They return together.)

Ah! *(to André:)* What will you say now?... I don't understand anything anymore! *(André laughs)*

(André:) Well, Satprem would like to know what's happening with his books....

Yes, and he's right.

Yes. And by the same token, it would be good if we could know—if someone in the Ashram could know—what exactly M. is doing with Sri Aurobindo's books.

Yes, quite.

The fact is, nobody knows anything. They're printing books, SABDA tries to sell them here and there—they have excellent promotional methods, but we have no idea what they are specifically. We don't know what's going on. It even goes ... I'll go further, Mother: for the last two years, I haven't been able to put my hand on the corrections made to the film negatives, I mean the offset reproduction of the Centenary edition [of Sri Aurobindo's works].

There were corrections made?

Yes, there were. I know there were because M. told me so. I asked him for a list....

What corrections? Who made corrections?

There's a boy working with him who makes the corrections.

But, look here, this is incredible! On the pretext that I can't see to this myself, they don't even show me!! They make corrections without telling me!

I don't know how serious these are, I have no idea.

Oh, but "serious" or not, they CANNOT make corrections without asking me!

True, Mother.

Good heavens!... So what can we do now?

(Satprem:) Yes, Mother, you absolutely must have some sort of control over these people. I think the best way would be to call B. [Sabda], M. and André together, and have André spell out all the points in black and white.

Oh, but André isn't combative.

(André:) Yes, I am Mother! [laughter] I am convinced, but....

No! I didn't say "convinced," I said "combative."

Combative? Oh, I am not at all combative, Mother!

I know. That's just what I said.

I am not at all combative, because ... I try to see through their eyes, and then I don't know who's right anymore!

Yes! *(laughter)* That's exactly the point.

(Satprem:) But the two basic things to ask them are their production and their distribution. That's all.

(André:) Yes, right.

Oh, yes! I ask them, you know. But they say I can't see anymore.... True, I can't see—I see, but ... it's a mixed vision. It's interesting (I wouldn't wish it on anybody, because the people who would see with it ...). I see what is true in things from the supramental point of view. And it's extremely interesting. I hear sounds that people don't usually hear, because these sounds have a supramental reality. I can see.... When people talk to me, I see at the same time not only what they think (that's old hat), but what's true from the supramental point of view. All the time it is like that. Both together. Because my body has no longer the same

241

... (what's the word?) ... I am strong, but the old type of energy is gone; and the one that replaces it is far more powerful—but I don't like to talk about it. When I do, I appear to be boasting. So I don't say anything. I tell you now so you'll understand.

I am no longer on this side but not yet on the other; I am in between—it's difficult. But I am still capable of controlling what these people are doing.... At any rate, they have no right to do whatever they want with Sri Aurobindo's books. And as for Satprem's books, I had said that he gave them to me personally...

(Satprem:) Yes.[1]

... and that they were under my personal control; but "under my control" doesn't mean they have a free hand!

(André:) Yes, Mother, that's right.... I'll tell you frankly what bothers me. What bothers me is that I know from experience that you're always right because you always see things from a higher plane than we. Also I know from experience that even if at the time I feel you say something that....

(Mother laughs)

... that doesn't match my own thinking, well, you're still right. And that's why I have a lot of trouble being "combative."

But don't you know! I don't "think," mon petit!

Well, yes, Mother, that's the point!

Exactly.

(Satprem to Mother:) Yes, but you do need human instruments to do things, don't you?...

Yes, yes.

---

1. In a letter to Mother dated June 13, a month earlier, I wrote, "My royalties from all the countries of the world have always been given to you to the last cent, but I would like to make sure that my royalties from India are also given to you directly and personally, and not lost in corporate accounts...."

And there are instruments like André who are trustworthy and can do certain things for you.

But, you see, he himself says he isn't combative!

(Satprem:) Yes, that's right! [general laughter]

There you are.

(André:) For instance, you see, when M. (and I believe he's being very honest in that case), when M. tells you how miserable he is, how everybody is after him, how everybody gives him a bad time....

Oh, M. is in a state.... He's like this *(gesture like a wet towel).*

Yes, precisely! So you really hesitate being combative with him.

But that's no reason why he should.... It would be much better to be frank with him, tell him exactly what we expect from him.

(Satprem:) Yes, that's right.

And put it in writing. And I'll tell him that I WANT to know.

(Satprem:) Yes, we have to put it down in a few lines on paper.

(André to Satprem:) Yes, what you did for your books was very good.

And if he doesn't comply, he'll be putting himself in the wrong —but I think he will.
(To André:) You don't understand?

(André, reluctantly:) All right, I'll draft a note and discuss it with you.

(Satprem:) Ask the same for Sri Aurobindo's books: what are their production and their distribution? And they must keep you informed of reprints, etc.

Yes. That's right.

(André:) And inform you in writing, otherwise....

Yes, not verbally.

(André:) They must supply a written statement, because he always does everything verbally.

Yes, I demand a written statement. I want a detailed and accurate report from him. A complete and genuine statement of what they do.

(Satprem:) M. and SABDA, both of them, isn't it.

Yes.

(André:) Actually SABDA is the most....

Yes, SABDA is....

(Satprem:) That's where the falsehood lies.

SABDA is far more difficult.

(Satprem:) Yes, exactly.

He's become.... B.'s mind is ... *(twisted gesture).*

(André:) Yes, THERE is the knot, because ... (how to put this?) that's where they conceal the most.

Both of you must put this very clearly in writing, and I'll sign it. I'll have to write something myself, so that it doesn't look like a mere signature.

(Satprem:) It can all be said in a few lines.

Yes, it need not be long. I want Satprem to be present when I sign it.

(Satprem) Oh, that isn't necessary at all, Mother!

I prefer it that way.

(Satprem:) All right! As you like [laughter].

So settle it among yourselves, prepare a text and come to have me sign it when it's ready.

(Satprem:) This very evening.

Tomorrow is what day?

(Satprem:) This evening itself, Mother, it's only a few lines.

Today is André's day, so you will come too.

(Satprem:) Yes, we'll come together.

(To André:) Do you say yes?

(André, resignedly:) I say yes! [laughter]

(Satprem:) It will be settled once and for all.

But don't at all think that.... *(Turning towards André)* You're doing your best—you said you were afraid of going against my thinking....

(André:) Yes.

But, mon petit, you've got to understand!!

(silence)

I can't explain it in words, you wouldn't understand. I don't even know how to express it.... I just know that even mistakes (what we call "mistakes") and difficulties are the result of the manifestation of the divine Consciousness helping us to progress towards the future perfection through ... (what's the word?) through continuous molding. That's what I see. And that's why....

(Satprem, aside to André:) ... We mustn't be afraid of making mistakes.

(André:) Yes, we mustn't be afraid of mistakes.

Each one has a role and plays his part.

(Satprem, aside to André:) We mustn't be afraid of our own truth, André.

The only important thing is to mix as little personal ego as possible with the divine vision. That's all.

(André:) Yes, right.

(silence)

It's difficult, I can't speak. But it's so wonderful when you see it! But I can't speak.

When I can say exactly how it is, then I'll say it.... Not quite yet.

You see, the sensation of my body is ... as if I were as big as the world and holding everything in my arms, truly the way a Mother holds her children—except it's a hundred times better than that! But that's it, that's how I live.

I can't explain.... Later.

Later.

All right, so prepare that text. I'll see you both this evening.

(To André:) Mon petit, I KNOW the truth of things, but I am powerless to express it. I can't say it just because I don't have the power of expression. But do as I said.

(Satprem:) Yes, Mother, certainly!

(André goes out)

Mon petit....[1]

(Mother gives Satprem
a kiss on the forehead)

---

1. As was to expected, all this conversation and the instructions signed by Mother came to naught: the businessmen went on with their business as before. The only result was to spark angry reactions, which fell on Mother, and on Satprem ... in time.

July 26, 1972

(In an attempt to bring the book distribution in line, Mother, on Satprem's suggestion, asked a young teacher from the school to be in charge of the copyright department. Mother first speaks of this young teacher.)

He's discovering skeletons!
Poor M. [All India Press director], he was so upset!

Naturally, for he isn't the real culprit in all this, you know, it's the other one behind, SABDA.

Oh, that's....

And that's why he is hurt—because he's more receptive. The other one is penned up in his falsehood.

The other one is a NO! *(Mother makes the gesture of something compact.)*
Anyway....

*   *
*   *

(Mother looks for something near her.)

I had something I wanted to show you ... *(Mother does not find it)*. I don't know, I thought I had kept some things for you, but I don't know where they are now.

You know, this *(Mother sweeps a hand across her forehead)* is almost emptiness itself. There's nothing here *(forehead)*—nothing. When I am perfectly quiet and still *(Mother raises a finger upward)*, some things come *(gesture above)*, some things get done or straightened out—it takes place above. When I am like that, after a while a whole world of things gets done, gets organized, but it's ... (what can I say?) it's another kind of reality, a more ... substantial reality. How is it more substantial? I don't know. Matter seems ... unsubstantial compared to that. Unsubstantial, opaque, unreceptive. Whereas that is....

247

The funny part is that people think I am asleep! I don't at all sleep. That's how I spend my nights: a Force at work.

And I am conscious ... but it's hard to put in words. Words are ... words distort. Really a new kind of consciousness is developing —how will it express itself? I have no idea.

So people are convinced that I am asleep, that I am deaf, that ... and on top of it all, I can barely speak *(laughing)*—so I must have become an old.... I hardly belong to the old world anymore, so the old world says: she's finished—I couldn't care less!

Yes, I should think so!

I am telling you because I can tell you things.

But it's probably better this way.

The trouble is, I am becoming an object of curiosity; that's a problem because.... A host of people come flocking here just for that: an object of curiosity.

But there's this odd thing: for EVERYTHING, for everything I do—for instance, I still take my bath, I try to eat (it's the most difficult—VERY difficult), for everything ... *(Mother stops short)*.

I wanted to tell you something, but it's gone.

Maybe it was not meant to be said.

Yes, you are obviously impelled by something else.

Yes, yes, that's right. Exactly.

So much so that sometimes, just after doing something, I wonder.... I suddenly ask myself, "Did you do this?"—and I've just done it!

That's how it is.

Yes, I quite understand. But when you act in that other, more substantial matter, how does it find its way into this old matter here? How is your organization up there communicated here?

(silence)

I don't know, there's almost an interdiction to speak; because whenever I try to express something, I suddenly find myself before a blank.

Yes, I can understand why.

Everything conspires to give the impression that I am falling apart.

Yes, but that doesn't matter!

Provided somebody knows it to be untrue is what counts—YOU know.

But still, a good number of people here, though not knowing, feel that way.

Oh?

More than you think.

Ah, the Force is tremendous, mon petit!

Those physically nearest to you are not necessarily those who feel it.

Yes, I know—because they just see this appearance, which is not so.... I tell you: I do things, and I don't know how I do them. There's a kind of.... Oh, but the most fascinating field of experience is food! I am not hungry, I don't feel like eating, food doesn't interest me by any means, yet they bring me my meal, and I "have" to eat—sometimes I eat (always in small quantity), but since I don't move and don't work, I don't need material energy, so I don't need to eat much, and I don't think I am losing weight *(Mother touches her arms).*

No, apparently not.

Apparently not, therefore....

But you aren't heavy! [laughter]

Oh, I've never been heavy!
But it's truly interesting, because I don't at all feel like eating, I am not interested in it, and yet something FORCES me to eat—not much, but it says, "Eat."
The same with speech. Things are so clear, there is such a clear vision! *(gesture above the head)* When I am silent and quiet for

249

hours, SO MUCH work is being done, and everywhere at the same time *(universal gesture)*. . . . But I can't express it.

This incapacity to speak is also rather special. . . .

(long silence)

There are so many things I would like to tell you. But a kind of will bars me from speaking. So I. . . .

Yes, I understand the danger of mentalizing things. I really understand. It's dangerous.

Oh, but mon petit, the mind is gone.

No, I mean mentalizing by expressing things.

Yes, exactly. It distorts.
We must be patient.
This *(Mother points to the garlands of "Patience" around her wrists)* is symbolic. Repeatedly it's: patience, patience, patience.

But the others, too, must be patient. And you, you must be very patient.

Yes, Mother.

Very patient—do you want my patience? *(Mother slips her garland around Satprem's wrist)*. And she too *(to Sujata)*: tell me, do you want my patience? *(Mother gives another garland)* Here.

(silence)

So what do you think could help you? Would you like some silence? . . .

Oh, that's. . . .

. . . or would you rather ask me questions?

(Mother plunges in)

July 29, 1972

What I told you last time is not to be published—it's all right for the *Agenda*. I mean what I said about the people around me.

Yes, Mother, of course, all that is strictly for "the Agenda."

Everything personal is for the *Agenda*.

Yes, yes, of course.

> (Mother unties a garland of flowers from her wrist)

Do you like patience?

I don't know if I like it, but it's useful!

> (Mother laughs and gives Satprem a garland)

I have plenty! *(two or three garlands around her wrist!)* What do you have to tell me?

Nothing. I feel the ... churning one is put through.

Oh! ...

Sometimes it feels as if something were ... raging ferociously.

Yes, exactly. As if to demonstrate that you have to go through death in order to conquer death. Exactly. And just as you are about to cross the threshold, suddenly it's all righted.
I thought I was the only one experiencing that, and I was happy to do it for everybody, but evidently some people feel it also—you feel it.

Oh, do I! Dash it all, it's ... I feel something ferociously raging.

Yes, that's right, quite. And it shows there's a sort of ... difference—a mere difference of attitude; a difference of attitude: the body can either fall apart or be transformed. And it's ...

251

almost the same procedure; only the attitude is different. If you have absolute trust in the Divine and feel to what point the Divine is everywhere and in everything, if you want to depend only on the Divine, belong only to the Divine, then it's perfect. But the least conflict . . . and it's like the gates of death suddenly yawning.

Yes.

Strange.

Yes. But unfortunately in my case, when this happens, when that fury rages, I am still at the stage where I am literally in a fog, I am completely engulfed in a cloud. Somewhere in the background there is still a sort of memory of the Truth, but at the time I am completely engulfed.

Oh! . . .

Entrapped in an opaque cloud . . . it's terrible.

But all you have to do is . . . feel that divine Presence within you, you know, stronger than everything. One feels It could revive all the dead if It wanted—just like that, you know. To that Presence . . . it doesn't make any difference.[1]

My body is learning to repeat unceasingly: what You will, what You will . . . *(Mother opens her hands).*

I have no preference: it's REALLY what You will. For a time, I had hoped to be conscious of "what You will"—but now there's only: what You will *(hands open).*

To be conscious of You.

To be conscious of You.

> *(Mother closes her eyes,*
> *palms upwards, and plunges in.*
> *Then her eyes open, immense, immobile.)*

---

1. Perhaps because the difference between life and death is not what we imagine!

August

August 2, 1972

The "Formation of Death"

On several occasions since the beginning of this year 1972—and actually even in a conversation of September 8, 1971, where some of Mother's words had a strange ring to them—Mother mentioned the "formation of death" she was up against. Today, again, in the following conversation, Mother speaks of that "formation."

In occult terms, a "formation" is a strongly "formed" thought, or a concentration of force with a specific goal and a permanent existence of its own. Formations can be negative or positive. In everyday life, for example, wills or desires or long-nurtured suggestions one day come to their happy or sorry fruition. The day, the success, or the "accident" were prepared by the constant repetition of insignificant little thoughts, which eventually exude their cancer or dazzling success. Thus Mother, who for long had had no "thoughts" or "will" of her own, except "what You will," was extremely sensitive and vulnerable to anything coming from the "outside," precisely because there was no more "outside" for her, she was directly and instantly bathed in everything: she was "in" people. "My body is excessively sensitive," she said, "and needs to be protected from all those things coming in. As if it had to work inside, as in an egg." (February 26)

We are here trying to find out what happened on November 17, 1973: the why of things. A "tragedy" does not occur at a particular minute or hour in History. It is the result of all the hours and little minutes that have prepared that particular minute or made it inevitable. As I said earlier, I was thunderstruck on that November 18, 1973. I was certainly the blindest of all the characters taking part in the tragedy, for they all seemed to know in advance that she was going to die—at least those in her immediate entourage. But that "knowing in advance" bears a terrible implication. Here we put our finger on the "formation of death" Mother was imbibing daily —"a perpetual discomfort," she used to say. In those repeated little minutes we can pinpoint the cause of what happened at 7:25 p.m. on November 17, 1973.

There is no better eyewitness than Pranab, Mother's "bodyguard" since he was almost constantly physically present and even slept in Mother's room. Asked about the cause of Mother's departure, this is what he stated in a public speech on December 4, 1973 [in English]:

"On one side She had to fight the onset of decay and old age and on the other She was fighting against this dirt that we were constantly throwing upon Her. But more the failing body I hold responsible for what happened. Often I have seen that She was trying to counteract these forces but when She saw that She could not concentrate much, She could not talk much, She could not write much, She could not see people, She could not do as She wanted, because the body was failing, and the dirt and dust that we were throwing upon Her was increasing, increasing and increasing, I felt and I have seen also some kind of despair...."

We know that all too well, alas: they thought she was old and disabled. But Pranab adds the following, which suddenly gives us the magnitude of the real tragedy—we could almost say the horror Mother had to face in her body. This is what he says, and let us remember we are today in August 1972:

"This thing which came now [in November 1973], I think She had prepared me enough for it from quite a long time back. Long before, say, in the year 1948, when Sri Aurobindo was still living, She told me, "I am not willing to go, I will not go, and this time there will be no tragedy: but if it so happens that I leave my body, then put my body under the Service Tree." ... And lately, say, AFTER 15th AUGUST 1972, I felt that perhaps what has happened was going to happen. I could not tell anybody and everybody, but to my close associates I said what I was feeling. Afterwards, I felt strongly that it was going to happen, I was counteracting this idea, saying that it should not happen. But behind everything the idea was there."

Thus, day in and day out Mother was imbibing their thoughts of death: she was GOING to die. And for her this was no "thought": things had become "concrete" for her. Her body, the consciousness of her body felt itself in the grip of death.

As in all tragedies in human History, there is not a particular person to blame. Humans only incarnate certain types of force or character—they come, die, triumph and vanish—but the forces remain and continue to animate millions and millions of unknown little humans here and there, who are silently "responsible" and the invisible actors in the drama. There is no one to put on trial here—except millions who are but ourselves. It would therefore be absurd to say that Pranab was the author, or the sole author, of that "formation" ("Everywhere, there are wills that it [the body] should die!" she said), but he certainly fostered it and transmitted it, and because he was physically present all the time, Mother had to breathe that horror constantly. Ultimately there remains this haunting question, the only one perhaps: Could it have been otherwise?

*
* *

Would you like a portrait of Sri Aurobindo?
Blue or all golden? Gold's better!

(silence)

There are two formations like this *(gesture confronting each other),* like two *wrestlers:* one formation is that I will die on Sri Aurobindo's birthday; the other formation is that I am undergoing the necessary transformation to span humanity to the Supramental. Both formations are as ... they're like this *(same gesture facing each other)* and....

When this formation [of death] makes itself felt, an awareness comes that there's hardly any difference between life and physical death, in that anything, at any time, can send you over to the other side. Then, with the other formation, there's a feeling that ... (how can I put it?) the body's frailty is due to a need for the consciousness to change so it can manifest the Supramental.

And I am like this *(gesture between the two).*

But the body has learned to remain quiet in either case.

(silence)

Why, but why am I not told what will happen? I don't know....
I think it's to insure a kind of very passive state.

(silence)

And you? How are you?

Well, I would really like to understand the mechanics of the subconscient's transformation. I just don't understand the word "transformation." "Dissolution," is understandable; I mean, some movements come to the surface (sometimes you even see them symbolically the night before), they rise to the

257

*surface, perform their little trick, their little mischief, you
more or less control them, then they come in contact with the
Light, and pff! sink back again. . . .*

(Mother nods)

*But at the first opportunity, they surge up again, and every-
thing starts anew.*

Horrid. It's just what is happening to me now.

*But then, how do you . . . ? You seemed to be saying that it gets
transformed by coming in contact with the Light. But it looks
like it isn't transformed at all: it simply sinks into the depths
and surges up again at the first opportunity.*

No, something is transformed, but it's slow, slow, slow. . . .

(silence)

It's like asking a rock to become air!

(silence)

*And what I find fascinating is that the more microscopic and
tiny it is, the more power it seems to have!*

Really! . . .

(Mother takes Satprem's hands
and plunges in till the end)

August 5, 1972

People know I don't eat anymore, so they've stopped sending
anything.

I've got all I need!

Yet I didn't tell anyone! I wonder how they came to know.

I've got all I need, Mother!

Really? . . . I don't want you to get thin! *(laughter)*
There are some interesting things. . . .

(silence)

What about you? What do you have to say?

No, Mother, nothing. What are the interesting things?

(after a long, smiling silence)

I see certain things, certain events, certain patterns of wills . . . I
see them coming like this *(gesture of a screen)*, I see them very
powerfully and distinctly. And at the same time the sense that:
this is how it will be with the Supramental.

But it's difficult to describe.

You can't describe it—it's a STATE of consciousness. It's a state
of consciousness, together with the knowledge that that state will
be part of the Supramental.

And all this happens within a VERY profound silence. So I can't
express it.

*(long silence
Mother touches her hands)*

It's like vibrations coming out of my hands, like this *(gesture)*.
My hands seem so powerful! They feel they can change things just
by doing this *(Mother makes a fist)*.

But I would rather you asked me questions or told me something, because . . . otherwise I instantly enter that state which is
so, so vast . . . peaceful . . . and so powerful—where things are
accomplished.

That's how they are accomplished.

But there are no words or explanations—nothing satisfying for
the mind.

(silence)

You don't have anything to say?

259

I am still looking for the key to infusing that Power I feel, that Force, that Truth into everyday physical activity. I find it quite difficult.... Yet when I stop all activity, the contact is instantly made, and very powerful and REAL it is, but the minute I go back to being active, everything recedes into the background.

Aah!...
Personally I am not engaged in activity.

Matter seems to feel it as something imposed, not coming from within; it isn't natural (in my case, at least).

But I now feel just the opposite! The body and matter (the part of matter under my control) seem to REFUSE to obey anything but That.

Let me give you an example: I see almost ... (it's an "almost" which sometimes is beyond almost, you understand: the extreme limit of "almost") almost as well with my eyes closed as with my eyes open. See, really SEE *(Mother touches her physical eyes).* When I have difficulty writing, for example, instead of peering and straining, I shut my eyes. And then ... I see.

And the same for everything, for all the senses. To swallow food, if I try to swallow in the usual way, I literally choke, but when I am in a certain state ... I find I've swallowed everything, and I didn't even notice it! And everything is like that.

So ... I seem completely impotent, yet I feel a tremendous power in me.

*(Mother plunges in for 40 minutes,
then opens her eyes
and speaks in English)*

It can go on for hours....

August 9, 1972

*(A news item originating from Boulder, Colorado, and dated
August 8, reports a solar flare covering over 2.8 billion square
miles of the sun's surface. Within an hour of the eruption, the
effect was felt on earth, causing a magnetic storm that seriously
disrupted communications in many parts of the world. In terms
of magnitude, the current sunspots are the greatest ever recorded
since at least 1964 [Indian Express, August 9].)*

Did you hear about the explosions on the sun?

Yes.

They say it's falling to the earth . . .

Ah?

. . . and it's going to affect humans. Did you hear that?

I didn't hear it was falling to the earth.

They say it will come to the earth and affect humans.

*I think it affects the earth atmosphere, the weather, but that's
all.*

I don't know.

*It affects the atmosphere; for example, radio transmissions are
scrambled. The atmosphere is affected, but that's about all.*

Is this today's news?

I don't know, Mother.

Because mine is today's latest news. They're rather pessimistic.

But what do you say?

261

I say that it must be the supramental consciousness—not "consciousness": the supramental SUBSTANCE. And those who are ready will thus have their new body.

That's my most . . . optimistic explanation.

Did you actually discern something outside of the official news?

Not quite.

For me, eating is getting more and more difficult—almost impossible. Clearly, something has to replace food.[1]

Almost, almost impossible to eat.

Feeling has nothing to do with it, there's no disgust or anything of the sort: I just can't swallow. It's like this *(gesture of choking).* Result: I take nearly an hour to absorb what would normally take five minutes.

(silence)

So you think these solar eruptions are some kind of precipitation of the supramental consciousness on earth?

Of the SUBSTANCE. The consciousness came long ago, but the thing is. . . . Because, for example, this body has the same needs it used to have; that's the way it is built: it needs to eat, but it can't eat. So when I was told these eruptions would affect even the human body, I thought: could it be the substance that will create the supramental body?

If the Supramental is to manifest on earth, something of it has to relate to the physical.

Quite!

(silence)

The body is in a curious condition *(Mother touches her finger-tips):* it feels a terrible Force—it is full of strength—and it can't do a thing!

It is in a bizarre kind of state.

---

1. In simple terms, we could say that all living matter on earth is "assembled" by the sun's energy (including and especially what we use for food); that same matter is then "disassembled" to release and provide us with that SAME energy. The question is, could one directly absorb those SAME energy particles without going through the intermediary process?

I can write, but the way I see what I write is different from before.

There you are.

And what's your feeling?

Well, I feel the Force is more and more ... imperative.

Imperative. Yes, it's becoming terribly powerful, in a body which is ... *(gesture of being miserable).* But the body does not feel weak, yet it isn't hungry. It isn't "hungry," that went long ago; but now, recently, it's become almost impossible to eat. How is one supposed to live, then?

So when I was told that this solar explosion was heading for the earth and would affect people, I thought: well, maybe that's what is coming to replace food?

It's *wishful thinking,* I can't say it's a knowledge. It just came to me like that.

Because, according to what Sri Aurobindo said, the supramental body will be immortal and sexless—that is, no procreation. So for those who live, if the earth is still there and they are to go on living, they will have to transform themselves constantly, otherwise they won't be able to last. Hence something has to replace food.

Food carries in itself a seed of *death,* of decay. So obviously, it must be replaced by something else.

(silence)

Do we know how much time it takes for the rays of the sun to travel to earth?

Oh, it's very fast,[1] Mother. It's already done, it has already entered the earth's atmosphere.

Really?

Yes, it takes a few minutes.

Ohh!

(long silence)

So the effect of the explosion is already....

---

1. Eight minutes.

Already here, yes. Radio transmissions, for example, have already been disrupted. Those solar eruptions occur in cycles. The phenomenon recurs at fixed intervals—I can't tell you exactly, I don't know if it's every ten or twenty years[1]....

Oh!...

But this one is particularly strong, it seems.

Oh, it's a recurring phenomenon....

Yes, cyclic. But I think its magnitude was quite extraordinary this time.... Very unusual.

(silence)

Do we know what the sun is made of, its substance?

Yes, Mother. It's a substance in a state of nuclear fusion; like a gigantic and incessant atomic explosion.

Oh!

It's in a gaseous state. With constant atomic reactions. It's a million times more powerful than the atomic bombs they have exploded on earth, and nonstop.

(long silence
Mother laughs)

So of course, if those explosions increase or decrease, the effects must be fantastic!

Certainly.... The sun is not really solid matter, you see, it's energy.

Yes, it isn't matter.

It isn't matter, it's energy.

(In an amused tone:) And that's what keeps us alive!

---

1. Eleven years.

Yes! [Laughter]

(silence)

Sri Aurobindo and all the Vedic Rishis have always likened the Supermind to the sun....

Yes.

So there must be some relationship, a correspondence.

Yes.... I personally find it very ... (what's the word?) significant that this should have happened this year [of Sri Aurobindo's centenary].

Yes.

(silence)

But do we know how long the earth has existed?

Yes Mother, it's been calculated.

Ah?

Yes, it was calculated: I don't know exactly how many billions of years—but it's billions of years.[1] And they have also calculated the end!

Ah! And?

I think it's still quite far ahead. But it appears the end of the earth is scientifically inevitable—because of progressive cooling and changes in the gravitational field.[2]

Théon used to say that up to now there had been ... that this was the seventh creation; there had been six creations before which were "reabsorbed"—just as you said. And this one was the seventh, but it wouldn't be reabsorbed, it would transform itself. There we are. Instead of that destruction by the sun which so far has ultimately led to the disappearance of the creation, this time the creation would go on transforming itself, to become again the Supreme and manifest Him.

---

1. Four and a half billion years, according to the current estimate.
2. It is said that in five billion years the sun will become a "red giant" and burn its planets. The cooling period would come much later.

265

Théon and Sri Aurobindo didn't know each other, you see, they never met each other, they didn't even know of each other's existence. Yet Théon proclaimed ... (I don't remember what he called the new world) what Sri Aurobindo calls the "Supramental." What's remarkable—interesting, you know, strikingly interesting —is that without knowing each other, with totally different approaches, they reached the same conclusion.

And we are precisely at the time when ... the other creations had come to an end; but instead of coming to an end, this one will be transformed. How? I have no idea.

The interesting thing in man is that materially speaking, he is ... a mere nothing, a second lost in eternity—a tangled web of weaknesses—but in terms of consciousness, he has the capacity to understand. His consciousness is capable of contacting the supreme Consciousness. So naturally there are all those who wanted to merge back into that Consciousness, but Sri Aurobindo said: the point is not to merge back into it but to make the world capable of manifesting that supreme Consciousness.

That's ultimately the whole point.

How did they arrive at the same conclusion? ... There must have been a reason for them to know the same thing at the same time, in totally different countries and without ever knowing about each other.

And I met one and the other.

Greatly interesting, obviously.

Greatly interesting, because this physical being [Mother's] was not born in an important position, quite the contrary *(gesture indicating an ordinary background)....* The only thing I remember well is when I was a little girl (five or six years old, I can't say exactly), a very little girl, seated in a little armchair made especially for me, and I would feel a GREAT Force *(Mother raises a finger above her head)* above my head. And already at that age (just the way a child can think, you know) I knew "that" was sure to accomplish great things.... I didn't understand anything, I didn't know anything.

(silence)

And now it's transformation instead of pralaya.[1]

(long silence)

___
1. The destruction or end of a world (apocalypse).

According to what was reported, it seems those explosions have liberated particles.... And I thought they said they were on their way to the earth; but from what you say, they're already here?

I didn't see this morning's papers. I'm sure there were atomic particles.

Yes.

Generally they're stopped by the density of the earth's atmosphere, so they affect only the atmosphere, not the earth itself.... The most immediate consequences are climatic.

Yes, it's terrifically hot here!...

(Mother plunges in.
Pranab comes in and says from
the far end of the room, "It's late."
Mother instantly comes back)

Is it time?

Yes, Mother.

August 12, 1972

Nothing to ask?

Is there anything new?

Oh, it's always new!
And you, what's new with you?

Nothing, Mother, I'm a little upset about my lack of consciousness during sleep.... I wonder what on earth I do at night!

267

(after a silence)

Does anyone see Pavitra at night?

(Sujata:) I see him almost every night.

Oh, you see him.... Me, I see him just as when he was here; and he's busy doing things—a totally conscious and active life. Last night, he was speaking to some people, organizing meetings, he was extraordinarily active.

Besides, he was among people who still have a physical body, who were sleeping, I mean who had come out of their body. He was so conscious! I've never seen anyone so ... so materially conscious, I could say. Exactly as if he were continuing his work. Mainly seeing people, talking to them, bringing them together....

You know that when he died, at the time of his death, he entered me?...[1] I did my best to prevent him from blending [with Mother]: I kept him like this *(gesture as an individual form)*. And after he recovered from the shock, he spontaneously came out and started to work. I see him almost every night.

I've never seen anyone remain so much like himself. It's truly remarkable.

(Mother plunges in)

(Sujata:) But, Mother, how does one get rid of sadness?... I see him very often at night, you see, almost every night, but I am still sad not to be able to see him with my physical eyes.... What to do, Mother?[2]

(Mother smiles) You see him, but there isn't any contact between you?

We work together, Mother, like we used to.

So? So?

Yes, Mother, but when I'm awake like I am now, I....

(Mother laughs) It means you are still quite young!

---

1. See *Agenda X*, May 17, 1969.
2. Sujata was Pavitra's personal secretary for thirteen years, from 1949 to 1962, and continued to work with him daily up to the end.

No, Mother!

Yes, you are.

For my elder brother too, you know, he lived far away, I didn't see him, but now that he has passed away, I know I will never see him again in the same form, so I am sad, very sad, Mother. What can I do?

Well, that's strange!

I don't know, it's like a pain in the heart, Mother. I can't get rid of it, you see. I don't know what to do.

You must go deeper. You feel sad because you are in a very superficial consciousness—you must go deeper, into a deeper consciousness.

You mean in the waking state? When I am awake like now?

Yes, oh yes! It's when you are awake that you must try to reach your psychic consciousness.
When you are in contact with your psychic consciousness, there's no more sadness.

(silence)

You're still quite young really! *(laughter)* How old are you?

I am forty-six, Mother.

You have a twenty-five-year-old's consciousness.

Ah!

(Satprem protests:) No, eighteen.

It doesn't matter! It doesn't matter....

August 16, 1972

(Today is the day after Sri Aurobindo's centenary. Hordes of people line up in Mother's corridors.)

This morning I am seeing two hundred people . . . two hundred!

How was it yesterday?

I'd rather not say anything because. . . .
According to what I had heard before,[1] according to that, it was a big victory. But nothing was visible. I didn't say anything to anybody. Even so, several people felt it was the beginning of something.
It's a long story. . . . Some adverse forces had banded together and decided that I was going to die yesterday. And it was true, it happened, there was an attack. In that sense a real victory took place at the balcony. But it was invisible.
Now if this . . . (what's the word?) this "news" is true, if it continues to be true, I should last till . . . I'll be this way *(gesture in suspense or between two positions)* till my centenary, that is, 1978, then (still assuming this voice is true), the supramental transformation of the body will begin.
Is it true? I have no idea. That's what I was told.
I have no idea.
I am like this *(hands offered upward).*

(silence)

Can my body follow? That's the question.
My body is constantly like this *(same gesture)*: what You will, Lord, what You will. . . . But it must nevertheless undergo a transformation.

And you, what did you feel yesterday?

I can't really say, Mother. There was too much turmoil in the atmosphere.[2]

---

1. Conversation of August 2 (the two rival "formations").
2. Ten thousand people in a carnival atmosphere amidst incense sticks and stalls reminiscent of Lourdes. Not to mention the "embellishments" to the Samadhi, the "embellishments" to Sri Aurobindo's room, whose floor—where he had walked so much that he had left on it the imprint of his footsteps—has been covered with glue and blue linoleum.

Oh, yes!

Difficult to say.... Sri Aurobindo's Presence, of course.

Oh, yes! Ohh, very strongly....

(long silence)

I am like this *(same gesture, hands open).*

(Mother plunges in
one can hear the humming of
the crowd outside and loudspeakers)

They told me I had to see two hundred people this morning
—two hundred. This morning.

Thank God you exist, Mother!

Mon petit ... *(Mother takes Satprem's hands).*
Next month it'll be better, we'll have more peace.
We'll have more peace....

August 19, 1972

(Mother looks very pale. She has just seen 175 people.)

What do you have to say?

And you, Mother? Would you say something?

I've just seen over a hundred people.

Yes, you're a bit tired.

Not tired, it's ... dazed, you know.

I am not saying anything.
But if you have something to ask?

You should rest a little, Mother.

I'll rest. But go on and ask me if you have something.

*I have a feeling I am not making the right movement inwardly.
I'm not going at it the right way.*

Ah!... You're too active.
If you could simply.... More and more I feel that unless one does this *(Mother opens her hands upwards in a gesture of surrender)*, and leaves it all to the divine Grace, with an INTENSE faith ... it's just ... impossible.
Like this *(same gesture)*.

> *(Mother plunges in
> then opens her eyes wide and looks at Satprem.
> The contemplation goes on,
> eyes open, unblinking.)*

August 26, 1972

Soup! *(laughing)* A rare thing nowadays *(laughter)*.

> *(Mother hands Satprem
> a packet of soup and some flowers)*

How are you?

Quite well, quite well!

Not too harassed?

Ohh, it's frightful ... 150 to 200 people every day—200 people every day.

272

The only days when it's less are your days.

Oh, is it!

(Mother sits gazing for a long time)

Nothing to ask?

What do you see, Mother?

(after a silence)

I feel like saying *(smiling)*: nothing! Nothing, I see nothing. . . .
There's no longer "something that sees," but I AM, I am a myriad
things.
I live a myr-i-ad things.
There are so, so many—so many—that it's like nothing! . . . I
don't know how to say it.

Yes!

(long silence)

The body is becoming aware of the Force passing through, like
this *(gesture through the fingers)*.
Like this *(same gesture)*.
Do you feel it?

Yes! Oh yes, of course!

(Mother plunges in)

August 30, 1972

How are you?

I think I'm well.

Well, so am I! *(laughter)*

(silence)

I can clearly see that instead of thought governing life, it's consciousness. And when the consciousness remains quietly open to the Divine, all goes well. A lot of things constantly come into the consciousness, from the whole world, it would seem *(gesture of being assailed from all sides):* all the things that negate or oppose the divine Action. They keep coming all the time like this *(same gesture).* But if I can remain quiet *(gesture of offering, hands open),* in an attitude of ... *(smiling)* nonexistence, a sort of ... I don't know if it's transparency—I don't know if one should say "transparency" or "immobility"—but it's something in the consciousness that's like this *(same gesture of offering, hands open).* When it stays that way, all is well; but as soon as it starts stirring, that is, as soon as the individuality comes to the forefront in any way, everything becomes detestable. Devastating, really.

You see, the physical body has a millennium of past experiences that says, "Why, that blissful state is impossible!"—this stupidity is what delays everything. It's as if the cells themselves, the cells of the body which are used to struggling and suffering, couldn't accept that things can be like this *(same gesture of surrender, hands open).* But when it IS ... then it's wonderful.

Only it doesn't last. It's not daylong. Constantly, constantly things keep coming *(same gesture of being assailed from all sides).*

But now I see quite well, quite clearly—it's very clear: consciousness replaces thought.

Yes, yes.

And ... (how can I put it?) the difference between the two: thought is something that goes like this *(whirling, restless gesture),* ever in motion ... whereas consciousness is like this *(gesture hands open, offered upward).* I can't explain it.

> *(Mother closes her eyes,
> her hands remain open)*

Do you have something to say or ask?

I was wondering what I could do to accelerate the process. Everyday life is beset by so many harassing things.... What can one do to accelerate the process?

If one could remain untroubled, it would make a big difference.

274

Yes.

A big difference.

You see, my body is beginning—just beginning—to know that the divine side means a life that's ... *(Mother stretches out both arms in the vastness)* progressive and luminous; but there's an accumulation of past experiences which says, "Oh, that's impossible!"—just like that. Well, that stupid "impossible" is what delays and spoils everything.

The basis of the fact is that as soon as the body steps out of the right attitude things get painful: everything aches and is laborious —you feel death and dissolution everywhere. And that's what reinforces ... Matter's stupidity.

So, really speaking, I'd rather not talk, unless it's to answer a specific question.

In my case, I wonder to what exact point I should apply myself?

(after a silence)

Do you feel you have gone beyond thought?

Oh yes, completely. The only thing left is mechanical thought, but otherwise.... I can say I never use the thinking process: I always feel I draw things from above. The speculative mind, for example, is just impossible for me.

Well, it's good then, you're on the right track.

Well, maybe! But practically speaking, one is struggling with everything and feels a bit ... submerged at times.

As for me, you know, all the things I used to rely on for action seem to be PURPOSELY collapsing (everything, even the smallest things) so I can say: what You will. It's become ... it's become my sole refuge.

I don't remember anything, you know! For instance, somebody says to me, "You'll say this to that person," I sincerely answer yes, but the next minute or so I no longer remember what it was! ...[1] I remember nothing—zero.

---

1. But if the slightest trace of deeper truth exists in what Mother is asked to say, she remembers it perfectly!

275

Sometimes I can stay for hours in a sort of peaceful and luminous contemplation, and think it's been only a few minutes.

To the ordinary and undiscerning eye, you must accept to look like a.... I am sure that ninety-nine people out of a hundred think I am ... *(smiling)* cracked.

No—no, Mother! No, that's....

It's UTTERLY unimportant.

I can see it in their consciousness, but it makes me smile. You have to accept that.

But there are also a good number who see the Light too, you know.

Possibly. *(Laughing)* Good for them!

(silence)

Often, very often I ask the Lord: how can I help now that I can't see so well, can't hear so well, can't speak clearly and need help to get around? This state is.... Yet the body doesn't sense any decline! It is convinced that if tomorrow the Lord wanted it to resume its regular activity, it could do so. The Force is there *(Mother touches her arms, her muscles)*, a terrible force sometimes! ... So why? ...

This state is intentional so that ... *(smiling)* so that people will leave me alone!

Yes, Mother, it's true, I really think it's true.

There you are. Otherwise people would never leave me alone.

You would be flooded in no time with truckloads of futile problems.

Yes, futile! Their problems are all futile! *(Mother laughs)* And how impudent: infidelity in marriage, lack of honesty at work! Things of that sort. Unbelievable—it's unbelievable. People ask me such questions ... *(laughing)* such improbable questions!

All the rules, you know—oh, all the moral rules seem to have been thrown to the winds. So the appearances are.... I'll give you an example: somebody [from the Ashram] opens a "Travel Agency," and when people give him money to buy tickets, he pockets the money and doesn't buy the tickets—what do you think of that? *(laughter)* What next!

(silence)

But, you know, I'm sure your condition is intentional, because as I can perceive it in my small mesure, I feel you are a kind of colossal power transmitter in your immobility.

Yes, I know. I know, it's colossal! Yes, a Force that's.... And even in my hands: an incredible power.

(silence)

(Smiling) Often, you know, I look ... (how can I put it?).... You are in the consciousness—you see, you are IN the consciousness —and so I look to see what place you occupy in the consciousness. Well ... *(Mother keeps her eyes closed, smiling).*

Mon petit, I don't want you to feel ... *(Mother makes a gesture of strutting)*, I don't mean to compliment you, that's not my intention. But you're always ... you're like a luminous garden ... with a distinct form *(Mother draws a kind of rectangle in the air)*, it's luminous and ranges from vivid pink to golden light. Exactly. And that's you—that's how I see you. Always.

There is a vast atmosphere—a vast atmosphere.... A vast atmosphere enveloped in Sri Aurobindo's aura: the blue, the luminous light blue which is his color. I see you in that ... you're like a distinct garden *(same gesture)* with colors ... it goes from vivid pink to ... a luminous, golden atmosphere. A lovely garden. That's what I see—I see it eyes open *(Mother touches her open eyes)*. And that's very good.

There remain a few spots of rigidity, I mean ... (what can I say?) fixities of a personal nature, but ... gradually, gradually, they are disappearing, they are being transformed. There. That's what I see.

*(Mother plunges in till the end,
then Sujata comes to her)*

(Sujata:) Mother, my uncle,[1] who came to see you yesterday with me, told me afterwards, "I don't know if you could see it, but I saw a Light coming out of Mother's face...."

(Mother laughs)

So I asked him, "But what effect did it have on you?" He said, "You know, I don't have any personal desire, nothing, I simply wanted to ... bow before that."

(Mother smiles)

---

1. Later this person was greatly instrumental in pleading Auroville's case with the government of India when the impostors tried to jail the Aurovilians and deport them from the country.

September

September 6, 1972

*(Mother calls Satprem and Sujata in at 10:30 A.M.
instead of 10:00.)*

On your days, the Wednesdays and Saturdays, I see only the Ashram *birthdays*, but we're now more than 2000, just fancy! So it's.... I see the other birthdays on other days and several at a time, but even so quite a few people come on your days—next Saturday in particular, the 9th (a mass of people in the Ashram were born the 9th).

All right, Mother, all right, I get the point! [laughter]

So I'll have to call you at 10:30 instead of 10:00.[1]
What about you, are you feeling better?

A little better [a problem with an eye].

The world seems to be engulfed in a sort of violent chaos. They're fighting at the Olympic Games!... An athlete was killed by bullets.[2] That's how it is.

Yes, they killed an Israeli.

Yes, the Arabs did it.

These Muslims really have something which is ... something that must disappear, Mother. They're so fanatical!

They are very violent.

Yes, fanatical.

Very violent.

I don't know what universal trait they symbolize, but they really seem to be....

---

1. Which means 11:00 instead of 10:30!
2. In fact, a dozen Israeli athletes were killed by Arab terrorists.

Force.

Force.... Well, they spend their time stabbing each other.

(after a silence)

You see, they firmly believe there's life after the body's death
—the body's death to them is in no way the end of life.

They only believe in some sort of heaven, that's all.

(Laughing) Yes, murderers' heaven!

(long silence)

Eating is becoming almost—almost impossible. Nor do I have
the faintest idea of what will replace food *(Mother sweeps her
hand across her forehead)*: I don't see anything.

Everything is becoming ... I can't say a suffering, but a discomfort: a discomfort, there's perpetual discomfort, as if my body
were made to live through every single thing that must disappear.
Nonstop. From time to time, for a few seconds there's ... *(Mother
opens eyes filled with wonder)*, but not even long enough to be able
to define it. And it's very rare. Whereas the other condition is
almost constant. Everything—external things, internal things,
things in so-called others, things concerning this body—all, all is
terrible, terrible, terrible....

That's certainly how Buddha saw things, and why he said that
life was a falsehood and had to disappear—but I know better! I
KNOW it isn't a falsehood. But it must change ... must change....
But in the meantime....

Only when I am *(gesture, hands open)* absolutely silent within
and everywhere ... does it becomes tolerable.

(silence)

I feel a fantastic Power *(Mother touches her fingertips)*, but ...
also sense a little person full of ... (how can I put this?) containing
all the things that must disappear. As if all the negations had accumulated here so that I do the work, and I don't know who that "I"
is anymore.

The body, this poor body, is not happy—it isn't unhappy either.
It has a sensation of nonexistence. Everything it encounters, the

282

entire organization of things, its entire life is the negation of what it sees as the ... Beauty to be realized.

That's all.

(Mother plunges in)

September 9, 1972

(This morning, someone told Mother he saw her in his sleep, and she was walking along in the street.)

... I'll walk along in the street when I am hundred years old.

* *

(Mother sits looking at Satprem, smiling, for more than fifteen minutes.)

Nothing to ask?

I very much felt Sri Aurobindo.

Aah!

(Mother plunges in)

September 13, 1972

I wrote this the other day *(Mother holds a piece of paper),* and Z told me, "Oh, this would be good for the New Year!" But it's in English.... Can you read it?

> "When you are conscious of the whole world at
> the same time, then you can become conscious
> of the Divine."

My idea is not that being conscious of the world automatically makes you conscious of the Divine, but when your consciousness is vast enough to see and be conscious of the whole world, then you become capable of....

How can I say it?... I don't want to be too specific. I mean I want each one to understand according to his capacity—you follow? Do you follow what I mean?

Yes, yes, Mother!

A person with a superficial consciousness will understand in that way, but one with a deeper consciousness will understand the real meaning.

Now I'll put it in French *(Mother dictates):*

> *Quand vous devenez conscient du monde tout
> entier en même temps, alors vous êtes capable
> d'être conscient du Divin.*

Is it all right?

Yes, Mother, but "alors" [= then] isn't necessary: "Quand vous devenez conscient du monde tout entier en même temps, vous êtes capable d'être conscient du Divin."

I purposely put "alors" [then] because otherwise it would mean that by becoming conscious of the whole world, you automatically become conscious of the Divine—which isn't true. It's but one aspect of the Divine. That's why I put "alors."

All right?

Yes, yes, Mother. But if you read it literally, it means you have to be conscious of the whole world ...

... in order to be capable of becoming conscious of the Divine. That's the idea. But I don't want to put it in those terms, you see. I want each one to ...

... to understand in his own way, from his own particular level.

Yes, because as the Work progresses, true consciousness develops
—but I don't want to say that.
But is it in good French?

Yes, yes, it's fine! It's very good! [laughter]

(silence)

And what about your own progress?

Well, I very much wonder!

(Mother laughs) Same here!

(silence)

But it's an incredible situation, you know: either true consciousness or the sensation of an impending and general danger. Everything—eating, taking a bath—is a danger, you see. The only thing
that's ... (Mother opens her arms and hands in a gesture of
contemplative abandon).
Except resting, at least up to now—resting is nice: it's relaxation
in the Divine. Both are nice: resting and silence—immobility (provided my body's position doesn't hurt too much), then I think I
could stay like that for centuries. Just being employed in ...
(What should I say? No work is involved): just letting the Divine
go through me, through this body. More and more, when someone
is here, in silence, it's ... (gesture indicating the Force flowing
through Mother) to reach the point where there's nothing but the
Divine.
Those two things are very good. The most difficult thing of all is
eating. There's ... no, neither disgust, nor dislike, nor anything of
the kind (no sensations are involved): a physical impossibility.
A real problem. Something to be found—but what?
I hope you haven't got that problem?

*Not for eating, no! But it looks as if progress means becoming
constantly aware of everything that's not good ...*

Yes, yes.

... everything that goes wrong or is defective.

Yes, yes, that's exactly it!

285

But then it's terribly negative, a drudgery.

Yes, but don't you . . .? *(gesture of interiorization)* Do you sleep at night?

Badly, not well.

Me, I don't sleep at all anymore, but it's . . . it's marvelous! The only marvelous moment *(immobile gesture, arms and hands open in total surrender)*. It's absolutely like bathing in the Lord, you know: like this *(same gesture)*. There's no active sensation, no . . . nothing. Nothing. Nothing but . . . a luminous peace.

This is certainly what will eventually replace sleep. Sleep, the fall into unconsciousness we call sleep, will disappear and be replaced by *(same gesture, arms open, smiling)*.

For the body, it's . . . we could say, bathing in the Lord.

There's not even a trace, not the faintest sensation of an individual person—utterly gone. It's a STATE of consciousness.

A state of consciousness.

> *(Mother plunges in,*
> *her arms and hands open)*

September 16, 1972

Here's a "Grace"—for both of you.

> *(Mother gives a white hibiscus)*

I had a practical question to ask you. . . . A thought occurred to me, and I'd like to know how you consider it. Two or three years ago, I sent my book, "The Sannyasin," to Europe; I asked P.L. to try to find a publisher for it in Europe. Now it's in the hands of "Auropress." When I sent it to Europe, P.L. asked me, "What terms do you have in mind for the book?" I wrote him what came to me at the time: "This book belongs to India,

I owe it to India, and if it generates any profit, that money belongs to India." But in Europe they didn't want it, and now it's in the hands of Auropress. So the financial question arose again: where will the profits go? Naturally my immediate reaction was: "All the money must go to Mother, it belongs to Mother." Then, my old thought about India came back: "This book must go to India, the profits belong to India." So, I'd like to know if this idea has any sound basis, or should I just leave it the way we normally do, that is, all the money from the book will be given to you?

(silence)

Naturally, I make no distinction between you and India....

Yes, yes! That's what I thought *(laughter).*

Evidently. Also, I am sure you will use the money much better than the government people possibly could.

Oh, indeed!

Without any doubt. But since that thought crossed my mind, I wanted to put it to you.

Well, I can't say, but it seems to me that ... I am the best representative![1]

Yes, Mother, undoubtedly!

(silence)

How is P.L.?

No news.

(Mother goes into contemplation)

---

1. The money simply ended up in the pockets of the manager of Auropress. From all sides they swindled. It is frightful.

September 20, 1972

(*Satprem's eyes are still in poor condition.*)

So, what about your eyes?

And you, how are you?

Me ... the consciousness is progressing.

> (*Satprem rests his head on Mother's knees.*
> *She puts her left hand over his right eye.*)

If you could stop everything for ten days ... don't use your eyes to read or write—not look at anything, just use your eyes to see what's indispensable, to eat or move about. I don't know, there's a kind of automatic vision that isn't tiring. It's when you "look" at something that it tires you. I wish you had ten whole days of that automatic vision.

You are now my eyes for the work, you understand, so you must keep them in good condition. Myself, I see everything ... through a sort of veil. But I've gained a new perception for it. I don't see in quite the same way; it's as if I saw more inside, I don't know how to explain it. That's increasing. Growing. But it takes long, so long....

September 30, 1972

I've found a very interesting quotation from Sri Aurobindo.

What is it?

This one:

"The principle of mechanical repetition is very strong in the material nature, so strong that it makes one easily think that it is incurable. That, however, is only a trick of the forces of this material inconscience; it is by creating this impression that they try to endure. If, on the contrary, you remain firm, refuse to be depressed or discouraged and, even in the moment of attack, affirm the certainty of eventual victory, the victory itself will come much more easily and sooner."

(Letters on Yoga, XXIV.1336)

Oh, this is very, very, VERY good! Oh, it's excellent! (Laughing) It's perfect for you![1]

(silence)

What's difficult is keeping the consciousness stable.

(Mother approves vigorously)

The minute you stop being active, it's very easy: everything becomes still and concentrated—the Force flows. But the moment you return to some activity, it all goes away.

(Mother nods vigorously)

I don't know what kind of power, or inner opening, would bring that automatic stability?

In my case, you see, it was a radical action: the mind and vital were simply gone. Therefore the body had to re-create little by little a new mental and vital activity. And it's very interesting, because it happened only when it was needed. So naturally, it's not perfect —speech mainly. That's the most bothersome, for I have trouble expressing myself; but the rest, oh!... (pointing to the silent forehead, then arms outstretched and motionless, as if everything were suspended in the immutable Eternal). As soon as it's like that, it becomes VAST, luminous, tranquil....

---

1. Mother is alluding in particular to Satprem's eye troubles.

289

And time no longer counts.

(Mother plunges in
until the end)

You must rest until you are cured—completely cured.

October

October 7, 1972

And your eyes?

I can't stop the work; everything is programmed. I'm not worried.

> *(Satprem reads to Mother some passages from the conversation of August 30 for the next "Notes On the Way.")*

That's all?

Will it do, Mother?... I've cut quite a few things out, but do you think what's left is all right?

It's very personal.

I've cut a lot already; but, you see, if you remove all the personal parts, nothing much remains....

(Laughing) Nothing at all remains!

For instance, when I answer your question about whether I still use the thinking process, I don't consider myself a "person," I'm simply a human "representative" whose answer may enlighten others. It may help other people.

Oh, certainly!

But that's all I have for the Bulletin, *I have nothing else.*

It's enough! The November issue is always thinner anyway.

Yes, but also you don't say much. You haven't spoken much about your experience lately.

I can't speak.
Besides, I have nothing to say.

!!!

What's here is just.... It's like this *(gesture of offering, hands open).* Truly that's how it is, I have nothing to say.

A possible formulation would be: constantly, constantly as if on one hand I were telling the Lord, "What do You want me to do?", and on the other hand....

> *(silence*
> *eyes closed*
> *hands opened*
> *in total surrender)*

Yes, like that.

The sensation is one of being as ... as transparent and impersonal as possible so the Divine can pass through and act. And here *(pointing to the forehead),* it's completely silent ... just this *(gesture, hands open and immobile).* That's all. My whole life is that way.

The more the body is able to do this *(same gesture),* the better its conditions of life. Truly. I mean ... "solicitude" isn't the word, we would need a special word.... In English, I could say: *The care the Divine takes of my body* ... (you understand?) is ... beyond all description. And above all beyond all the body's physical shortcomings.

There you are.

But all words belittle—they belittle ridiculously.

I'd like to stop talking.

> *(meditation)*

October 11, 1972

> *(After inquiring about Satprem's health.)*

And in general is it better?

Yes. I don't know, how do you see it yourself?

(Mother laughs) I mean, is it better on the whole? ... Can't you hear?

Yes, yes, of course I can hear! You mean the whole of ...

Of you?

Oh, me.... I don't know, I'm a speck of dust ... that is trying to be a little useful, that's all.

(Mother nods her head)

But I don't know what "me" is. Whenever I see that "me," it seems quite ridiculous and dark.

(Mother laughs)

Everything good in me isn't "me" at all.

That I understand!

So I really don't know.

That's very good.

Yes, but the person I "inhabit," if I may say so, seems so dark, so small, so ... oh, so uninteresting!

Listen, it's the Divine who made us the way we are....

Yes, Mother.

... Our unconsciousness is what prevents us from knowing it, otherwise we would always be in a kind of luminous peace, and simply: what You want, Lord, what You want ... *(Mother opens her hands in a gesture of total surrender).* Like that.

For me—I mean, for this sort of ... for this *(Mother pinches the skin of her arms),* which has lived so many years but doesn't know anything anymore, and can't do anything anymore, there's only ... *(same gesture of surrender, hands offered to the Lord).*

Whatever conscious will is left is used to remain attentive—attentive, absolutely still and peaceful *(gesture of listening to the above).* To try not to obstruct or distort what the Lord ... *(Mother corrects herself)* what the Divine wants. That's all. And not a personal Divine: the Divine Consciousness at work in the world.

We know nothing, we know absolutely nothing, we are totally stupid really, but if we can be like this *(gesture, hands open)*: receptive—receptive in a silence ... a silence that worships ... Light, Light ... a perfect Knowledge and unerring Will....

*(Mother opens her hands
long silence)*

You have nothing to say?

No, Mother.

Or ask?

One always has a feeling of ... yes, of always being full of all sorts of problems. There's a hiatus, an increasingly painful chasm between a life you know is tranquil and vast, and a person who is.... You feel the disparity between the two is getting more and more poignant.

Yes, that's exactly what I am living through.
But then I've learned that there's only one way:

(Mother opens her hands)

That is it. Do you understand?

(Mother plunges in)

October 14, 1972

So the 30th is your birthday?

Well, yes!

What's your birthday wish?

Liberation.

Good.
How old will you be?

Forty-nine.

Baah! ... *(as if to say: still a child)*

(Mother plunges in,
then she "looks")

Did you see something in me?

I find you are going well.
There was Peace, a luminous Peace *(enveloping gesture)*. I find you are going well.
All is going well, it's good.

October 18, 1972

(This is the season of "pujas," the time of rituals to the Universal Mother.)

Do you want some silence?

Yes, Mother, if you like.... I'm tempted to ask you if Durga won a victory this year?

We shouldn't talk about it.
I think it was a REAL victory.

(Mother plunges in till the end.
Then Sujata draws near her)

Did I give you the [blessing] packets yesterday?

Of "Victory," yes.

(To Satprem:) Did he get the Victory?

(Satprem:) Yes, Mother, I hope so! [laughter]

(Sujata:) Which victory, Mother?

Which victory? But there is only one, my child.

297

Which is?

Which is THE Victory . . . we can call it what we like: the Victory of Truth over Falsehood, the Victory of the Lord over his creation.

Which means the creation will now go consciously towards the Divine?

Ohh!

Eh, Mother? No? Not yet? . . . Not quite yet?

Well, that Victory is still only for a few.

The creation consciously going towards its divine Origin and ready to manifest that Origin is still only for a few. I think it will take centuries until it becomes general—oh, centuries, maybe millenniums!

But what matters is for us to be the few who are conscious, who consciously . . . *(silence, Mother opens her hands)* . . . manifest the Divine. That is our victory, for a few of us, which we can and must win and embody—by "win," I mean overcome the material resistance in the body *(Mother pinches the skin of her arm)*. That we can and it is our duty to overcome—I mean all the stupid unconscious resistance. That must come to an end. This is our work, and it must be done here *(pointing to the body)*.

(silence)

You say it will take centuries or even millenniums. But, for instance, would it not go faster by contagion? No?

We'll see, mon petit! Let's first do what we should do. Let's concentrate on that.

Let's do what we should do.

Yes, Mother.

298

October 21, 1972

Look how lovely!

(Mother gives Satprem a white lotus)

And you, Mother, how are you?

(after a long silence)

You see, I would either have to describe every single thing that keeps happening, or say nothing at all.

When I say nothing and just stay like this *(gesture, open hands)* ... in an attitude of absolute *surrender,* things go on well. But if the SLIGHTEST thing pulls me out of it, I feel ... as if I were about to die.

Extraordinary.

When I am in that position, I get the feeling that ... life is eternal.

(silence)

And when I come out of it, there's a horrible discomfort. That's my condition.

(silence)

Well, what do you want?

What you want.

(Mother plunges in till the end)

No news? Tell me whatever you like.

David, the young Italian who made a documentary on Sri Aurobindo, now wants to film "The Gold Washer." But he wants to do it in the true spirit, with your help, showing how it inevitably leads to Sri Aurobindo and you.

Oh, very good! Very good.

October 25, 1972

> *(Satprem gives Mother a flower,*
> *and Mother gives it to Satprem.)*

It's "Power of Truth in the Subconscient."

How are you?

Physically I'm well, I think.

The governor [of Pondicherry] is coming here to say good-bye, but he hasn't arrived yet. I've asked to be informed of his arrival; you'll just sit over there while I see him, and then you'll come back.

> *(after a silence)*

All possible contradictions are accumulated in the subconscient.

Yes.

And it keeps coming up like this *(gesture gushing out)*, all the time, all the time. And ... you feel you are completely stupid, unconscious, obdurate.
All that is ... *(same gesture rising from below)*.
But the consciousness here *(gesture around the head)* is peaceful, extraordinarily peaceful ... *(Mother opens her hands)*: let Your Will be done, Lord. So "that" exerts a pressure on what rises from below.
As though the battle of the world were being fought in my consciousness.
It has come to a point that forgetting, forgetting the Divine for just a single minute is catastrophic.
How about you, how are things for you?

Well, the cleansing of the subconscient seems just endless, Mother.

Yes, because it isn't one person's subconscient: it is THE EARTH's subconscient. It's endless. Yet we must....

300

Stopping that would mean stopping the work. Going on with it means it will take ages.... I don't know ... it's endless.

Although clearly, quite clearly, stopping it would mean stopping the work. As if this consciousness *(gesture around Mother)* were the meeting point and the center of action.

So my sole means is to remain quiet—very, very quiet ... *(Mother opens her hands upwards).* To feel that the individuality is nothing, absolutely nothing—so the divine rays can pass, pass through it. It's the only solution. It must be the Divine who ... who fights the battle.

(silence)

Last time you said, "It will take centuries, perhaps millenniums, before humans consciously turn to the Divine." But....

Maybe not.

One's impression is that this time, something decisive should occur.

Yes.... You know, my impression is that the individuality is like an image to focus the attention (humans need something —they have always needed something on their scale to focus their attention), so the body tries its best not to obstruct the divine Force from passing through, it tries to suppress all its own inter-ferences, but at the same time it sees itself ... as an image humans need to focus their attention.

(At this point, Governor J. enters the room, sits silently before Mother, remains a few minutes in meditation, then does his pranam and leaves the room.)

(Mother plunges in till the end Sujata comes up to Mother)

(Sujata:) Mother, you know, I saw you yesterday morning be-tween 4:00 and 4:30, and you were giving your blessings to everybody. You were sitting on a very high seat, dressed in a white sari (if I recall correctly), and I was among the first to approach you for pranam. I knelt before you, brought my hands together, and bowed my head. Then you held my head, and suddenly I noticed I couldn't raise my head anymore! And

301

I realized you were forcing my head downwards: you know, with your hands you were pressing, so my head kept going down and down and down. Finally I saw your feet—I was very close to your feet—and what lovely feet they were, Mother! All white and ... wonderful. Translucent almost.[1]

(Mother smiles and caresses Sujata's cheek)

October 28, 1972

What would you like? ... Nothing?

Do you think I'm soon going to pass into another life?

Another life?

Yes, another consciousness, let's say.

(after a silence)

I wanted to ask you something. You know the mantra I gave you, I don't remember if the last word is Bhagavatee or Bhagavateh?

Bhagavateh, Mother.

Ah, Bhagavateh! ... (Mother repeats the mantra) OM Namo Bhagavateh ... like that.

Yes, Mother.

(meditation)

Did you notice how strong the mantra is on the subconscient? It

---

1. The feet are the symbol of matter.

has a great, great power over the subconscient.

I told you what a nuisance the subconscient is, didn't I? ...

Oh, yes!

But, repeating that mantra has a great, great effect on it.

(silence)

One mustn't ... one mustn't ... [get impatient]. If people can have trust....

Eating has become almost an impossibility, mon petit. In my case it's all right because I don't do anything, I am immobile all day, so if I don't eat it doesn't matter too much, but people who work and move and come and go must take care.

(Imploringly) Let me do the work.

I hope ... I hope it will be useful to others.

It's become ... it's become an almost unsolvable problem *(Mother holds her throat):* at times I can't even swallow.

(silence)

I've found but one solution: What You want, Lord, what You want.... And what comes up from the subconscient is constantly met by: OM namo Bhagavateh, OM....

(meditation)

October 30, 1972

(The last birthday)

Ah, happy birthday, happy birthday, happy birthday! ...

(Mother gives some presents)

These are pens....

And these are the chocolates!

303

(Mother holds Satprem's hands in hers)

Mon petit....
(To Sujata:) Naturally the chocolates are for you!
The biscuits for him.

(Sujata gives Mother flowers)

This is "Divine Grace" ... and this is "Power of Truth in the Subconscient."

(Mother gives Satprem Sujata's flowers)

Yes, Mother, yes, Mother....

Happy birthday, happy new year.

November

November 2, 1972

(Mother sees Sujata)

How is Satprem?

Quite well, Mother, I think.

And you, how are you going?

But I wanted to ask you: how is Mother going these days?

Mother isn't "going"! There's no longer any person to "go."
Mother goes where the Lord wants her to go.

(silence)

Do you understand my condition? One minute the body feels it is going to die; the next minute it feels immortal. So after that, one can't ... one can't possibly say "how it's going."
Do you understand?

Yes, little Mother, I think I do. Only, Mother, it's you who carry us along. So when we feel that things are working out for you, they work out for us also. That's how it is, isn't it?

Things always work out. I am convinced that whatever happens is willed by the Lord. It's only our impression that gets more or less warped by our ignorance.

Yes, Mother.

(silence)

My feeling is that all words, even when they sound very wise, are just stupidities. That's all. It would be far better never to say anything *(Mother puts her hand over her mouth)*. It belittles things so much, so, so much....

November 4, 1972

The whole subconscient is ... *(gesture of something rising up en masse).*

(silence)

And then ... how can I put this? ... It isn't sensation or knowledge, it's a kind of ... *(Mother feels the air between her fingers)*, you can't even say conviction: it's a certitude—a certitude in the perception—that Bliss is there ... right there, WAITING FOR US, but a whole world of contradictions that have been repressed in the subconscient keeps rising up from the subconscient to prevent us from feeling it. So ... you could say it's a battlefield, but in a perfect calm.

It's impossible to describe.

Impossible to describe.

When I remain still and enter that Consciousness, time flies with fantastic speed, in a kind of ... luminous calm. But the slightest thing that pulls me out of it seems to pull me into hell. Exactly.

The discomfort is so great one feels one couldn't last a minute or a few minutes like that. So one ... one calls the Divine.... You feel like curling up in the Divine.

And then it goes well.

(Mother plunges in
but after a while she seems ill at ease)

November 8, 1972

For a moment—just a few seconds—I had the supramental consciousness. It was so marvelous, mon petit! ... I understood that if we were to taste that now, we would no longer want to exist differently. We are in the process of ... *(gesture of kneading dough)* of changing laboriously. And the change, the process of change seems. . . . Yet you can grasp it in a kind of indifference (I don't know how to express it).

But it doesn't last long. As a rule it's . . . laborious.

But that consciousness is so marvelous, you know!

It's most interesting because there's a sort of EXTREME activity within complete peace.

But it lasted only a few seconds.

(silence
hands turned upwards)

And you?

Is it a total consciousness?

It's fabulous! Like a harmonization of all opposites. Yes, a total, fantastic activity together with . . . perfect peace.

But these are mere words.

(silence)

Is this consciousness material?

The action is a material one—but not done in the same way, of course.

(silence)

What helps make the contact with "that"?... What exactly makes you go across there or be there?

I don't know because I am constantly—my WHOLE consciousness, including that of the body, is always turned to the . . . *(gesture of offering)* to what it feels as the Divine.

And without "trying," you follow?

Yes. Yes.

(Mother plunges in)

November 11, 1972

(Mother does not look too well.)

We'll need a message for the November darshan.

*(Mother remains silent
then writes with her eyes closed)*

Beyond all preferences and limitations,
there is a ground of mutual understanding where
all can meet and find their harmony:
it is the aspiration for a divine consciousness.[1]

(With a charming smile) Nothing to ask?

*(Satprem shakes his head
Mother keeps her eyes closed)*

November 15, 1972

(Mother seems very impersonal and faraway.)

So?

I have a feeling I sometimes see you at night.

(Mother nods: yes, yes)

And you, the work, Mother?

---

1. Original English.

What?

Your work?

"My" work....
Poetically, I could say: a few seconds in heaven and ... hours in hell.
It's better not to speak about it.

(Mother moans while in trance)

November 18, 1972

I wish I could disappear to do the work better.

(Mother remains within the whole time)

You'll be better over there [at Nandanam].

November 22, 1972

What do you wish?

Well, you know, I always wish to ask you how things stand.

Oh! ... Better not speak about that.

Yes. I understand it's a process ...

Oh! ...

... that's infinite and....

Yes. Either I say everything or nothing at all. And saying every-thing is.... You know, there's both a constant effort and ... *(Mother opens her hands)* every minute a discovery. So describing it would be endless, and also uninteresting.

Well, I'm not so sure about that! I'm not so sure!

Therefore....

(silence)

The body consciousness is beginning to be wise, it too is saying with a great, great ... more than sincerity, "Let Your Will be done." People and their opinions and their way of seeing things seem so very ridiculous to it!

Yes, I can understand that.

Let Your Will be done.

Yes, to your vision, we must be swimming in an utterly absurd world.

Absurd, an absurdity!

That I can understand very well: this whole physical world is absurd. Without a doubt.

And even the people! ...

Yes!

... whom you thought were wise, or people who have known you for so many years—their reactions seem so absurd!
So ... *(Mother opens her hands)* let Your Will be done.

Naturally the body understands very well (it never doubts that His Will will be done: it is ALWAYS done), but let us be ... let us not be an obstacle to that Will or a complication: let us allow things to be done luminously and peacefully—consciously, luminously, peacefully ... all-encompassingly.

Let us not be part of the obstacles. Let us be ... *(Mother opens her hands)* let the supreme Wisdom pass, pass through ... something that is not an extra obstacle. That's all.

(Mother plunges in)

November 25, 1972

(The day before, Mother came out on her balcony for the November "darshan.")

How was it yesterday, on the balcony?

(Mother returns the question) How was it?

I don't know.... Seemingly quite good, in any case!

Where were you?

At the door of Sujata's house, downstairs. And for you, how was it?

(long silence)

(Smiling) The apprenticeship of personal nonexistence.
I don't know....
It's difficult.

Yes.

A growing sensation that without the Divine there's no existence.

Forgetting the Divine even for a minute is becoming catastrophic, you see.

Now and then, for a few seconds, the true beatific consciousness comes—but only now and then and for a few seconds. That's all. Otherwise, I am like this (gesture, fists clenched to stand firm in the struggle).

(silence)

And you?

I have a lot of difficulties with my outer consciousness. I seem to be unable to open it up.

(Mother vigorously nods her head)

And so it's very painful, you know, everything is very painful.

That's it, exactly that! One quite feels the inability of the outer consciousness to participate in the experience ... to be up to the mark.

Yes! Exactly, absolutely.

Well, that's my continuous condition.

How to ...? And then once a day—once, twice, for a few seconds (tone of amazed wonder): "Oh! ..." And it's gone.

Is this ... this body to be left and another one built? I don't know.... It doesn't fit with.... I have not been told that it has to be that way.

No.

Although I haven't been told either that this body is capable of transformation. So I don't know.

But Sri Aurobindo did tell you that you would do the work.

(In a dubious tone:) Yes, he told me....

Because if you left, what would we do here? Truly, we are completely useless, there's nothing else to do but leave. Because the only place....

314

But it has no desire to leave.

Yes, I know, Mother.

It doesn't know, that's all. And . . . I can't exactly say I suffer but there's constant discomfort.

There's obviously discomfort for you, but for us, the only moments we feel truly alive are those spent with you.

Oh, mon petit . . . *(Mother takes Satprem's hands).*

It's true, the factual truth. I know the Grace it is to be here.

> *(long silence*
> *holding Satprem's hands)*

That is the conviction the body needs to have: that INDEED it serves some purpose.[1]

Oh, but of course!. . . But of course, it does!

> *(silence)*

You see, being here, with you, is the only moment when one feels . . . ah, this is IT. IT, you know.

> *(Mother plunges in*
> *still holding Satprem's hands)*

---

1. That is what Mother needed so much. When they closed Mother's door on me, they condemned her to death. It is the plain truth. But not one understood that, or even tried to. Not one. What was their heart made of then?

November 26, 1972

(A Note by Mother in English)

Before dying falsehood rises in full swing.

Still people understand only the lesson of catastrophe. Will it have to come before they open their eyes to the truth?

I ask an effort from all so that it has not to be.

It is only the Truth that can save us: truth in words, truth in action, truth in will, truth in feelings. It is a choice between serving the Truth or being destroyed.

December

December 2, 1972

> *(Mother has just spent an hour and fifteen minutes*
> *eating her "breakfast.")*

Do you have something?

No, nothing in particular, Mother.

Then I'll give you only ten minutes. Something strange is happening which I don't understand—and it's getting stronger and stronger: it took me more than an hour to eat my breakfast, yet when I started I told myself: I must finish this in twenty minutes. And I really thought I had finished in twenty minutes!

Time ... I have completely lost the sense of time.

I was convinced I had finished in twenty minutes and it took me more than an hour—to eat nothing!

I take a bite or a sip, and then ten minutes, twenty minutes go by *(gesture showing the glass or spoon in midair while Mother goes off)* ... I don't know where, I don't know what.

But what's extraordinary is the disparity: usually I don't think about the time, but since it was your day and it was already late, I told myself: I must finish in twenty minutes—and it took me more than an hour!

There's something there I must understand. Clearly, the standard of time changes. But it's very impractical.

But is this consciousness you go into ... (what's the word?)
active or immobile?

(Mother closes her eyes for a moment) I feel I am in a light. A light that's. . . .

If I go into it, it will last an hour!

The same at night: I don't sleep; at first, as I lie in bed, I have a pain here, a pain there. . . . Then I enter the consciousness where pain disappears, and suddenly I wake up (I am not "asleep," I am in ... a light, a formless light), with the impression I've been in bed an hour, while in actuality it was five or six.

I just go into ... *(Mother closes her eyes)* oh, I tell you it can last ... I have but to do this *(Mother closes her eyes)* ... I could keep you here for an hour and not know it!

But today I am so late, I shouldn't keep you.
I regret it; but something has to be found.

But is this light active? Or are you just....

Oh, yes! It does PLENTY of things.... But not, not in the usual
way. It's....
(*Mother closes her eyes for a moment*)

Did you feel something?

Yes, Mother![1]

Well, that's how it is. And hours go by unnoticed.
One day I must take you there with me.

Yes, Mother.

Not today. But one day when I am not late, we'll go there
together, and perhaps you'll know. Yes.
One must be patient, mon petit.

(*Satprem hands Mother a garland of "Aspiration"*)

Oh, how nice it smells!
What day is today?

Saturday.

What date is next Wednesday?

The 6th, Mother.

The 6th, there will be a lot of people probably....

And the 9th there's also a meditation.

So we'll have to postpone it for the week after. What date will
that be?

---

1. Always that same massive power which seems to rise from within and seize the
whole being in a kind of solid fire.

December 13.

(To the attendant:) Put as few people as possible on the 13th.

(The attendant:) I don't put anyone!

I want to try an experiment.

(The attendant:) I won't put anyone ... extra.

Good. So let's be patient!

> *(Satprem rests his forehead on Mother's knees)*

It's completely, completely new.... Something completely new, which I don't understand.
We'll see. I would be interested to do it with you and see your sensation. But we must wait a little.
Au revoir, then.

December 6, 1972

(The night of the 5th, a violent cyclone struck Pondicherry. At Nandanam, in the middle of the devastated garden, a white hibiscus bloomed. Satprem places the flower on Mother's knees.)

A "Grace" flower bloomed in the thick of the cyclone, Mother.

> *(silence)*

(One can hear the axes hacking away at the broken branches of the great yellow flame tree called "Service," which spreads its foliage above Sri Aurobindo's tomb.)

The tree that gave me all my "Transformation" flowers [from

Satprem's garden] is broken. The "Service" tree also: some of its branches have been torn off.

Usually it didn't come this way....

The consciousness must have sunk a lot ... quite a lot.

(silence)

Some curious things are happening: the consciousness is clearer and vaster than it has ever been—a vast, vast vision ... and very precise: I know things happening at a distance (without thinking: they just come). But my memory is ab-so-lu-te-ly gone. I don't know —half an hour later, I've already forgotten what I did. Absolutely forgotten.

(silence) ·

The consciousness of the Presence—the Presence everywhere, in everything....

(Mother plunges in
then comes back to give Satprem the "Grace" flower)

Mon petit....

I would like the Grace of belonging exclusively to you.

December 9, 1972

(Mother caresses the flowers Sujata has just brought her.)

I still have my cold....

(Satprem:) But you look better, Mother.

Yes. It isn't really a "cold."

322

Yes, I am sure. . . . I felt there was a cyclone . . . a real cyclone within.

(Mother laughs) There WAS a cyclone within.

(silence)

Obviously, everything is designed so that the only . . . (I can't find the word in French) *reliance,* the only support is in the Divine. But I am not told what the "Divine" is—how do you like that! . . . Everything else is collapsing, except the . . . the . . . the what? The Divine . . . something—what? . . .

One feels it. It can't be described or defined in any way—absolutely not.

(silence)

It's like an attempt to make you feel there isn't any difference between life and death. There. That it is something else than life or death—neither what we call death, nor what we call life—it is . . . something.

And that . . . is Divine.

Or rather it is our next step towards the Divine.

December 10, 1972

(Mother sees Sujata, who reads her a letter from Satprem.)

December 10, 1972

Mother,

For the past several nights, my body seems to have been physically tortured all night long. I keep tossing and turning in pain. Also I feel as if my stomach is being clawed. I am afraid that if this goes on, I am actually

going to fall ill. In the morning when I come out of it, I
feel as if my body were full of poison.[1]
May I become entirely and exclusively your child.

Satprem

For me life is a torture if I am not exclusively turned to the
Divine. That's the only remedy; otherwise, it's true, life is a torture. Existing becomes intolerable.

The only remedy is to be like this ... *(gesture, hands turned*
upward in contemplative silence) ... when time ceases to exist.

December 13, 1972

Weren't we supposed to have a meditation?

A meditation?

Yes, Mother, you said you wanted to try an experiment with
me. You said you wanted to take me with you into that con-
sciousness....

Would you like to?

Yes, if you'd like to!

Well, personally, I am always there. So.... What's difficult for
me is to become conscious of the world as it is.
What did I tell you last time?

You said you wanted to try an experiment. You wanted to take
me with you into that consciousness to see my sensation.

---

1. I now wonder whether I was not, in my own measure, beginning to learn the
painful lesson of oneness, which starts with all the ambient ill-will. Now I understand fully well that there must be no more "person" in order to withstand all that.
If there is "somebody-who," it is painful—and dangerous.

Ah! Very good. Now?

Yes, rather!

Give me your hand.

> *(Mother takes Satprem's hand for a moment*
> *then plunges in for a full hour)*

How do you feel?... Did you feel something?

First, a lot of power, a lot, as always. But only towards the end
did I feel a kind of ... something eternal—I don't know. Do
you think I followed you a little?

(Mother nods her head) Yes, quite well. Quite well.

December 16, 1972

> *(Mother gives Satprem an egg)*

I have nothing.... I've become poor!

Then the world is poor!

(Mother laughs) How are you?

Quite well, Mother, yes, quite well.

Inside, I know.

What does the world look like to you from that other
consciousness?

> *(Mother does not seem to have heard the question)*

As I told you: I am happy—are you satisfied?

Oh, yes! Certainly!

Well, there you are; it's true.
I find you are making progress.

Ah, God willing!

Shall we go there together?

Yes, Mother! But I'd like to be able to follow you.

>   *(Mother smiles,*
> *making a gesture of pulling Satprem with a rope)*

Hem!... I'll pull you!

Good, then!

>   *(meditation*
> *then Mother opens her eyes*
> *as if she were about to speak)*

What is it, Mother?

(Smiling) I saw you: you had become very young. Like a twenty-year-old.

>   *(Mother plunges in again)*

December 20, 1972

Do you have anything to ask?

I had a question about Sri Aurobindo. I was wondering what stage he had reached when he left—what stage in the transformation? For instance, what difference is there between the work you are doing now and what he was doing at the time?

He had accumulated a great deal of supramental force in his body, and as soon as he left he.... He was on his bed, you see, and I was standing beside him, and all the supramental force that was in him passed quite concretely from his body into mine—so concretely that I thought it was visible. I could feel the friction of the passage. It was extraordinary—extraordinary! It was an extraordinary experience. It went on for a long, long time like this *(gesture of the Force passing into Mother's body)*. I was standing beside his bed, and it passed into me.

Almost physical—it was a physical sensation.

It lasted a long time.

That's all I know.

But what I want to understand is at what stage he was in the inner work—for example, cleansing the subconscient and all that? What difference is there between the work he had done at the time and where you have reached now, if you will? I mean, is the subconscient less subconscious or ...?

Oh, yes! Certainly, certainly!

But that is the mental way of looking at things, you see—I don't have it anymore.

Yes, Mother.

(silence)

Perhaps the difference lies in the general or collective intensity of that Power, that Force?

There is a difference in the POWER of the action.

He himself—he himself has a greater action, a greater power or action now than when he was in his body. Besides, that's why he left—because it had to be done that way.

It's very tangible, you know. His action has become very tangible. Of course, it isn't something mental at all. It is from another region. But it isn't ethereal or—it's tangible. I could almost say material.

I've often wondered about the right inner movement needed to go into that other region. There are basically two possible movements: a movement inwards in the direction of the soul, as it were, and a movement of annihilation of the individuality,

327

in which you are in a sort of impersonal vastness.

Both are needed.

Both?

Yes.

(Mother plunges in)

December 23, 1972

Time sense is completely topsy-turvy—when I think five minutes have passed, it's an hour, and when I think an hour has passed, it's five minutes! It's completely, completely.... And I am puzzled, I am truly puzzled as to what causes it. Another standard of time. And it doesn't follow my conscious will: I'll start eating, thinking, "I want to be finished in twenty minutes"—and it takes me an hour! On another occasion, I don't think of time: I finish in twenty-five minutes. I don't understand.
From an outward point of view, I am starting to look crazy!

!!!

At night (I have long nights, but I don't sleep), I feel it's over in one minute!... I go to bed saying to myself: ah, this will last a while—and it's over in five minutes, it seems to me.
Another time, I want to go fast, and it takes ... almost an hour. I don't understand.

Do you still have activities at night?

Yes, but they are not "dreams," you see. I mean ... it's not that kind of thing at all.
Sometimes I am identified with some people, and I thoroughly feel—I don't feel it's "another" person: I feel it's myself. And sometimes it's people I don't know. There are all kinds of things.

The consciousness is VERY vast. It isn't limited to one person or even a few persons: it is very vast.

(silence)

But I am perplexed by what's happening with clock time.... I thought it was not quite nine o'clock, and I was told it was already ten. I have no idea how that happened.

I start my breakfast telling myself: Ah, I'll eat fast, I am late—it takes me an hour!

But I don't say anything because people are so stupid they would say I am going crazy. That's not it ... I simply live in another consciousness.

It's probably necessary for your body to live in a kind of timelessness.

Oh, yes! I feel, I know—I know positively that my body is being accustomed to something else.

Because, certainly, the sense of time must bring wear and tear.

(silence)

So my one external resource—EXTERNALLY—is to say the mantra: OM Namo Bhagavateh (it's an external part of myself that says it); but inside, I am like this *(Mother opens her hands upward in total stillness)*. And now if I remain like that, hours may go by, and I won't know it.

What's the time?

Half past ten, Mother.

If you wake me ("wake me" is a way of speaking, of course!) at eleven, I'll give you an example!

Yes, Mother!

Would you like to?

Yes, of course, Mother.

329

*(Mother plunges in for forty minutes,
Satprem slightly touches her hand to call her back)*

Did you feel something?

I feel very comfortable.

(Mother laughs and takes Satprem's hands)

Yes! The trouble is that everything else is rather unpleasant!

December 26, 1972

*(Mother sees some teachers from the school. Towards the end
of the meeting, Pranab enters Mother's room in his customary
manner, heads straight for Mother, and launches into a violent
diatribe against some French television reporters—whom
Mother had received the day before—because they filmed
Sri Aurobindo's tomb "in spite of his orders."
Mother tries to calm him down.)*

When they [the reporters] cannot get something from one
person, they go to somebody else—and it works. In any event, I
won't see them anymore.

*(Pranab explodes:) If I meet them again, I'll smash their
cameras.*

I don't want any violence or nasty scenes here.

*(Pranab retreats to the other end of the room,
muttering angrily)*

(Mother sits with her head in her hands) I have worked all my life
so people would become a little conscious. But this violence....

(Mother turns to one of the teachers
with a kind of distress in her voice)

People say that I am old, that I can't speak, that I am senile, but the consciousness has never been so clear.... One minute of silence and....

(the teachers leave the room silently,
Mother remains alone with
her bodyguard and the attendant)

December 27, 1972

(Champaklal hands Satprem the French and English texts of
the Christmas message so Mother can put it
in her own handwriting.)

(Satprem:) You've put:

> We want to show to the world
> that man can become a true
> servitor of the Divine.
> Who will collaborate in
> all sincerity?

(Champaklal, in English:) Mother, shall I give you paper? Mother will write now? To send to Press?

(Satprem:) Is it necessary?

But I can't write....

(Champaklal is upset)

... I'd better write it.

> *(Mother spends twenty minutes*
> *copying the message by hand,*
> *then she holds out her hands to Satprem*
> *and plunges in)*

December 30, 1972

> *(Mother distributes presents)*

So, a new year is coming....

Do you have a feeling about the new year?

> *(after a silence)*

Things have taken an extreme form. There's a sort of lifting of the whole atmosphere towards an almost ... inconceivable splendor, but at the same time, there's a feeling that one can ... die any moment—not "die," but the body could dissolve. Both things together make up a consciousness in which ... *(Mother shakes her head)* all past experiences seem puerile, childish, unconscious. And this ... is stupendous and wonderful.

But the body, the body has a single prayer—always the same:

> Make me worthy of knowing You
> Make me worthy of serving You
> Make me worthy of being You

There.

I can barely eat anymore, and I am not hungry. I feel a growing strength in me ... but new in quality ... in silence and contemplation.

Nothing is impossible *(Mother opens her hands upward).*

> *(silence)*

So if you don't have any questions to ask.... If you want silence ... conscious silence ...?

But am I making the right movement, I'm not sure?

Well, when you want to come into contact with the Divine, what movement do you make?

I place myself at your feet.

> *(Mother smiles,*
> *takes Satprem's hands*
> *and plunges in for half an hour)*

Did you feel something?

I was offered to the Sun.

1973

CHRONOLOGY OF WORLD EVENTS

1973

January 1	– Denmark, Ireland and Great Britain formally join the Common Market.
January 28	– A cease-fire negotiated by Henry Kissinger ends direct involvement of U.S. ground troops in Vietnam.
February 7	– Creation of a Senate committee, chaired by U.S. Senator Sam J. Erwin, to investigate Watergate.
	– Dr. Kissinger visits Peking, Hanoi and Tokyo.
February 12	– Secretary of the Treasury George Schultz announces the second devaluation of the dollar in 14 months.
February 21	– *Mother is ninety-five.*
March 15	– Devastating drought in the Sahel in central Africa.
March 29	– The last U.S. troops leave Vietnam.
April 4	– Student revolt in Barcelona, Spain.
April 8	– Death of Pablo Picasso.
April 17	– President Nixon admits that, unknowingly, the White House might have been involved in Watergate
May 9	– East and West Germany establish diplomatic relations.
May 14	– Launching of the first American Skylab.
June 1	– Abolition of the Greek monarchy; Greece becomes a republic.
June 22	– Nixon and Brezhnev sign a treaty to limit nuclear war.
June 27	– China explodes its 15th thermonuclear bomb.
June 29	– President Nixon tells Congress that "America faces a serious energy problem."
July 5	– A statement from the Holy See reaffirms the Pope's infallibility.
July 16	– It is revealed that all of Nixon's conversations in the White House are on tape.
July 17	– Coup in Afghanistan; the king is deposed and the republic proclaimed.
	– In the Soviet Union, the Russian historian Amalrik is condemned for slandering the Soviet state.

July 23	– President Nixon refuses to release the tape recordings of his conversations.
August 3	– In Iran, the Shah nationalizes the oil companies.
August 5	– In Greece, Palestinian commandos fire at tourists at the Athens airport.
August 6	– Vice-President Agnew is charged with tax evasion.
August 10	– Mr. Bhutto becomes president of Pakistan.
August 15	– Under pressure from Congress, Washington stops the bombings of Cambodia.
August 18	– Campaign of violence in England by Irish extremists.
August 21	– Press conference by Soviet academician Sakharov and interview with Aleksandr Solzhenitsyn warning the West against "the illusions of detente."
August 22	– Henry Kissinger becomes U.S. Secretary of State.
August 28	– France explodes 5 nuclear devices in Polynesia.
	– India begins the release of 90,000 Pakistani prisoners of war held since 1971.
September 1	– Nationalization of the oil companies in Lybia.
September 11	– Coup in Chile; reported suicide of President Allende.
September 28	– In Austria, Palestinians attack a train transporting Jewish Soviet emigrants to Israel.
October 6	– Beginning of the Yom Kippur War against Israel by Egypt and Syria; Egyptian forces cross the Suez Canal.
October 10	– Vice-President Agnew resigns; he is replaced by Gerald Ford.
October 13	– Bloody repression of students in Bangkok, Thailand.
October 17	– Kuwaiti oil embargo against the U.S. and the Netherlands "until Israel withdraws from the occupied territories."
October 20	– Attorney General Elliot Richardson resigns in protest against President Nixon's refusal to release his tapes.
October 25	– U.S. forces are put on "precautionary alert" following information about a possible Soviet intervention in the Middle East.

November 11	– Cease-fire between Israel and Egypt.
November 14	– Student revolt in Greece.
November 16	– The Nobel Peace Prize is awarded to Henry Kissinger.
November 17	– *Mother leaves her body.*
November 29	– Mr. Brezhnev visits New Delhi; military and economic agreement between India and the Soviet Union.
December 3	– Pioneer 10 passes near Jupiter.
December 17	– Palestinian attack on Fiumicino airport in Italy.
December 23	– OPEC doubles the price of oil.

January

January 1, 1973

(Message for the year)

When you are conscious of the whole world at the same time, then you can become conscious of the Divine.[1]

January 3, 1973

(After the work)

(Sujata:) Mother, I have something to ask you, I have a prayer.... Satprem is very tormented, you know; so I pray that you will take his torment away.

Why tormented?

(Laughing:) That's his nature, Mother!

(Satprem grimaces)

You know, me, I have but one solution—always the same for anything: this *(gesture, hands open)*. To abolish all personal existence, to be like this *(same gesture)*, something that lets everything pass through and is ... set in motion by the Divine. That's all. Then everything is fine.

(Mother takes Satprem's hands, and plunges in with a sweet smile)

---

1. Original English.

January 10, 1973

Good morning, Mother!

> *(Mother hands a basket to Satprem)*

This is mouthwash! And these are eggs.
Now what do you have to tell me?

Me, nothing.

Nothing?

No, it's difficult. A difficult period.

For me too.

Yes.

> *(silence)*

So ...

Where does that come from?

... we can go in the silence if you like?

Yes, Mother, certainly! But I was asking where it comes from.

> *(after a silence)*

In my own case, I know: it's because everything that needs to be transformed is rising from the subconscient, and it's in-ter-mi-na-ble.... It keeps rising and rising and rising....

And with each little thing looms the possibility of catastrophe. So you live in a constant suggestion of catastrophes—I know where it comes from, I know what it is, but it isn't pleasant.

No.

And there's a new kind of malaise. Something new. As I was

telling you, there's a new and wonderful joy that comes! But it comes the way you disclose something, you know ... *(Mother dangles an imaginary lure between her fingers)*: "See, this is what you could have." Exactly like that. "It could be like this," and brrrt, it's gone!

So really, I'd rather not talk about it.

Yes, Mother.

> *(Mother plunges in for twenty minutes, then goes out of her room and comes back)*

Would you like to stay a little more?

You'll be late, Mother, no? It's already eleven.

You were called in late.

That doesn't matter!

Have you got some work to do?

No, Mother, not at all! But YOU have some work to do!

Oh, me ... *(Mother raises her arms)*. I live in a constant contradiction—constant, constant ... With all sorts of suggestions: "This way, you could die; that way, you could die...." So I simply reply, "I don't care!" Then it calms down.

My consolation was that I thought I was doing this for everybody; that once I had done it, it would be done—but evidently a lot of people are in the same difficulty.

Yes, but when you have finished, it'll be finished for them too.

Let's hope so....

> *(silence)*

To comfort me, there is a kind of assurance from above, that if I reach my centenary, I will start going uphill again. But it's still far off. How many years left?

Five years, Mother.

Oh, mon petit! Five more years in this hell!...

We'll try to go with you to the end.

Oh, you.... *(After a silence)* You will go to the end.

Oh, Mother.... But I can go to the end only if you go there also!

(Mother laughs
silence)

But you know, at the same time, I am aware of the divine forces going through like this *(gesture through the body)*. I try to obstruct as little as I can. And it gives some extraordinary results: constantly, there are ... what people call "miracles."

But to me, things are not yet as they could be—as they SHOULD be.

The possibility of suffering, for example—suffering from pain, suffering ... a purely physical fact (all the nonphysical things are: *Mother makes an immutable and peaceful gesture to indicate the inner states),* but something purely physical: really, the capacity for suffering must disappear. Not that I don't want to suffer, but ... it isn't a nice gift to give people!

Five years....

The years are long, long, long, long....

It's like this: two or three hours can go by in a second, and half an hour can last for hours. Everything, but everything is upside down.

(Mother gestures: what to do?
silence)

And then—oh, I haven't told you: yesterday or the day before, I don't remember, all of a sudden, for two or three minutes, my body was seized by the horror of *death*—the idea of being put like this *(gesture of being tossed into a hole)* in a tomb was so horrifying! Horrifying.... I couldn't have stood that more than a few minutes. It was HORRIFYING. Not because I was buried alive, but because my body was conscious. It was considered "dead" by everybody for the heart had stopped beating—yet the body was conscious.

(silence)

That ... that ... that was a horrible experience.... I was displaying all the signs of "death," you know, the heart wasn't working, nothing was working—but I was conscious. The body was conscious.

(silence)

We must ... we must warn people at least not to rush to ... *(gesture into a hole).*

Yes, Mother.

Oh! ...

No, we won't let that happen, don't worry. We just won't let it happen.

(silence
Mother hold Satprem's hands,
she smiles)

You are sweet.

Oh, Mother!

(Mother looks at the table beside her) I would like to give you something that you like.

I would like your presence with me, always.

Oh, that ... more and more!
(To Sujata:) How are you, mon petit?

Quite well, little Mother.

Yes?

Yes, Mother
  Yes, Mother
    Yes, Mother.

January 13, 1973

(Mother receives Satprem and Sujata fifty-five minutes late.)

Nothing to be said.... It's chaos!
The Supermind has obviously nothing in common with our regular time.

(silence)

I feel I am being pulled in opposite directions by the old world and the new....

(Mother shakes her head and plunges in)

January 17, 1973

We need a message for February 21, Mother.

Do you have it?

No! [laughter] Z proposes two texts from Sri Aurobindo, but I feel it would be better to have something from you.

Yes. Do you have something?

Well, no, Mother! Won't you rather say something yourself?

(after a silence)

Plus on avance, plus le besoin d'une présence divine devient impérieux et ... inévitable. [The more we advance, the more the need of a divine presence becomes imperative and ... inevitable.]
"Inevitable" isn't the word, it's....

"Indispensable"?

Yes, that's it, indispensable.
Is it all right?

Yes, Mother.

(Mother writes the message in French)
February 21....

1973.

(then she signs it)

How do you want to put it in English?

We should put: "The more we advance on the way, the more the need of a divine Presence becomes indispensable—imperative and indispensable."

(Mother writes the message with her eyes closed)

A dot on the "i" here [Satprem guides Mother's hand]. That's all. And just put a period at the end, and your signature.

Is my handwriting all right?

Yes, it's quite good, Mother, it came out very well.

(Mother goes into contemplation)

(Sujata:) Mother, you are going to see the Dalai Lama tomorrow, aren't you? Satprem would be very interested to know your impression—what you have felt.

What day is tomorrow?

(Sujata:) Thursday, Mother.

On Saturday then? I'll tell you if I had any particular impression.

January 20, 1973

(On January 18, Mother received the Dalai Lama. It should be noted that Mother had long ago admitted a number of Tibetan refugees to the Ashram and Auroville.)

Anything to say?

I'd be curious to know what you felt with the Dalai Lama?

A truly benevolent man. Buddhist benevolence, you know, and he practices it marvelously.
He seems to have no ... *no selfishness* in him (there's no word for it in French). I mean, a constant concern to do the right thing.

(silence)

Very active [mentally]—there wasn't much of a deeper contact. That's all.
He was happy with his visit, I was told. Did you hear that too?

Yes, I heard he was happy.

Didn't you see him?

No, Mother, no.[1]

He is a young man....

Though I had seen him in a "dream" a few months ago.

Ah?

Yes, we met. Why, I have no idea.

---

1. Satprem had no fondness for crowds, and that day the entire Ashram had thronged the place. The Dalai Lama had expressed the wish to see Mother alone, but the Ashram's dignitaries were literally glued to him and stayed in Mother's room throughout the meeting. It was hard to have any "deeper contact" under those circumstances.

Very benevolent—he's very benevolent.

I was told something (I don't know if it's true), he is reported to have said, "Sri Aurobindo and the Mother are the most important personalities in the world today"—I don't know if it's true.

He seems to have been pleased with his visit. He was very happy to see the school and the children.

But on the plane where I live . . . he doesn't seem to be very conscious THERE. . . . I don't know. I don't know, but in any case he has a very light presence, very light—he doesn't impose himself at all.

I sensed a very strong man—very strong. And harmoniously strong; his right arm was bare, you know, it gave the feeling of a strong and quiet force. But . . . I didn't have much of a deeper contact. . . . I can't say.

That's all.

What about Tibet, did you see anything—do you see anything for that country?

I told him Tibet would become independent again. He asked me when. I said, "I don't know."[1]

Sri Aurobindo's idea was an independent Tibet within a sort of great federation with India. But when will that happen? I don't know.

Tibet was locked in a lower form of Tantrism; the Chinese probably came to free them from their imprisonment . . .

Yes.

. . . in that lower Tantrism. When that cleansing is over (with much damage, unfortunately), maybe they'll be free again?

(Mother nods her head)

He gave me this *(Mother shows a Tibetan Buddha in brass)*. It's a Buddha. Is there something written there [under the statue]?

Yes, Mother, there are some inscriptions.

---

1. Mother replied, "All depends on the world's receptivity to the supramental consciousness." We publish in the *Addendum* an account of the Dalai Lama's questions and Mother's answers.

I think it's Tibetan.
Very nice.

Yes, it has a good face.

(silence)

You didn't see him?

No, Mother, I only saw pictures of him. Something akin to Pavitra, was my impression.

Oh, really!

Yes, in the same "line," if you will.

*
* *

ADDENDUM

(Account of the Dalai Lama's visit. The Dalai Lama's questions were put to Mother by Kireet, the Registrar of the Centre of Education, who in turn conveyed Mother's answers back to the Dalai Lama.)

(original English)

(Dalai Lama:) It is my dream to have the perfect economic development of Tibet, the perfect organization, the efficiency that we find in Communism, but all this based upon, founded upon the Buddhistic qualities of Compassion and Love, so that the people in power do not degenerate into corruption. What is Mother's view of this dream, and whether such a thing will be realized in Tibet?

It is not a dream. It will naturally be. But the time it will take, I do not know. This is something like what Sri Aurobindo has said about the Supramental.

Truth, Love, Compassion will give a basis to the new creation. It is not birth but the value of men that should give the right to authority.

If the teaching of Sri Aurobindo can spread over the world, and if there is the full manifestation of the Supramental, then the Supramental will be the power of the liberation of Tibet.

It is bound to come, it will come; but if it goes as it is going now, it will take hundreds of years. But if the Supramental is manifested, it may come quick. Quick does not mean ten or twenty years—that would be almost miraculous.

(Kireet:) But the Supramental is now working very powerfully.

It is, it is working. It will be manifested with enough power when the right people have the authority.

For the moment, it seems that the opposition, the falsehood attacks with full power before dying. Never, never have men lied as much as they are doing now. It seems the old habit comes spontaneously. But it must be broken.

We are at a very—what we could call an unpleasant moment of the history of the earth. It is interesting because the action is very powerful, but I can't call it pleasant.

But I have told you that already; I wrote it.[1]

(Kireet:) Yes, Mother. The Mother has given the message.

(Dalai Lama:) As for myself, I have no desire to continue in power in the Government. For I feel that the Government involves so much of conflicts of parties, and the necessity of taking sides with one party against the other....

One can govern without taking sides. That is the mistake of all the governments; they reduce their capacity tremendously.

But beyond the mind, there is a higher and deeper consciousness —they would find a Consciousness in which one can make use of all the capacities. It is a question of the consciousness being broad enough, so that each capacity can be put in its place in order to make a general harmony.

(Dalai Lama:) There is good will, there is sincerity among people all over the world, but the number of such people is not large. Will they be able to have an effect to change the conditions of the world?

---

1. Message of November 26, 1972: "Before dying, falsehood rises in full swing. Still people understand only the lesson of catastrophe. Will it have to come before they open their eyes to the truth? I ask an effort from all so that it has not to be. It is only the Truth that can save us; truth in words, truth in action, truth in will, truth in feelings. It is a choice between serving the Truth or being destroyed."

It is bound to change; it is bound to change. Only, if the people are sincere it will shorten the time; it will go faster if the people are sincere.

The first and indispensable step is to stop all falsehood. Falsehood is all that contradicts in us the Presence of the Divine.

January 24, 1973

Do you have something?...

No.

The farther I go, the more contradictions I discover in myself —sharp contradictions. They look like impossibilities.

No, not impossibilities—it probably means you have to go deeper or higher to their meeting ground. That's how it works: the opposites get increasingly vehement until we find the point where they ... where unity is established.

One must go deeper and deeper, or higher and higher—it's one and the same thing. It's the same thing.

(silence)

All our old ways of understanding things are WORTHLESS—worthless.

All, all our values are WORTHLESS.

We are on the threshold of something truly marvelous, but ... we don't know how to keep it—it comes like this *(gesture imitating a passing bird)....* We just don't know.

Never, never before have I had such a sense of ignorance, of impotence, of ... of being a jumble of frightful contradictions, and I know, I KNOW—deep down, beyond speech—that it's because I don't know how to find the place where they ... they harmonize and unite.

I can do absolutely nothing, I know absolutely nothing—in fact, I am nothing but a ... false appearance, that's all.

I don't remember anything, I even forget what I have said before.... Everything is ... *(gesture of crumbling).*

And strangely, almost at the same time, there's torture and bliss —almost at the same time. There you are.

(Mother coughs
silence)

Only, what's odd is that human nature as it is constituted seems to understand torture more readily than bliss.

There's a curious phenomenon: because books [by Mother] are published, I am put in contact with things I said before, and of course when I said them I was very convinced, but now ... I tell myself: how could you say that!

Well.

There is "something" ... *(Mother opens her palms upward).*

(long silence)

There is only one, one will left: may the Divine express Himself without deformation through this body. This is constant, constant, constant, constant....

Tell me, what is the mantra?

OM....

OM Namo Bhagavateh?

Bhagavateh, yes, Mother.

(Mother plunges in.
The clock strikes an eternal hour)

January 31, 1973

(Long silence, Mother shakes her head several times as if
at a loss, she tries to speak and plunges in again.)

355

The same identical circumstances, occuring at the same time, can cause a marvelous bliss—marvelous, as I have never felt before —or sheer hell. The very same circumstances, and at the same time.

For hours on end it's enough to drive you mad, and for a few ... (maybe hours, maybe minutes—the sense of time isn't the same, but anyway ...) a wonder. A wonderful Presence.

It doesn't really depend on circumstances: the circumstances are always the same, and yet....

And in this new consciousness, time has a completely different value: I feel I have spent a few minutes, and I am told it's been almost an hour. That's how it is.

(silence)

So it's as you want. If you want to meditate....

Personally, I have a strange impression. In the past, years ago, I used to feel that a part of my consciousness was vast, was ... this or that; but now I understand fully well what you mean by an "old piece of bark" (you know, "There's only an old piece of bark left"), I feel I am only a mass of flaws, of imperfections, of dark elements and so on, but the other part of myself completely eludes me. There is only this sort of facade full of unpleasant and clashing and false things. While the other part, the other "me"... I don't know, it eludes me completely. I know it's there, but I am mainly conscious of all this that's in front of me.

(Mother plunges in)

February

February 3, 1973

Time is no longer the same.... And I can't eat anymore. Well.... What's going to happen, I don't know.

Very good things!

> *(Mother laughs and takes Satprem's hands)*

You're sweet.

But I'm sure, Mother!

Of course! So am I! *(laughter)*

> *(Mother shuts her eyes,*
> *and feels with her hand the flowers near her)*

What is this one?

"Grace," Mother....

Then it's for you.
Oh, that....

> *(Mother opens her hands upwards*
> *and plunges in)*

I can't speak.
Can't speak anymore, can't eat anymore.... And time goes by like lightning.

> *(Mother plunges in again)*

February 7, 1973

(Regarding a text given by Mother for the next "Bulletin":)

There is only one solution for falsehood:
It is to cure in ourselves
all that contradicts in our consciousness
the presence of the Divine.

(December 31, 1972)

I am very keen on this! It's very true—very true. It may not be easy to understand, but it's VERY PROFOUNDLY true.

All in us that veils or distorts or prevents the manifestation of the Divine IS the falsehood.

It means a whole lot of work!

That's what I am doing all the time—every day and all day long, whenever I don't ... even when I see people. It is the only thing worth living for.

February 8, 1973

(This is an extract from a meeting with a few teachers from the school. We owe these recordings to the kind cooperation of one of them.)

What is the best way of preparing ourselves? For one clearly feels that all this is going to require a rather extensive preparation.

To broaden and enlighten your consciousness, naturally. But how to do that? ... How do you broaden and enlighten your consciousness? If each one of you could find his psychic being and unite with it, all problems would be solved.

The psychic being is the Divine's representative in the human being. It's true, you know: the Divine isn't something far-off and out of reach; the Divine is within you, but you aren't fully conscious of it. You have rather ... so far it is acting more as an influence than a Presence. It must become a conscious Presence, so at each moment you can ask yourselves how ... how the Divine sees.

That's how it is: first, how the Divine sees; then, how the Divine wills ... then, how the Divine does. It has nothing to do with going off to inaccessible regions: it's RIGHT HERE. Although, for the moment, all the old habits and the general unconsciousness have put a sort of lid on it, which prevents us from seeing and feeling. We must ... we must lift that, lift it off.

Basically, we must become conscious instruments ... conscious ... conscious of the Divine.

Normally it takes an entire lifetime, or even several lives in some cases. But here, in the present conditions, you can do it in ... a few months. Those who have an ardent aspiration can do it in a few MONTHS.

(Mother remains concentrated for a few moments)

Did you feel anything?

(One of the teachers:) Was there a special descent?

There is no "descent"! That's another wrong idea. There is no "descent." It's something that is ALWAYS here, but you just don't feel it. There is no descent, that's a completely wrong idea.

Do you know what the fourth dimension is?

We have heard about it....

Have you experienced it?

No, Mother.

Oh, but it's precisely the best example modern science can offer —the fourth dimension. The Divine is the fourth dimension for us. It ... belongs to the fourth dimension. It's everywhere, you see —always everywhere. It doesn't come and go: it's always there ...

361

everywhere. It's we, it's our stupidity that keeps us from feeling it. There's no need to go off anywhere . . . no need at all, none at all.

To be conscious of your psychic being, you must be able to have felt the fourth dimension, felt it once, otherwise you cannot know what it is.... Oh, Lord!

It's been seventy years since I've known what the fourth dimension is—more than seventy years.

(silence)

Indispensable, it's indispensable. Life begins with that. Otherwise, you are in falsehood—in a hodgepodge of confusion and ignorance.... The mind! The mind! The mind!

Otherwise, to be conscious of your own consciousness, you must mentalize it. It's dreadful, dreadful!

There you are.

This new life isn't the continuation of the old one, is it Mother, it has to spring up from within.

Yes! Yes!

There is no common ground between the two....

There is—there is, but you aren't conscious of it. You must . . . you must . . . it's the mind that prevents you from feeling it. One must BE, you see. All you do is mentalize everything—everything. What you call "consciousness" is thinking things out; that's what you call consciousness. But that's not it at all! That's not consciousness. Consciousness . . . should be wholly lucid and WORDLESS.

(Mother closes her eyes)

Like that . . . everything becomes luminous and warm and . . . STRONG!

And peaceful . . . a true peace, which is not inertia or immobility.

Mother, can we give this as an objective to all children?

All . . . no! They are not all the same age, even when they are the same physical age. Some children are primitive. One should.... You see, if you yourself were fully conscious of your psychic being, you would know which children are psychically developed. Some children have only an embryonic psychic—the age of the psychic varies enormously. Normally, it takes several lives for the psychic to become completely formed, and it's the psychic that passes from one body to another; that's why we aren't conscious of our past lives—because we aren't conscious of our psychic being. But sometimes, at some MOMENT the psychic being participated in a particular event, it became conscious; and that creates a memory. Sometimes you may find you have a partial recollection of something, the fleeting memory of a circumstance or event or thought, or even of an action.... It's because the psychic was conscious of it.

(silence)

What would you, I am nearing my hundredth year—it's only five years away—and I started my effort to become conscious when I was five. It's a fact. That's telling you.... And I am going on, and it is going on. Now, of course, I have come to doing the work in the cells of the body, but the work started long ago.

I don't mean to discourage you, but only to tell you it isn't done in a wink!

The body ... the body is made of a substance that is still very heavy. It is the substance itself that must change for the Supermind to manifest.

That's all I can say.

February 14, 1973

(Regarding the poor translation of Sri Aurobindo's texts in the "Auroville Gazette." Mother had asked Satprem to check a few issues and try to rectify the situation with the collaboration of his friend Luc in Auroville. This triggered off reactions which were unmistakably ... sharp.)

... But, Mother, I've seen it: all the translators, whether

French, English, German or whatever, have a translator's
COLOSSAL *ego; the minute you touch their translation, it's as if*
you were ripping their little selves apart. Whether it's Y., T., C.S.
or any of the people I have dealt with, translators are simply
not-to-be-touched. This is the truth. Well, let's leave them alone.
A veritable grace is needed to make them understand.

But I myself wasn't satisfied with my translations.

It's very difficult, Mother! I am well aware of it. But the
minute you touch a translator, it's like touching dynamite!

(Mother laughs) Let's just leave it, then.

Yes, Mother, it's hopeless. I'll inform Auropress that your note
is cancelled.[1] Amen. She [the translator] will have to change
from within—you have to change us all from within, that's the
crux of the matter.

I think (that's what she told me) that when she finds something
difficult, she'll ask me. She said, "If I have doubts, I'll ask you."

But the trouble is, most often they have no doubts!

(Mother laughs)

No, no, Mother, I say this in all humility, because I've been
doing this work for ... eighteen years now; and I see how
many years it took me, how many blunders, and how much
help Sri Aurobindo gave me until I really started getting into
the proper spirit. So I have compassion for these people, I
quite understand why they make mistakes. What annoys me is
how they can be so sure of themselves. 'Tis a pity.

Sometimes people understand a poor translation better than a
good one.

Yes, Mother, possibly!... But still, sometimes it plainly doesn't
make any sense.

---

1. Mother had sent a note to the *Gazette* to the effect that all translations of Sri
Aurobindo's texts had to receive the Copyright Bureau's approval before publication.

I can't personally read through everything, it takes too much time.
Manage with them the best you can.

Bah, bah, listen! Nothing short of a grace could do something!...
For me, it means more responsibility, more complications, it
means an extra load—I'm by no means looking forward to it,
you know.

Well, once in a while, if it really makes no sense at all....
I think we have to be a little....

Yes, Mother, I also feel we should forget about it—people must
understand from within, and that will be that.

I am hearing (through Nirod[1]) certain things that Sri Aurobindo
said, and he says that even he contradicted himself a great number
of times ...

Yes, yes, Mother!

... and that, of course, the two or three different approaches
are all true. So we can afford to be as ... as wide as he is!
Truly speaking, his comprehension of things was very supple—
very supple. Listening to certain things he said, I felt I had understood very little of what he meant. Now that I am more and more
in contact with the supramental Consciousness, I see how supple
—supple and complex—it is, and how it is our narrow human consciousness that sees things ... *(Mother draws little boxes in the*
air) fixed, cut and dried.

Yes, of course.

So.... we are under the mind's sway, and the mind is rigid like
this *(same little boxes in the air)*. But I see that as soon as you go
beyond the mind, it's ... it's like waves on the sea.
In a word, we have everything to learn. We try to understand in
the mental way, so we understand nothing. We simply demarcate
things *(same gesture of drawing boxes)*, and that's what we call
understanding.

---

1. *Correspondence with Sri Aurobindo.*

When we have thoroughly put everything in boxes *(same gesture),* then we say we have understood!

(Mother plunges in)

February 17, 1973

*(Mother remains absorbed for a long time,
then shakes her head....)*

Oh!... I have to cope with everything that contradicts the Divine in the past and the present, and it's.... In this body. I mean, all the past is surging up from the subconscient, and now even everything that was repressed.... It isn't something I "feel" or "experience," but it's a perception. The perception ... yes, of how all our notions of good and evil, right and wrong are futile for the Divine vision, absolutely futile—unreal.

All human notions are so narrow and limited, so partial and tinged with moral preferences.

As if I were being shown everything in the consciousness that opposes the ... immensity—the divine immensity. Everything is so narrow, so small....

(silence)

What time is it?

Ten-forty.

Would you like to stay?...

(Mother plunges in)

February 18, 1973

*(Extracts from a meeting with the schoolteachers. One of them
complains that the first signs of violence are showing up
in the children.)*

Violence is necessary as long as men are ruled by their ego and
its desires. But violence must be used only as a means of defense
when you are attacked. The ideal towards which humanity is
moving and which we want to realize is a state of luminous understanding in which each person's needs as well as the harmony of
the whole are taken into account.

The future will have no need of violence because it will be
governed by the Divine Consciousness, in which all things are
harmonized and complement each other.

For the moment, we are still in a stage where weapons are
necessary. But it should be understood that this is a transitory
stage, not a permanent one, and we must strive for the other one.

Peace ... peace and harmony will be a natural outcome of the
change of consciousness.

You see, in India there reigns the Gandhian concept of non-
violence which has replaced physical violence with moral violence,
but it's far worse!

But if you dare speak against Gandhi, everyone will immediately
... oh!

You don't need to mention his name, you can explain to the
children that replacing physical violence with moral violence is no
better. Lying down in front of a train to stop it running is a moral
violence that can ultimately cause more disorder than physical
violence.

There would be a lot to say.... It depends on each case. I
myself very much encouraged the practice of fencing because it
gives you skill, control over your movements and discipline in
violence—I very much encouraged fencing at one time. I learned
how to shoot; I used to shoot with a rifle, because it gives you
steadiness and skill and a very good eye; and it forces you to
remain calm in the midst of danger. All these things are.... I
don't see why one should be *hopelessly nonviolent*, it only makes a
spineless character.

Turn it into an art! An art for cultivating calm, skill and self-

367

control. There's no need to cry out indignantly as Gandhi would. It's useless, useless, absolutely useless—I am not at all in favor of it! One should master the means of self-defense, and one should cultivate them in order to do so.

Above all, make them understand that moral violence is just as bad as physical violence. It can even be worse, that is, at least physical violence forces you to become strong and control yourself, whereas moral violence is.... You may be like this [apparently quiet] and harbor the worst moral violence in yourself.

February 21, 1973

Mother is ninety-five.

February 28, 1973

(For the last ten days, the "conversations" have been spent in silence and contemplation—I have the impression that Mother wants me to understand something by another means. But what? Furthermore, the attendant is now almost constantly in the room. She no longer bothers to pretend being in the bathroom. She breaks in on the conversation, offers her own comments—of course, since Mother "can't hear."... People go in and out of Mother's room as they please, and continue their own conversations. The atmosphere is quite changed. This is perhaps why Mother tries to establish another type of

*communication with me, another kind of link. But silence ...
is very silent. And I did not realize what was fast approaching
before my very eyes.)*

So?... How are you?

I don't know too well.

Not too well?

I don't know.

(Mother laughs)

*One feels one doesn't in the least know what path one is
treading.*

Neither do I!... Neither do I.
But I know it's on purpose. I am not worried, because I know
it's on purpose. We have a mental way of knowing, which is worthless—truly worthless. As Sri Aurobindo said, it goes from falsehood to truth—whereas the Supramental goes from truth to truth.
And it has nothing to do with the mental approach. That I know.
When I am completely still, with no one here and none to disturb
me, then ... *(Mother closes her eyes)* a certain condition comes ...
and you feel that if that developed, it ... *(Mother smiles silently)*.
You enter a luminous immensity ... devoid of any questions.

*(Mother takes Satprem's hands
and plunges in)*

March

March 3, 1973

We have nothing for the next Bulletin, no "Notes."

(silence)

One would like to know if one is on the right path....

What path?

Your path, the path to the new consciousness.

(Mother indicates that she does not want to talk)

For the moment, the real Force—the real Force—is in silence.

(Mother plunges in)

March 7, 1973

How are you getting on?

Well, I really can't say.... You must know better than I.

(Mother laughs) Personally, I keep hearing: peace, peace, peace....

(Mother plunges in,
holding Satprem's hands in hers)

March 10, 1973

What do we do about the Bulletin, Mother ... the "Notes on the Way"?

Do you have something?

Almost nothing, just two small pieces.

Go ahead, read them.

(Satprem reads)

Is that all? . . .

Yes [laughter]. . . . Obviously, you don't feel like talking anymore.

No. I can't talk, it doesn't come out clearly.

But that's not true! It does! It comes out very well.

If you have a question, we can try.

I don't know, whenever I try to come into contact with that Consciousness, I always sense a sort of luminous immensity, as you say. . . .

Yes.

But I feel it's stationary, you see; I am in it and could stay in it forever, but. . . .

Exactly. That's my own sensation too.

But is it enough to let That permeate one? Isn't there anything else to be done?

Yes, I think so. I think it's the only thing to do. Personally I keep repeating, "What You will, what You will, what You will. . . . Let it be as You will, may I do as You will, may I be conscious of what You will."

And also: "Without You, it's death; with You, it's life." By "death," I don't mean physical death—it might happen, it might be that if I lost the contact now, it would be the end—but that's impossible! I feel that ... I AM THAT—with some resistances the present consciousness may still have, that's all.[1]

And when I see somebody ... *(Mother opens her hands as if she were offering that person to the Light)*, regardless of who it is: like this *(same gesture)*.

(silence)

It's funny, I constantly feel like a little baby curled up—curled up in ... (what term to use?) an *all-embracing* divine Consciousness.

(Mother remains immobile)

And the slightest contradiction that enters the atmosphere causes me such discomfort, I feel I won't be able to stand it.

There, that's how it is.

Just now I had gone off like that, you see, but I suddenly felt uncomfortable and that pulled me back. It isn't expressed mentally, it is neither an idea nor even a sensation, it's ... I don't know what it is. It is like a negation, a painful negation. Which really makes me feel an acute pain, and I am pulled back into this physical consciousness.

*(Mother plunges in, then seems uncomfortable.
Champaklal comes and rings the bell)*

---

1. This "if I lost the contact" and "that's impossible" leads us back again to the same perplexing question. And we recall Mother's words: "Only some violence could stop the transformation, otherwise it will go on and on and on...." (December 4, 1971, *Agenda XII*)

March 14, 1973

(Extracts from a meeting with the schoolteachers. The subject is the school squabbles and rivalry among groups of teachers.)

I can't make head or tail of these things. . . . I can no longer be of any help, you see, because all these mental combinations don't make any sense to me anymore.

A spirit of confusion has entered the school, I find.

They all mean the same thing, but they use different words, and the words . . . clash. Personally, I know they have very similar aspirations, but each one speaks in his own language, and the languages are at cross-purposes, so they quarrel over nothing. That's the situation!

I think the best would be for everybody to keep quiet for a while.

I too never had any problems with the people around me, but now we seem to speak different languages.

(silence)

But the effect on me is odd: I have the impression that I am ill —there's nothing wrong with me, I am in good health, yet I have a constant impression of being ill.

The truth is, it's the transition from the ordinary mental consciousness to the supramental consciousness. The mental consciousness panics in the presence of the supramental consciousness. The vibration is so different I feel one could die every minute. Only when I am very tranquil do I. . . .

The old consciousness (which isn't at all a mental consciousness, but anyway . . .), the old consciousness keeps repeating its mantra—there is a mantra—it keeps repeating its mantra, which makes a sort of backdrop, a contacting point. It's very peculiar. But beyond that, there's something full of light and force, but it's so new that . . . it causes almost a panic. And if it does that to me, with the long experience I have . . . if it has the same effect on others, I think we'll all end up lunatics! Well.

I think we have to remain very tranquil if we don't want to lose the thread!

(There follows a long discussion by the teachers)

But our language is ... there's like a cloche over it, a mental cloche it doesn't want to free itself from.

It is truly a difficult time. I think we should be very, VERY TRANQUIL—very tranquil.

(Mother turns to one of the teachers
and to all the teachers)

I will tell you my old mantra. It keeps the outer being very tranquil: OM, Namo, Bhagavateh.... Three words.

To me they meant:

> OM: I implore the Supreme Lord.
> Namo: I obey Him.
> Bhagavateh: Make me divine.

(silence)

This, I found, has the power to calm everything.

March 17, 1973

I had a question I wanted to ask you.

What is it?

I was wondering about the difference between.... You remember, in the past you used to go into trance, into the inner states. I wanted to know the difference between the trance you knew in the past and the one now?

Completely different.

So it isn't a "trance."

No.

No, it's another type of consciousness. The difference is such that I wonder ... sometimes I wonder how it is possible—at times, it is so new, so unexpected it's almost painful.

Aah!...

So I ask myself, "What?" And externally I see but one solution: externally—I repeat OM Namo Bhagavateh. Constantly—that's for the outer being. And inside ... *(gesture, hands open in immobile contemplation) ...*

(silence)

... an extraordinary silence. I think I've been in it for a few minutes, but sometimes it's an hour.... And the opposite too: I feel time drags on and on, and it's been only a few minutes. Which means that time is different. But then, if the value of time changes.... Our time is based on the sun, you see, but there, it is another reference.

So, in other words, you don't actually go out of Matter?

No, not at all.

It's a new condition IN Matter.

Yes. Yes, yes, exactly. And ruled by something other than the sun —I don't know what.... Probably the Supramental consciousness.

(silence)

At mealtime, for example, sometimes I think I have eaten very fast, and it has taken me more than an hour. Other times, I feel it took a long time—it took just a few minutes. So if you look at that from an ordinary standpoint, you feel that ... people will think you're crazy. So there's a sort of recommendation: silence, silence, silence, silence....

Not too much with me, please!

(Mother laughs)

I wanted to know if personally ... if personally I was in the right direction.

(Mother is absorbed for a few seconds)

The answer was immediately YES, but it wasn't I who gave the answer.

> *(Mother is absorbed again*
> *and comes back almost immediately*
> *with a movement of suffocation)*

You see how it is: now, as soon as I try to know something, I feel such a suffocating heat I think I am going to die. There. Do you understand?

Yes.

That's how it is.

Yes, Mother. Yes, one shouldn't "try to know," that's the point.

> *(Mother plunges in)*

March 19, 1973

(A note from Mother)

Here we have no religion.
We replace religion with spiritual life, which is truer and both deeper and higher, that is to say, closer to the Divine. For the Divine is in all things, but we are not conscious of it.
This is the immense progress that men must make.

March 21, 1973

What's up?

I saw you last night.

(In a delighted ton) Aah!

*Oddly enough, I was trying to devise—to invent or construct
—a new bed for you, as though yours wasn't comfortable. A
bed that would allow you ... yes, to be a little more comfortable. I've no idea what it means!*

I do. It's very good! *(laughter)*
Very good.

(silence)

What's the time? ... What would you like?[1]

Whatsoever you like.

No! ... *(laughing)* I am at your disposal!
You don't have anything to say?

*I've noticed I am becoming extremely sensitive. The least
disturbance in the atmosphere and I get blows.*

Oh, me too! And to such an extent that it makes me ill.
Yes, quite annoying it is. But there must be a radical remedy, I
mean something that shelters you completely. That would be....
Personally, my solution is to curl up materially in the Divine.
Only it's difficult. It's.... It can be done, but all this *(zigzagging
gesture in the air)* makes a constant disturbance.

*(Mother plunges in
holding Satprem's hands)*

---

1. Mother means contemplative silence, naturally.

March 24, 1973

Good morning! . . . Do you eat caviar?

Caviar!

It is a very good food. . . .

I'm sure!

   I used to eat it, but now I can't. . . . Not so long ago I used to eat it, but it made my eyes swell.[1] So I've stopped.
How long since you last ate caviar?

Oh, at least . . . thirty years!

(Mother laughs) Try some, and see what you think.

Right, I will see!

(silence)

I brought you a flower from the garden: "Surrender of Falsehood."[2]

Oh! . . .

(Mother immediately takes the
flower and puts it on her forehead,
where she holds it a long time,
silently)

I take it in the largest and most profound sense. . . .

(silence)

Nothing to ask?

No—may falsehood disappear.

---

1. All salted food, the doctor said.
2. Double red laurel flower.

Look.... As I understand it, when Falsehood is gone (even in a single person—when not a vestige remains ...), there must be Light, Peace ... *(Mother stretches her arms out)* ... Vastness ... perfect understanding ... the TRUE vision of our world and things, and union, a conscious union with the divine Consciousness.

(Mother plunges in)

March 26, 1973

(Excerpts from a conversation with the teachers. One of them complains about the "lack of coordination.")

Coordination! ... But that's because people are accustomed to using the mind to organize things, that's all they know: organization as devised by the mind. While we here are trying to change that pattern. We seek a change of government—but the new government isn't very well-known yet, that's the difficulty.

Maybe I want to go too fast.

I see clearly ... I tend to go too fast, possibly.

March 28, 1973

(That day, Satprem had the inner perception that a new phase was beginning, that Mother was "withdrawing" more and more within. Effectively, a few days later, on April 7, she stopped seeing almost everybody, except the few regular disciples.)

Are you eating enough?

Yes, Mother.

What news?

Are things progressing?

I suppose so.
I turn my consciousness towards myself as little as possible,
because ... the sensation is VERY unpleasant.
Things are tolerable only when I am turned exclusively towards
the Divine and the material consciousness repeats, OM Namo
Bhagavateh.... Like that. Like a backdrop to everything.
OM Namo Bhagavateh....
You know, a backdrop you can use as a physical support.
OM Namo Bhagavateh....

(Mother plunges in for 40 minutes)

March 30, 1973

Excerpts from a meeting with the teachers.

*(At the end of a long and distressing conversation that exposes
the grudges of a particular individual against her neighbor,
then angry remarks, then finally a request for "blessings" for a
new trucking company, with a photo of the truck on the back
of which Mother is asked to write something, one of the
teachers announces that an epidemic of chickenpox and
mumps has broken out at the school among the students and
teachers, and that one of them has typhoid fever. Mother
listens to all that.... This will be the last meeting
with the teachers.)*

I hope you're not bringing any of that here?

(the teachers laugh, uncomprehending)

Have you taken all the necessary precautions?... Otherwise it would be a real catastrophe.

(silence)

I hope you took every precaution not to bring me any of it here?...

*(silence,
one of the teachers explains
that the incubation period lasts from 3 to 4 weeks)*

If you haven't, it's really a crime *(there is almost anguish in Mother's voice)*, because.... There's nothing to explain. It's a crime. I am not AT ALL protected.

March 31, 1973

So, what would you like to tell me?

First, how are you?

I can't hear you. Are you asking how I am?...

Yes—you "can't hear"!

But what does it mean? I can only be well when ... there's no I.

I have been asking myself a question.

Ah?

About that new consciousness. I can grasp (or guess) its contemplative or passive aspect, but not so well its dynamic or active aspect. I don't quite see how it ACTS—I understand the contemplative part, but how does it act?

I don't know. I have no idea.

But do you act or are you simply in ...?

Yes, I act. But what exactly do you mean? ... Yes, I act!

For example, when you are inside, in an inner state....

But I act much better than when—I appear to be inside, but that's not so. Everybody makes the same mistake.

Yes, but I fully understand.

When I am concentrated in that way, it's not that I am inside, I am in another kind of consciousness.
And it's vast, vast, vast, vast—vast.

Yes, but it's the active side of that consciousness that I don't....

But it doesn't have any side! It's a consciousness *(gesture of pressure from above)*.... It has no side, it isn't passive or active —it's a consciousness ... *(same gesture of pressure)* a consciousness pressing on the world.

(silence)

You see, you're trying to translate it mentally, which is impossible—impossible. You have to enter that consciousness ... then only will you know what it is. There's no active or passive, no inside or outside—all that is replaced by something else ... which I can't describe.... There are no words for it.

But for instance, personally, whenever I try to go there, into that consciousness, my main impression is of nonexistence.

Ah, no!

Individual nonexistence, I mean.

No....

It's wide, it's vast, but there's no more person, no more individual.

No. That's not it.... For me, all that is the past ... *(silence).* Yes, I quite understand what you mean....

(Mother plunges in)

April

April 7, 1973

(The last few days, Mother saw very few people. She remained absorbed within. The previous meeting, on April 4, was spent in complete silence. Mother gives me flowers, holds my hand in hers and remains silent for a while. She is so white....)

I seem to be gathering all the world's resistances.... They come to me one after another, and if I weren't.... If I stop calling the Divine for a single minute, intimately feeling his presence within me, the pain is unbearable, mon petit! To such a point that I now hesitate to speak of "transformation" to people, because if that's what it is, one really has to be a hero.... You see, there's something in the body that would almost howl nonstop.

Yet it looks to me that there is something VERY simple to be done to make it all right.... But I don't know what.

(silence)

Sometimes I wonder, "Does the Lord want me to leave?" I am quite ... *quite willing*, you know, so that's not the point; but does He want me to stay?... No answer. No answer except "Transformation." And that is....

I truly, truly sense there is something to be done that would make everything go right—but I don't know what it is.

(long silence)

What about you?

Well, I was asking myself many questions about you....

Ask, I don't know if....

No, no, I mean questions concerning YOU.

Me?

I sense there's an increasingly faster movement that's ... that's absorbing you.

Yes, yes, it's quite true.

You see, I have a solution for the transformation of the body, but ... it's never been done before, so it's extremely ... hard to believe. I cannot, I cannot believe that that's it. Yet, it's the only solution I see.... The body has a wish to go to sleep and awake ... ("sleep" in a certain sense, of course: I remain perfectly conscious in consciousness, in the movement) and awake only after it is transformed ...

(Satprem, wordlessly:) Sleeping Beauty!

... but people will never have the patience to stand it, to take care of me. The task is colossal, a herculean task; they're nice *(Mother points to the bathroom)*, but they're already doing their utmost, and I can't ask for more.

That's the problem.

Yet, it's the only solution to which the consciousness assents: "Yes, that's it."

For, you see ... there's a certain state—yes, a state like this *(Mother closes a fist)*, self-absorbed, in which you are ... at peace.

But who? Who? To ask that of the people who take care of me is almost impossible.

I don't know, but lately I've had a sort of feeling that you were going to "withdraw" in some way; that you were more and more absorbed and that, well, you would have to have less and less contact with the outside world for a certain period.

Yes. Yes, but then everyone will think it's ... it's the end, and they won't take care of me anymore.

Oh, come on! Of course not!

(Sujata:) Oh, no!...

(Satprem:) That's not possible! People will understand. At least a few will.

What?

A few people will understand—and especially those who are here with you.

They are the ones who can understand.

Yes.... I'm sure they do.

But I can't ask them.

Well, we can tell them—I can tell them.

Yes.... Will he[1] believe you?

(Perplexed:)... Well, I think so!

(Sujata:) In any case, they're right here, they're listening.

(Satprem:) But I feel this strongly. Plainly you wish to have less and less contact with a host of external things which are of no use to your real work.

But we must, we must ... *(Mother gasps for breath, she moans, silence).*
He is going to come. If you stay here long enough, he'll come, and you can tell him.

Pranab?... All right.

I could—perhaps I could say to him, "I have asked Satprem to explain to you...." And you'll explain to him in detail.

Yes, yes, Mother, certainly.

I can tell you they're absolutely wonderful already; they do their utmost, that's why I don't dare ask him. You'll tell him I told you so.

Yes, Mother.

(silence)

I appear to ... *(smiling),* I appear to be *"fanciful,"* totally whimsical: I say yes, and the next instant I say no. So people get the impression....

No, no, Mother! No, no.

---

1. Satprem had heard, "Will THEY believe you?" But Mother did say "he" = Pranab.

But my head, my consciousness is clear, clear, clear.... But I can't talk anymore.

(long silence)

Tell me when he comes, because I want to tell him right away.

Yes, Mother.

(Mother is about to plunge in but notices she has flowers for Sujata on her knees. Sujata comes near her and gives her a lotus)

What is it?

A white lotus, Mother.[1]

Ah!...*(Mother gives the lotus to Satprem)* Here.
What do you prefer: to have my hand [to meditate] or not?

(Satprem:) On the contrary, I like very much that you hold me, Mother!

You like it?

Yes, hold me TIGHT.

Good.

(Mother plunges in)

What do you feel: am I drawing some force from you or giving you some?

(Satprem, a little flabbergasted:) But you fill me! You ... you make me wide, you overwhelm me!

Oh, good.

But, Mother, it's a real....

Yes, it's in the consciousness, I know—it depends on the receptivity.

---

1. The white lotus of the divine Mother (the pink lotus is Sri Aurobindo's flower).

Why, it's a fantastic Grace!

> *(Mother plunges in again,*
> *then comes back rather abruptly*
> *and says in a voice from above)*

If I ask you to come more often, would you be able to?

Anytime, Mother, at any moment!

Every day.

Yes, Mother.

Around eleven o'clock, like now.

Yes, Mother, certainly.¹

Naturally, she comes with you if she wants to.

> *(Mother plunges in again)*

(Enter Pranab. The attendant briefly explains to him that "Satprem has something to tell him on Mother's behalf." She had in fact listened to the whole conversation. Instant outburst of anger from Pranab. He shouts from the other end of the room:)

(Pranab, in Bengali:) Nonsense! Nobody can fool me. I know everything.
(Then in English, quoting a Bengali saying:) Our bed is sea, what do we care for this dew?

> *(Mother comes out of her concentration,*
> *she speaks to Satprem:)*

Tell me if you're tired.

(Satprem:) No, Mother, but Pranab is here.

---

1. The next time, after the intervention of Mother's attendant ("There are still too many people"), and perhaps other persons from Mother's entourage, the "every day" was reduced to three times a week, then two, then none.

Oh, he's here! Call him.[1]

(Pranab, in a dreadful tone:) Yes, Mother?

I have. . . . I can't speak.

(Pranab:) Don't speak Mother! [The attendant laughs.]

I have asked Satprem to explain to you what is happening—why I must make a change. . . .

(Pranab:) Mother, I am not interested, Mother.

No?

I am not interested—whatever happens, happens. I am there to stand up to the last—whatever happens, happens.

(Mother tries to speak,
Pranab cuts her short)

. . . I am neither reasoning nor doing anything. And I don't want to listen also, Mother. [The attendant laughs.] I understand fully. And let me go on with my own light—own conviction, own faith, own strength, own will. [Pranab raises his head as if he were talking to a crowd.] And I don't want to listen, Mother, anything from anybody.

But you don't want to know? . . .

No, Mother, I don't want.

(silence
Mother is perfectly still,
her hands folded on her knees)

(Pranab:) It's perfectly all right. I have come with something, I stand by something, and if it does not come, I don't mind—I am a sportsman, Mother. And I don't want to listen to any explanation. Because whatever explanation is given, if the object for which I came does not materialize, it is the same thing to me.

---

1. The rest of this conversation took place in English. The entire conversation, including the beginning in French, is available on cassette.

No, it's because there is an attempt to transform the body....

*That will happen—when it happens, we shall see, Mother....
Why to predict?*

*(Satprem:) No, no, meanwhile, for this work, she may have to
go as if in an inner sleep....*

(Pranab:) Let her go! What is there!

(Satprem:) So then we have to....

*(Pranab:) That she has told me. Long before Mother has told me.
It is not a new thing, Mother! You had told me, explained to me.*

Then, it's all right.

*(Pranab:) I don't want to listen to anything, Mother. Let it
happen—what will happen will happen, and we shall do the
best. That's all.*

*(Satprem:) No, the thing is that people should not disturb her
too much.*

> *(Now Pranab explodes.
> Half standing, half kneeling,
> his fist on one knee,
> he pours out a torrent on Mother.)*

*WHO is disturbing her? If anybody is disturbing you, Mother,
amongst us, he can be off! [The attendant laughs] Nobody
disturbs.*

(Satprem, appalled[1]:) No, no!...

> *(Mother tries to say something,
> Pranab cuts her off)*

*Mother, don't, don't tell anything. You go on: eat, sleep and
work, and don't try to make anybody explain me. I know what
it is, what everything is.
   Better everybody keeps quiet!*

---

1. Appalled at what is being thrown on Mother.

All right. All right, then.

I don't want to hear anything from anybody.

All right, then.

> *(Pranab goes to the other end of the room.*
> *He shouts for the benefit of Dr. Sanyal,*
> *Champaklal, Mother's attendant and Vasudha,*
> *who are all present.)*

(Pranab:) I have my faith, I have my conviction, I have my purpose, and even if I am in the dark....

(Satprem to Mother:) Shall I come tomorrow at eleven, Mother?

(Pranab:) All that humbug, I don't like.

Yes, mon petit, you'll leave a little before [Pranab's arrival] ... that's all.

(Satprem:) Shall I come at eleven or a little before?

A short while, till 11:25.

(Satprem:) Right, Mother. Understood, Mother. Goodbye, Mother.

(Pranab:) All those who like fuss, let them continue with the fuss.

> *(Satprem stands up to leave,*
> *Mother takes his hands.*
> *Her voice is like a child's)*

So. Thank you.

(Pranab:) There are many people to do fuss—I think most of them.

> *(Sujata lays her forehead*
> *on Mother's knees)*

Mon petit....

(Satprem, in a choked voice:) Goodbye, Mother.

(Pranab:) In thirty years I've seen enough—enough of humbug!

*
* *

(Satprem leaves the room. He holds the white lotus tightly in his hands. Something terrible has just happened, he does not know what. It was not a man who was standing in that room.... On his way out, he meets Sujata's brother and spontaneously, as if he suddenly saw it all, tells him, "One day they are going to close Mother's door on us.")

April 8, 1973

(The next day, as agreed, I came to see Mother. From now on, the attendant was barely visible anymore, but she secretly recorded our conversations.[1] The whole time of this meeting is spent in meditation. I keep having the feeling that Mother is trying to build another kind of bridge with me. Towards the end:)

Will I see you tomorrow?

It seems there are "still too many people"....

All right, Mother.

And....

(Mother plunges in again)

---

1. Mother was well aware of it and had even said to her son, "She records when she isn't supposed to."

April 10, 1973

Pranab declares to P.B., one of the Ashram's trustees, "Get ready for Mother's departure." P.B. has Satprem asked what it means.

April 11, 1973

(Mother looks for Sujata.)

Is she here?

(Sujata:) Yes, Mother!

(To Satprem:) How are you?

Quite well, Mother.... Mother, you have to give us a message for the Darshan [of April 24].

(after a silence)

This is what comes to me:

> Beyond man's consciousness
> Beyond speech
> O thee, Supreme Consciousness
> Unique Reality
> Immutable Truth ...

(Mother hesitates and corrects herself)

Divine Truth.[1]

(Mother plunges in)

---

1. This is Mother's last message.

April 14, 1973

(Mother is very short of breath, she seems to be in pain.)

My nervous system is being transferred to the Supramental. It feels like ... you know, what people call "neurasthenia"[1]—they have no idea what it is; but the entire nervous system is.... It's worse than dying.[2]

Yes, Mother.

But I think ... I think I can transmit the divine Vibration.

Oh, yes, definitely!

Will you tell me if you feel it?

But, Mother, being with you is fantastic—it's being ... it's a torrent ... it feels like a purifying fire, it's.... It widens you, it fills you—that's IT, in a word!

So, would you like to stay [to meditate]?

You know, Mother, ever since you've become supposedly powerless, I have started to feel the supreme Mother. When you had all your powers....

But I know it's my body ... this body.... Look, I have accepted —the Lord asked me if I wanted to *undergo the transformation,* and I said yes (I would have said yes in any event), but it's ... to the ordinary human consciousness, I am going mad.[3]

Yes, I understand, Mother. I understand.... Anyone else would have left umpteen times, rather than sit through all this. I really understand.

---

1. Mother may have used this term in its original Greek root meaning: "strengthless nerves." Unless she meant "neuralgia" in its broader sense.
2. We recall Mother also saying, "When people come into my room with ill thoughts, all the nerves are tortured."
3. See the *Addendum.*

What about you, are you all right?

Yes, yes, Mother!

What do you feel when we sit like this [in meditation], is it all right?

Oh, Mother, I feel at the very Goal of my life!

Good. What's the time, tell me?

It's 10:25.

So up to ... I don't know, 11:00 or 11:10 ... I'll keep you with me.

Yes, Mother, keep me!

(Mother plunges in)

*   *
*   *

ADDENDUM

A Grain of Rice?

"... To the ordinary human consciousness, I am going mad." What happened on November 17, 1973? Or rather, what IS happening? I have pored over Mother's every word for so many years, I have LIVED them all with a pounding heart—or a broken heart. What actually happened? And why?... I can never accept the idea that she left because the attempt failed—we may as well say that evolution has failed, or that she quit the game, or that it was too difficult —nothing was too difficult for her, she fought like a lioness. To say—as they all said—that "the body failed" because it was too old, or due to one thing or another, demonstrates that they never felt or even grazed that Power: "That" can revive a dead man and all the dead ... without its making any difference. So ... what happened? There was one moment when Mother lost the contact with her body, or rather, when THAT lost the contact with Mother's body. Did she not say (on March 10), "If I lost the contact—but that's impossible!" Another day in 1971 (on December 4), she had said, "Only a violent death could stop the transformation, otherwise it will go on and on and on...."

Therefore, there can be only two solutions to the mystery—I was about to say "murder mystery," but can one call it by any other name? What other term could better elucidate the enigma? Assuredly, Mother had that horrid entourage, but it was in no way exceptional, neither in good nor in bad: the people around her exactly represented the average humanity and the ordinary physical consciousness, for which what she was doing was just questionable dreams and hallucinations. They all believed her old, senile or even "insane," and on the brink of death—but could the beliefs of human pygmies get the better of that Consciousness? Of that Power? Of that Will? Could the attempt fail because of our belief or disbelief?

Thus she was alone among them—she was soon to be truly alone, from May 19 onward, exactly thirty-five days after the present conversation. I still hear Mother's son artlessly asking me, a few days after that May 19, "How will we communicate with Mother now?" "There will be NO MORE *communication," I replied. He was flabbergasted—not I.* WHO *could she "communicate" with? But as I said, I was positive that the experience would continue with or without communication: Mother was going to sever the nutrient link to the old physiology—they did not let her. There remained cataleptic trance, the fairy tale, Sleeping Beauty—they did not want it. I can still hear the voice of the Brute: "No, I don't want to."*

So?...

Did she decide to leave? No one will ever convince me that Mother "decided," or that she was old, or insane, or incapable.

Did "the Lord decide"? Well, of course, it is He who decides in any case. But He also uses human instruments—otherwise this world would have never existed—and these human instruments have a freedom of choice, they are not mere puppets in the hands of "God." Or rather, to be more precise, they have a choice between being the Divine's puppet or the devil's—and maybe BOTH *ways conspire to lead us to an unforeseeable goal.*

Hence, humans decided. They said no to the trance, no to the experience, no to the fairy tale; they could not stand it anymore—it had to stop.

A particular fact has haunted me for the past seven years, a particular passage in Pranab's speech which he delivered a few days after Mother's departure. (Once again, I am not accusing anyone: I am chronicling History; I would like to report the facts, the words, the characters as accurately as I can—I am Mother's scribe, that is all ... and I love her, because it's lovely to love.) Now, in that

*speech, we find a small remark, the kind of remark one makes in
passing, as the most "natural" thing in the world. Pranab is describing the "last days." You call them the "last days" AFTERWARDS,
when the story is over—in the meantime, it's just life as usual:*

(original English)

"At night [on November 14], She said, 'Make me walk.' We
were very hesitant, but as She insisted, we lifted her up from
the bed. She could not walk, staggered a little, almost collapsed.
Seeing this, we put Her back in bed. We saw that Her face had
become absolutely white and the lips blue. Then we decided
that whatever She said, we must not take Her out from the
bed again to walk. She took about 20 minutes to recover; She
started saying, 'Lift me up again, I shall walk.' We refused.
She asked why we were refusing. We said, 'Mother, you are in
such a weak condition that it will do you harm.' Then She
said, 'No, lift me up.' We did not. She began to plead, sometimes shout. All this continued until fifteen minutes past one.
At that time we thought we would give Her some sedative, so
that She might rest quietly. Then we gave Her SIQUIL as the
doctor had prescribed. It took Her about 45 minutes to
become quiet and She slept from 2 to 4 o'clock, but after getting up She started saying, 'Pranab, lift me up and make me
walk. My legs are getting paralysed; if you help me to walk
again, they will become all right.' But we did not listen. She
went on entreating till about 6 o'clock when She fell asleep."

*Yes, she fought like a lioness—till the very end. Is this the plea of
someone "who has decided to leave"?*
This was on November 14, three days before the "end."

"On the 15th," Pranab reports, "at night again … She
wanted us to help Her to walk, we refused to do that. We said,
'Mother, you should not walk.' She immediately obeyed us....
From that day She became absolutely obedient."

*How long had they been giving her SIQUIL? And what is SIQUIL, in
the first place?[1] A doctor friend of mine had explained to me: "It's
a dangerous drug." But I could not believe in that kind of thing, it
was simply too horrible.*

---

1. SIQUIL is the Indian brand name for triflupromazine hydrochloride, which is
manufactured in India by Sarabhai Chemicals, and by Squibb in the U.S. (under
the brand name VESPRIN).

Seven years later—it took me seven years—one day in September 1980, as I was passing a small local pharmacy on my way back from Madras, I decided to get to the bottom of it. I went in, asked for SIQUIL, *pulled out the "directions" from the box and . . . read, dumbfounded:*

> "Studies have revealed that over-sedation is not always necessary to benefit such psychotic symptoms as agitation, delusions, hallucinations or delirium. SIQUIL greatly simplifies home management of emotionally deranged patients, many of whom might otherwise previously have been hospitalized. These patients adopt a more realistic behavior, become less of a burden to their families and are more easily approached for training purposes and eventual rehabilitation.... SIQUIL is especially indicated in the treatment of severe acute and chronic mental disorders, such as schizophrenia, mania, depression, delirium, senile psychoses and psychoses caused by organic brain disease."

So, that body . . . whose cellular consciousness had been prepared, refined, trained by decades of yoga....
There is simply nothing to say.
They had had enough. They were unanimous.
I now recall a "dream" I had twelve years earlier, in which Mother seemed dead "because she had eaten a grain of rice." What kind of "rice" was it, that minuscule particle capable of breaking her body?
Yet, even if we find the physical cause of her departure, we will not have found the true reality—for the Divine uses everything, including our human errors, to turn it into his unforeseeable Honey.
I recall Sri Aurobindo: "the Eternal's dreadful strategy."[1]
Indeed, Mother's "end" is not the end. "Wait till the last act," she had said.
But still....

---

1. *Savitri*, I.II.17.

April 18, 1973

What would you like?

Stay like this.

> *(Mother takes Satprem's hands*
> *and goes off immediately)*

April 25, 1973

> *(For the last ten days, all the meetings have been spent*
> *in contemplation.)*

How are you getting on?

It's not easy.

No—it's more than difficult.... I am sorry, I thought I was suffering for everybody—but I see it isn't the case.

> *(silence)*

What would you like?

I'd like you to keep me.

Yes, but materially? You mean keep you like now?

> *(Mother takes Satprem's hands*
> *and prepares to meditate)*

Yes, Mother.

Are you comfortable?

Yes, Mother, very!

You shouldn't have any ache anywhere.

> *(Mother plunges in for half an hour,*
> *then suddenly moans[1])*

Sometimes, I feel like howling.

> *(silence)*

What do YOU feel?

Like a fire melting into your Fire—into what you are.

But what do you feel?

I don't know—the great Power.

Why do I feel like howling?

Well, I wonder if it's not me giving you pain.

No, mon petit! All the time I feel like that—it's not you, not at all.

Something.... It isn't really painful, it's just ... I think—I think it's something so new that the body is frightened. That's the only explanation I see. I start howling, but ... it's no use—the only thing to do is stop howling and change.

Something which....

Yes, that must be it: something so new that the body ... doesn't know how to take it.

> *(silence)*

You don't perceive anything in particular?

No, Mother, what I feel is first that great Flame merging with yours, and then a kind of vast immobility—a powerful immobility.

Ah, that's it! That must be why! Yes, the body must be getting alarmed. Yes, that must be it.

---

1. Coincidentally, Mother's former assistant, who has a cancer, enters the room at this moment.

(Mother plunges in,
Champaklal rings the bell)

Is it time?... Oh, mon petit....

(Satprem rests his head on Mother's knees)

April 29, 1973

(Mother sees Sujata. Sujata enters Mother's room after sitting
a long time outside, in front of Mother's door, engrossed in the
English translation of the "Sannyasin." Mother
takes her hands.)

Your contact is most pleasant, my child, I can tell you that.
Most pleasant.

April 30, 1973

Do you want to ask anything?... Tell me....

I don't know.... One would like to have the certitude one will
pull through all this....

(Mother raises her arms
silence)

Certitude of what?

Of the outcome of the battle.[1]

(Mother raises her arms)

The ultimate outcome is obvious.

Yes, Mother, it's obvious. But sometimes, when one is in the thick of it, one really doesn't know, one doesn't understand what's going on....

No, you mean whether we'll see the outcome of the battle in this body—is that what you're asking?

Yes, in this life.

If we'll see the outcome of the battle IN this body?

Yes, in this body and in this life.

(Mother plunges in)

---

1. I was thinking of my own personal battle in the subconscient, not of Mother's battle, of whose outcome I had not the least doubt.

May

May 5, 1973

(One day—it was on May 2—while walking in Auroville's canyons as I did every evening, I decided to force the Mantra into the body.)

Would you like to.... [meditate]? Or do you have something to say?

I'm endeavoring to force the Mantra into the physical mind.

(Mother starts repeating the Mantra—thirteen times—until her voice is nothing but a halting breath, like a child's whimper.¹)

OM Namo Bhagavateh
OM Namo Bhagavateh
OM Namo Bhagavateh
OM Namo Bhagavateh
OM Namo Bhagavateh
OM Namo Bhagavateh
OM Namo Bhagavateh
OM Namo Bhagavateh
OM Namo Bhagavateh
OM Namo Bhagavateh
OM Namo Bhagavateh
OM Namo Bhagavateh
OM Namo Bhagavateh

(then she sinks into a deep contemplation for half an hour)

What is the time?

Ten past eleven, Mother.

(Satprem rests his forehead on Mother's knees)

---

1. The recording of Mother repeating her mantra is available on cassette.

May 9, 1973

*(Today Mother is very late, she has Satprem and Sujata called in
before the other disciples. She immediately takes Satprem's hands.
It is heartrending.)*

Something's wrong. Something's wrong. I see you. . . .
Something's wrong.

What's wrong, Mother?

I feel like screaming. . . . But. . . .

(silence)

I am eating less and less, so I am constantly uncomfortable—and
so weak!¹ Yet, I feel so strong! . . . But there's. . . . That's how it is.
When I am still, I have such a power—an almost limitless power.

Yes. Yes, it's very tangible.

Like that.
But when I am in my body, I feel so uncomfortable. . . .

Yes, Mother, I understand.

And then everything takes up so much time! I haven't seen
anybody this morning. They're all here [waiting at the door]. What
can I do, mon petit?

Oh, Mother. . . . We love you, Mother.

Eh?

We love you.

---

1. That day, I felt that the movement was going to accelerate and a time would
come when a radically different way would have to be found—perhaps the supreme
Pressure of death is necessary to release the "almighty powers shut in Nature's
cells" that Sri Aurobindo mentions in *Savitri*? As though the supreme Power could
only be released by the supreme contradiction of power—and Death shall reveal its
mask of immortality.

What?

We love you, we have much love for you.

I don't even know what you're saying!

I'm saying that I love you.

Oh, mon petit....

> *(Mother plunges in*
> *holding Satprem's hands.[1]*
> *Then Champaklal's bell rings,*
> *twice, three times.*

What is the time?

Eleven o'clock, Mother.

Ten o'clock?

No, Mother, eleven.

Thank you, mon petit.

Oh, Mother....

Thank you, mon petit.

We need you, Mother.

Thank you.
Oh!... Oh, thank you, mon petit....

Ah, Mother, what Grace to be here with you.

> *(Satprem rests his forehead on Mother's knees)*

Goodbye, Mother.

---

1. During that meditation, I was trying to pass all my life force into Mother's body.

May 14, 1973

And you?... How are you?...

And you? [laughter]

All the time I have to keep a grip on myself not to howl.... From time to time, there's a marvelous moment—but it's short! Most of the time I am like this *(gesture clenched fists)*, to keep myself from howling.

(silence)

What do you like: holding my hand or not?

(Satprem takes Mother's hand)

What do you prefer?

This way is good!

*(Mother plunges in,
Champaklal rings his bell insistently)*

Oh, they are ruthless!...

May 15, 1973

(Mother sees Sujata)

Your hands are so cool!
Do you have something to tell me?

I love you.

You're sweet *(Mother caresses Sujata's hands)*.

We all love you.

Me too.
But me ... *(vast gesture, above).*

> *(Mother keeps caressing
> Sujata's cheeks
> silence)*

My God.... My God....

> *(Mother presses Sujata's cheeks)*

Goodbye.

Goodbye, Mother.

May 15, 1973

KRISHNA IN GOLD

(A vision of Sujata's on the afternoon of May 15)

(original English)

A place similar to the Playground. A few people, here and there, are talking or going about.
I am standing somewhere in the middle of the ground, in front of Mother's door.
From the main gate enters a vehicle—half-cart half-cab—drawn by two bullocks. It comes to a stop a few feet away from me. The driver makes the bullocks kneel down. Out steps a gentleman. The cart is driven away.
The gentleman is dressed in white, Indian-fashion (dhoti, punjabi). He is round-faced and fair-skinned. Reminds me of a Zamindar [landlord] from the North. In fact he is the new proprietor coming to take possession.
The doors behind me are locked. He has the keys.
But he is not supposed to open one particular room: the one I

415

thought was Mother's. But he goes straight there and unlocks that door.

He enters. I too, as if I had the right to do so.

We weave our way to the bottom of this room. I have a vague impression of a small window on the end wall. And in the left corner, is a richly decorated high throne. Seated in it is a Divinity.

He is quite small in that huge throne (about two feet or so).

He is made of solid gold.

At his feet are signs and objects of worship.

As we approach him, a sort of intense prayer or aspiration takes hold of me. We stand in front looking at him—my whole being is one intense prayer or invocation. The Divinity comes alive. He smiles slightly, then steps down.

He barely reaches my breast and seems to me like a little boy of eight or ten.

The three of us come out of the room. The scene has changed. Now it is a countryside. A vast, unlimited expanse stretches in front. A few plots are cultivated, but most of the land is untended.

We walk. We walk on a narrow ridge by the side of a cultivated rice-field, which is to the right of us. It is green. I am nearest to it. The gentleman is the farthest. The Divinity is between us. He has a funny walk. He is so heavy (being made of solid gold) that he seems to lurch from side to side. I feel concerned and hold his arm to help him. I feel a tenderness also as for a child.

Then I turn my face towards him to reassure him. But instead of me looking down it is he who looks down on me! I am really astonished to see how tall he has grown during this short walk of but a few steps! Now it is I who reach hardly his shoulder. He seems to have grown to a lad of 13 or 14.

As I look up, he looks down at me and smiles. Ohh, what a smile! Utterly sweet and full of mischief. It contained a world: "You see, I am quite all right. Now you will see what fun we have!"

We walk on. To our left, sitting cross-legged, head bent, is M. [a disciple very learned in Sanskrit texts]. As we advance, I think, "What a pity, we shall pass right in front of him, but he would not even know WHO passed by!" But as we near, he raises his head and sees. I feel glad for M.

We walk on. Now the scenes change fast. We meet more and more people. Trees. Roads. Still more people. Wherever we go there is trouble, disturbance, confusion. As if the Godhead were sowing disruption everywhere. The Zamindar gets annoyed. He had brought out the Divinity to show people what a fine fellow he was!

Everybody should have great respect for him, obey him, for is he not the Proprietor? But the God had just the opposite effect! He should no longer be abroad. He must be put back where he belonged, and relocked.

So we return to the sanctuary. This time I remain outside. The Zamindar takes the God inside. And tries to shut the door.

But the Godhead will not be shut in.

I can see the gold God growing, growing.

The ceiling falls in. The god's head and chest go through the ceiling. He rips off the walls and throws bricks everywhere. The Zamindar has disappeared under the debris.

The gold God grows. Taller and mightier. And will brook no resistance. With His mighty hands, He pulls down the walls of His old sanctuary.

When I woke up, I called Him "Krishna in gold."

May 19, 1973

The last meeting

(Sujata gives Mother a pale yellow, slightly golden hibiscus with a red heart. Mother holds the flower without seeing it. That day, I don't know why, I was full of questions.)

What is it?

It's "Ananda in the physical."

!!! We badly need it!

Yes, Mother!

And you?

I was thinking about something Sri Aurobindo wrote.... In

417

"Savitri," he clearly says, "Almighty powers are shut in Nature's cells." [IV.III.370.]

In ...?

In Nature's cells.

Ohh! . . . Oh, that is interesting!

ALMIGHTY powers.

(silence)

He doesn't say anything else?

No, not on that subject.... The consciousness of the cells seems to be awakened but not the power.

(Mother did not hear well)

You said the consciousness of the cells is ... missing? No?

No, the consciousness is there. The consciousness of the cells is awakened, but the power isn't.

Ah! . . . You said "awakened"?

Yes, Mother. Because had the power been awakened, there wouldn't be any weakness in your body.[1]

No.

But it is THERE, Sri Aurobindo says it clearly: it is THERE, inside, within the very cells.

Yes, there's no need to seek elsewhere.

But how to awaken it?

Through faith, our faith.

---

1. But everybody around would be flattened! "Smashed egos." What I failed to understand was this infinite Compassion veiling itself ... to avoid casualties.

If one knows that and has trust.... But you see, my physical, my body is deteriorating very rapidly—what could stop it from deteriorating?

Mother, I do NOT believe it is deterioration—it's not. My feeling is that you are physically being led to a point of such complete powerlessness that the most complete Power will be forced to awaken....

Ah!... you're right.

That Power will then be COMPELLED to come out.

Or else I could ... I could leave this body, no?

Ah, no, Mother! No, Mother, it must be done NOW.

(silence)

It must be done now.... You see, I am certain it's NOT disintegration, not at all. It is NOT disintegration.[1]

(Mother nods approvingly)

You know, I have always seen that the other pole springs up from the most extreme opposite. So the supreme Power must spring up from the sort of apparent powerlessness you are in. By no means is it a disintegration.

(long silence)

What would you like now?

To stay with you, Mother, naturally.

Like this? *(Mother takes Satprem's hands)*

Yes, Mother.

(Mother plunges in
for about ten minutes)

---

1. I was fighting with all my strength against the suggestion of death that was in the atmosphere. That day, the "formation of death" was palpable.

419

For me, you see, the question is food. More and more I find it impossible to eat. Can this body live without food?

Mother, I truly believe that you are being led to the point where something else will be FORCED *to manifest.*

I can't hear.

I think you are led to the point—the point of helplessness or powerlessness where something ELSE *will be forced to manifest.*

Ah. . . .
Maybe.

As long as that point . . . of impossibility has not been reached. . . .

Oh, it's almost the point of impossibility.

Yes, Mother, yes, that's also what I feel. I feel you're reaching that point, and something else is going to emerge.

(silence)

It is not at all the end; quite the contrary, it will soon be the beginning.

I was told that the beginning would take place when I am a hundred; but that's a long way off!

No, Mother, I don't think it will take that long. I don't think so. I really don't think so. Another type of functioning is going to set in. But the end of the old has to be reached, and that end is the terrible part!

Oh . . . I really don't want to say *(Mother shakes her head)*, I don't want to insist, but . . . truly . . . *(Mother speaks with her eyes closed, all the pain of the world is in the shake of her head).*

Yes, Mother. I understand, Mother, I understand. Yes. . . .

The consciousnes is clearer, stronger than it has ever been, and I look like an old. . . .

Yes, Mother, it's "normal," if I may say so. We're going, you're going to pass into something else, I sense it—it isn't faith in me that speaks, it's something else deep down, that understands.

(silence)

I don't speak out of "faith," Mother; it's really like something telling me: that's THE WAY.

(Mother plunges in, she moans softly, leans forward and seems to be looking for something, then takes Satprem's hand again and goes off.)

What time is it?

Five to eleven.... Goodbye, Mother.

(Then the door was shut)

And Now

Then the door was shut.

She was to live for another six months, 182 days.

Two days before the "end," she kept repeating, "I want to walk ... I want to walk...."

Before my eyes, they drove twenty-five screws into her coffin. There was a ray of sun on the nape of her neck; her hands were tightly clasped together—there was such strength in those hands! Such power in that supposedly dead body. And then that fierce concentration.

She wore a white silk dress and a small blouse with gold buttons.

The long saga unfolds before my eyes—so many years with that young girl's laughter rippling through everything, and the silences of snow, the beating of wings through boundless space, and the solid fire enfolding the body like concrete love. So many mysteries. "Death is the problem given me to resolve."

Already night and silence have fallen over the little actors, their good and evil, their sorrow and petty affairs. Tomorrow this scribe, too, will return to the flame of love whence he came, and she, to the sweetness of the Ganges. But what about men? What about History? Still millions and millions of men destined to die? Still sorrow upon sorrow? When will there be undying love? When a lovely earth?

Is it once again put off?

"A new way of dying ought to be possible," she said in 1963. She spoke so much to me about "death"—Savitri, too, went into death to release Satyavan. But what is death? ... That coffin? This tomb of gray marble where they go to place their flowers and light their incense, while going on with their petty affairs? But there, within ... a mighty silence, there is a body molded of power, whose every cell has repeated year after year, second after second: OM Namo Bhagavateh, OM Namo Bhagavateh....

So, is that all? Is this the end of the story?

But Krishna in gold has shattered the chains of the old sanctuaries; rolling and frolicking, he strides along the roads of an old, laggard world, sowing chaos and dissension and confusion everywhere—the inanity and illusion of everything: science and religion, ideals and medicine to patch up the old distressed carcass; everything is crumbling and collapsing; people speak a thousand languages but no one understands anybody; the heads of states look like clowns and clowns look like seers, and everything is the same in black or white, in Chinese or Russian or American. But Krishna winks: "Just wait...." The bomb? No. It would be too childish. The end of all illusions, the end of the human illusion —this is more serious and very upsetting. What if everything was a deception? Medicine and the Holy See, Aristotle and Euclid and the perpetual duplication of the molecules of deoxyribonucleic acid—what if things did not work that way at all?... An earthquake more earthshaking than all the Hiroshima bombs put together. The mental boat shipwrecked once and for all, and man flung on an unknown shore?... The periwinkle out of its shell. The world looked so complex and awesome and mathematical in that shell. No more shell, no more "mathematics"—just ... just what?

The most revolutionizing revolution in the world.

Alexander and Lenin and Pompadour (and Einstein and the latest Nobel Peace Prize laureate) were so awesome ... in a shell. But without the shell, it's something else.

A stupendous SOMETHING ELSE. "I am on my way to discovering the illusion that must be destroyed so that physical life can be uninterrupted.... Death is the result of a distortion of consciousness."

What if everything were "distorted" in the mental waterhole we live in? What if all our science of life, our every step, our distance, our time, our eyes were all false? The eyes of a ladybug, then of a periwinkle, then of a man—and then the eyes of tomorrow.

Krishna in gold is breaking the old shell—the shell of good and evil, hope and despair—the shell of life and death. What if there were no more "life" and no more "death"?

Quite a staggering new look.

But unrepentant men go on reciting the Gospel of the periwinkle and burning incense on gray-marble tombs and making babies and more babies, while Krishna in gold is pulling down the ceiling —how are they going to awake from it all?

In that tomb, some thousands and millions of cells are repeating the Mantra, tirelessly, relentlessly—a new vibration is wearing down the partition walls of the world. Alone in that mighty silence, a small human form with her hands clasped together repeats the prayer of the world, repeats the cry of the earth, repeats. . . . They did not want her alive—she is conquering death.

The veil of illusion shrouding an unknown reality.

She is wearing down death from within.

When our illusions are wholly gone, "that" will come. "I am walking a very thin line. . . ." The world is walking a very thin line. Will it fall on this side or that side?

It is perhaps time to decide what we want.

My gaze is so intense, my heart so grieved that, at times, I seem to penetrate that tomb. And I seem to discern something very still staring at death straight in the face, and an indomitable will—waiting.

Waiting for our prayer to join hers.

Mother, what do you have to say to these human offspring?

On that November 18, 1973, she said something. I was stunned, aching from head to toe amid those hundreds and thousands of people staring at a "dead body." The fans were droning, the neon lights were glaring; there was a scent of incense and jasmine in the air; they were making her coffin with all dispatch. But my heart was filled with such an enormous "This-is-not-possible," as if the entire earth and all the sorrowful men of this earth were crying out in my heart. So then, this was the "end," as it always was—as at Thebes and Babylon and Buchenwald. It was the end. And we start all over again. It was so overwhelmingly not-possible. Never, ever will I go through it again. Never, ever will there be "another time" with its sorrow and prayers and fruitless pain of being. There were a thousand men in my heart, all alike, who had waited and waited for THAT MOMENT. And there was no moment. We will have to come again in another life and learn again about Euclid and the law of gravity, and sorrow and "happiness"—and end up in a hole again? I was so broken, shattered on that November 18—there was only a splitting headache and a blank look staring and staring at that procession of dead people. But, suddenly, I had the most stupendous experience of my life. I who had so much complained to Mother of never having any "experience"! I was in no condition to have an experience, or concentrate or pray, or will anything—I was nothing but a headache, an aching body, a kind of frightful nonentity staring at a small white form. An unintelligible masquerade. It was false, screamingly false. A dream. Not real.

All of life was not-real.

Then she lifted me in her arms. She lifted me above my headache, lifted me above that crowd, above all those meaningless little bodies. And I was in a sound-burst. I entered a stupendous peal of bells—vast as the universe, exceeding all universes, all lives, all bodies, and yet WITHIN—a colossal ringing that swept away the worlds, swept away the pains, swept away the whys and the hows; I was one with that formidable SOUND ringing over the universe:

NO OBSTACLE, NOTHING WILL STOP
NO OBSTACLE, NOTHING WILL STOP
NO OBSTACLE, NOTHING WILL STOP . . .

. . . ringing and ringing. The whole world was ringing in a torrent of rapturous, irresistible, triumphant joy. NOTHING WILL STOP. . . .
It was the inevitable new world.
Here.
Done.
My whole body was trembling.

June 21, 1981
Land's End

Completed [in French] July 12, 1981
with love

SUMMARY

1972

January

April

July

September

October

December

12.2 – (An hour and fifteen minutes for breakfast.) I thought I had finished in 20 minutes and it took me more than an hour. Completely lost the sense of time. I take a bite or a sip, and ten or twenty minutes go by ... I don't know where, I don't know what. There's something there I must understand. (Sat:) "Is this consciousness active or immobile?" (Mother:) A light 319
– The same at night: a pain here, a pain there, then I enter the consciousness where pain disappears, and five or six hours go by . 319
– (Sat:) "Is this light active?" (Mother:) It does plenty of things, but not in the usual way. One day we'll go there together, perhaps you'll know. Something completely new, which I don't understand .. 320
12.6 – (Cyclone: the Samadhi tree devastated.) Usually it didn't come this way. The consciousness must have sunk a lot 322
– A vast, vast vision and precise: I know things happening, without thinking: they just come. But my memory is absolutely gone. Half an hour later I've forgotten what I did 322
– (Sat:) "I would like the Grace of belonging exclusively to you." 322
12.7 – ARMISTICE BETWEEN INDIA AND PAKISTAN IN KASHMIR; RETROCESSION OF THE TERRITORIES OCCUPIED DURING THE 1971 WAR.
12.9 – Everything is designed so that the only reliance is in the Divine. But I am not told what the "Divine" is. Everything else is collapsing, except the ... the what? The Divine, something—what? . 323
– Like an attempt to make you feel there isn't any difference between life and death—it's neither life nor death, is is ... something. And that is the Divine 323
12.10 – (Mother sees Sujata.) Life is a torture if I am not exclusively turned to the Divine. The only remedy: to be like this ... when time ceases to exist 324
10.13 – (Sat:) "You wanted to take me into that consciousness...." (Mother:) I am always there; what's difficult for me is to become conscious of the world as it is 324
– (Meditation) Sat: "A lot of power, and towards the end something eternal." 325
12.16 – Shall we go there together? (Sat:) "I'd like to be able to follow you." (Mother:) I'll pull you! 326
– You had become very young, like a twenty-year-old 326
12.20 – (Sat:) "What stage in the transformation had Sri Aurobindo reached? What difference with the work you are doing now?" (Mother:) He had accumulated a gread deal of supramental force in his body. All that force passed into mine so concretely that I thought it was visible. I could feel the friction of the passage. A physical sensation 326
– (Sat:) "Perhaps the difference lies in the collective intensity of that Power?" (Mother:) A difference in the Power of the action 327
– Sri Aurobindo has a greater power of action now than when he was in his body; that's why he left. His action has become very tangible 327

1973

January

February

March

May

List of Publications

Mother's Agenda

VOLUME I — 1951-1960

This first volume is mostly what could be called the "psychological preparation" of Satprem. Mother's confidant had to be prepared, not only to understand the evolutionary meaning of Mother's discoveries, to follow the tenuous thread of man's great future unraveled through so many apparently disconcerting experiences—which certainly required a steady personal determination, for more than 19 years!—but also, in a way, he had to share the battle against the many established forces that account for the present human mode of being and bear the onslaught of the New Force.

Satprem—"True Love"—as Mother called him, was a reluctant disciple. Formed in the French Cartesian mold, a freedom fighter against the Nazis and in love with his freedom, he was always ready to run away, and always coming back, drawn by a love greater than his love for freedom. Slowly she conquered him, slowly he came to understand the poignant drama of this lone and indomitable woman, struggling in the midst of an all-too-human humanity in her attempt to open man's golden future.

Week after week, privately, she confided to him her intimate experiences, the progress of her endeavor, the obstacles, the setbacks, as well as anecdotes of her life, her hopes, her conquests and laughter: she was able to be herself with him.

He loved her and she trusted him. It is that simple.

September 1980
$6.95 (U.S.A. & Europe)
Rs. 48/- (India & Asia)
Paperback · 540 pages
ISBN 2-902776-04-7

Mother's Agenda

VOLUME II — 1961

The course of 1961, the year of the first American voyage in space, touches the heart of the great mystery—"It is double! It is the same world and yet it is ... what?" In one world, everything is harmonious, without the least possibility of illness, accident or death—"a miraculous harmony"—and in the other, everything goes wrong. Yet it is the same world of matter—separated by what? "More and more, I feel it's a question of the vibration in matter."

And then, what is this "vertical time" which suddenly opens up another way of living and being in matter, in which causality ceases to exist, "A sort of absoluteness in each second"? A new world each second, ageless, leaving no trace or imprint.

And this "massive immobility" in a lightning-fast movement, this "twinkling of vibrations," as if Mother were no longer experiencing her body at the macroscopic level, but at the level of subatomic physics. Sixty years of "spiritual life" which crumble like a "far more serious illusion" before ... a new Divine ... or a new mode of life in matter? The *next* mode? "I am in the midst of hewing a path through a virgin forest."

Volume II records the opening up of this path.

May 1981
$8.95 (U.S.A. & Europe)
Rs. 48/- (India & Asia)
Paperback · 460 pages
ISBN 0-938710-01-X

Mother's Agenda

VOLUME III — 1962

The course of the year 1962 ... the year of the Kennedy-Khrushchev confrontation over Cuba and the first Sino-Indian conflict: "Could it be the first sign of something really ... momentous? It seems to have profoundly disrupted something central." The entire earth is disrupted. It is the year when Mother, in her body, emerges into a "third position," neither life nor death as we know them, but another side of the "web" where the laws of our physics no longer hold and which strangely resembles the quantum world of Black Holes: times changes, space changes, death changes. Could this be the material place, in the body, where the laws of the world—which exist only in our heads—become inverted and where evolution opens onto an unthinkable bodily freedom, a third position, that of the next species on earth?... "The body is beginning to obey another law. The sense of time disappears into a moving immobility.... A mass of infinite force, like pure superelectricity.... An undulating movement of corporeal waves, as vast as the earth.... All the organs have changed, they belong to another rhythm. Such a formidable power, so free! It's something else ... something else! I don't know if I am living or dead.... The nature of my nights is changing, the nature of my days is changing.... The physical vibration is becoming porous.... No more axis—it's gone, vanished! It can go forward, backwards, anywhere at all.... Ubiquity, or something of the sort."

And then this cry: "Death is an illusion, illness is an illusion! Life and death are one and the same thing! It's merely a shifting of consciousness. Why, it's fantastic!" And this simple discovery in the flesh: "The closer you draw to the cell, the more the cell says, 'Ah, but I am immortal!'" "A third cellular position in which you become incapable of dying because death no longer has any reality."

Has Mother, at the age of 84, discovered another material reality? "There, behind, it's like a fairy tale.... Something very beautiful is in preparation, ineffably beautiful—a lovely story that Sri Aurobindo was trying to bring down on earth, and it is sure to come!"

April 1982
$9.95 (U.S.A. & Europe)
Rs. 48/- (India & Asia)
Paperback · 532 pages
ISBN 0-938710-02-8

Mother's Agenda

VOLUME IV — 1963

The year of Kennedy's assassination; the beginnings of the Sino-Soviet split. While the destructive race between the superpowers intensifies and science questions the laws of the universe, Mother is slowly hewing out the path to the next species on earth. "The path I seek is ever descending," into the consciousness of the cells. Will it be global death then, or, just as the birds followed the reptiles, the beginning of a new world? "I am on the threshold of a stupendous realization, which depends on a very tiny thing." She is 85 this year. Will it be a more "intelligent" species within the framework of our physics, or one endowed with *another* kind of intelligence capable of changing the laws of physics, as the frog changes the laws of the tadpole in its fishbowl? In the course of this descent towards the cell, Mother suddenly veers into another *physical* universe: "Everything looks as though you were seeing it for the first time, even the motion of the earth and the stars.... There is no distance, no difference, there is not something that sees and something that is seen.... You become a mountain, a forest, a house.... You see simultaneously thousands of miles away and up close—a kind of cellular ubiquity." And then, too, this astounding realization: "The body is everywhere!" Is the next species ubiquitous? What happens to the laws of the old physics when the fishbowl is shattered, when distances and "elsewheres" are abolished? "All the usual rhythms have changed ... a universal movement so tremendously rapid that it seems motionless.... A true physical which lies behind." And where is death for one who escapes the wear and tear of time inherent to the fishbowl? "If this condition becomes a natural thing, death can no longer exist!... It would be a new phase of life on earth." And there is no need to look far for it: "The field of experience is right here, at every second ... people strive to enter into contact with something that is right *here*." A new cellular consciousness which will be a new kind of physics and perhaps the earth's next biology?

Scheduled for 1984
ISBN 0-938710-09-5

Mother's Agenda

VOLUME V — 1964

"The only hope for the future is a change in man's consciousness. It is left to men to decide if they will collaborate to this change or if it will have to be enforced upon them by the power of crushing circumstances." As the new force gradually infiltrates Mother's body, it is the earth one wonders about. How is earth going to digest "this vibration as intense as a superior kind of fire"? "I see very few bodies around me capable of bearing it.... So what's going to happen?"

It is the year of the first Chinese atomic bomb. Mother is 86. "A tiny, infinitesimal, stippled infiltration—the miracle of the earth!" A catastrophic miracle? Isn't the butterfly some sort of catastrophe to the caterpillar? "Death is no solution, so we are here seeking another solution—there *must* be another solution." Imperturbably, Mother descends deeper into the cellular consciousness, and deeper still: "A kind of certainty, deep in matter, that the solution lies *there....* It is at the atomic level that a change must take place; the question concerns the state of infinitesimal vibrations in matter." Time veers into something else: "Perhaps it is into the past that I go, perhaps the future, perhaps the present?..." And even the laws of matter change: "As soon as you reach the domain of the cells, that sort of heaviness of matter disappears. It becomes fluid and vibrant again. Which would tend to show that heaviness, thickness, inertia have been *added on*—it's false matter, the one we think or feel, but not matter as it really is."

So what, then, would true matter be, the matter of the next species? "I am on the threshold of a new perception of life, as if certain parts of my consciousness were changing from the caterpillar state to the butterfly state...." And the earth groans and protests ... at what? "The whole youth seems to be seized by a strange vertigo...." Are we going to move on to a next species, or not?

ISBN 0-938710-10-9

Mother's Agenda

VOLUME VI — 1965

"A whole world is opening up." It is the year when Mother reaches "the mind of the cells," buried under the old genetic coating which seems to want to keep men forever harnessed to death: "There, there is such a concentration of power . . . as if you had caught the tail of the solution." Another power of consciousness in matter capable of undoing the old program: "A kind of memory being elaborated from below"—a new cellular memory, which is no longer the memory of decay, illness, death, gravity and all our "real" world?

And at the same time, at that cellular level freed from the old laws, Mother discerns "two worlds one inside the other: a world of truth and a world of falsehood, and that world of Truth is PHYSICAL; it is not up above: it's MATERIAL. And that's what must come to the forefront and replace the other: the true physical." Mother called that replacement the "transfer of power."

Is it really conceivable that a marvel of physical freedom lies concealed within our cells, while we strive and toil outside with illusory panaceas: "If even a tiny aggregate of cells could experience the total transformation, all the way, that would be more effective than any big revolution. But it's more difficult. . . . You must overcome death! Death must cease to exist, it's very clear."

Is the entire earth not in the process of going through this "transfer of power," just as one day it passed from the reign of the animal to the reign of the mind? "Everything is escaping, there's nothing left to lean on, it is the passage to the new movement . . . and for the old, that always creates a dangerously precarious balance."

Mother's Agenda

VOLUME VII — 1966

"Humanity is not the last rung of terrestrial creation. Evolution continues and man will be surpassed. It's up to each one to know whether he wants to participate in the adventure of the new species." This was 1966, the year of the Cultural Revolution in China. A far more profound revolution was taking place in a body which, on behalf of all the little bodies of the earth, was seeking the one solution that would change everything: "We are seeking the process that will give the power to undo death. . . . The mind of the cell is what will find the key."

It is the perilous transformation from a human body animated by the laws of the mind to the next body animated by a still nameless law buried in the heart of the cell: "A coagulated vibration, denser than air, extremely homogenous, of golden luminosity, with a fantastic power of propulsion. . . . Everything, but everything is becoming strange. . . . The body is no longer dependent on physical laws. . . ." Isn't this the sensation the first vertebrate must have had when it emerged from its watery milieu into another, nameless one in which we breathe today? "Each part of the body, the moment it changes, feels it's the end. . . . All the supports have been removed. . . . I have no path to follow!" For what is the path to the next species? "A few have got to open it up."

At times, though, the other "milieu" suddenly appears: "An instant marvel. . . . A state in which time no longer has the same reality, it's very peculiar . . . a multitudinous present. Another way of living."

Eighty years earlier, a little girl had undergone her first revolution of matter: "When I was told that everything was made up of 'atoms,' it caused a sort of revolution in my head: Why, nothing is real, then!"

A second revolution takes place at the level of the cellular consciousness: the old matter and its apparent laws change into a new world and a new way of being in a body.

Mother's Agenda

VOLUME VIII — 1967

This year, all the features of the yoga of the cells become clear: "A growing conviction that a perfection achieved in matter is a far more perfect perfection than any other. The consciousness expressed in transformed cells is a marvel: that legitimizes all these centuries of misery. Oh, what a fuss all those gods make."

This year marks the discovery of "true matter" ... without fuss: "In that cellular limpidity, there are no more problems: the solution precedes the problem. That is, things organize themselves automatically." It's another mode of life on earth—"such a natural way of being"—in a body freed from its mental shackles and the laws of false matter: "An extraordinary impression of the unreality of suffering, the unreality of illness.... It does not cure illness: it annuls it—it makes it unreal.... And then you see: as the functioning gradually perfects itself, it necessarily, inevitably means victory over death."

Meanwhile *Surveyor* is digging the ground of the moon with its mechanical arm, but our own secrets remain buried in a little cell: "We can travel anywhere, we know what's going on anywhere ... but we don't know what's going on inside ourselves."

War is raging in Biafra, the Israeli troops are marching toward Suez, American planes are bombing Haiphong, China explodes its first thermonuclear bomb ... and so on. "A tremendous conflict over the earth." At stake is a new earth, or the return to the old fiasco: "A local and momentary manifestation is not ruled out, but what is needed is a collective transformation sufficient to create a new species on earth.... This fact is certain."

Will we understand where the real way out is, and the marvel concealed in a human body?

Mother's Agenda

VOLUME IX — 1968

A fire spread across the world that year, from Warsaw to
Columbia, from Nanterre to Alexandria: "There are long periods
when things are being prepared, but a moment comes when something happens; and this something is what will bring about a new
development in the world. Like the moment when man appeared
on earth: now it is another being."

This is the second turning point of Mother's yoga. She is 90.
Auroville has just been founded: "A center for accelerated evolution." Martin Luther King is assassinated, and Robert Kennedy.
Russia invades Czechoslovakia—what is going on? "I have the
strong impression this is an attempt to make us learn something
like the secret of the functioning °of man, of the earth©. The process we have learned is constantly shown to be false, not adapted
to reality, and there is a will to make us find the true process, but
through experience."

As if the earth were shut in a bowl, prisoner of a "false matter":
"Like a sort of web over the entire earth, and the body is being
taught how to get out of it.... Little by little the consciousness of
the cells is breaking away from that hold." And on the other side of
the web all of a sudden: "Never in my whole life have I seen or felt
anything so beautiful!... The most marvelous hours ever possible
on earth—why do people go looking up above for something which
is right here!" The short-lived miracle of 1968 seems to be
swallowed up, while the walls of our bowl are slowly but inex-
orably being shattered in every country, every continent and every
branch of human knowledge. "A considerable amount of time still
seems necessary for everything to be ready to change. And yet,
there is almost a promise that a sudden change is going to take
place." Could it be that, one fine morning, one last pressure of
circumstances will throw us headlong into a new consciousness?

Mother's Agenda

VOLUME X — 1969

Now Mother has found the "passage," what she calls "the new consciousness," the one capable of opening up a new world to us, just as the first breaking of the watery mirror by an amphibian opened up a new air to us: "I don't know what's happening, there's a state of intense vibrations, like waves of lightning rapidity, so rapid that they seem motionless. And then I go off to America, to Europe.... This body has never been so happy: these cells, other cells, it was life everywhere, consciousness everywhere, all bodies were this body!..." And all our physiological misery vanishes by the same token: "There is a sort of dilation of the cells, the sense of boundaries lessens, fades away, and the pains vanish *physically*."

And it isn't "another world," it is this earth, our earth, but lived otherwise: "As if we had entered an unreal falsehood, and everything disappears once you get out of it—it simply does not exist! And all the artificial means of getting out of it, including Nirvana, are worthless. SALVATION IS PHYSICAL! It is *here*, right here. All the rest, death included, really becomes a falsehood—there is no such thing as 'disappearing,' no 'life vs. death'!..." And as she breaks through the walls of our bowl, the whole world is in revolt—including Mother's entourage—as if it were under the pressure of a new air: "A considerable number of desires for it to die [Mother's body]; everywhere, they are everywhere!... The whole gamut of feelings around me, from anxiety, eagerness for it to be over quickly, to impatient desires: free at last!... I don't want to be put in a box, the cells are conscious.... What is going to happen? I don't know. It runs contrary to all habits." A new species is quite contrary to the old habit of the world—will the world accept it, or wind up killing it off?

Mother's Agenda

VOLUME XI — 1970

The beginning of the terrible years.... There was the feeling that Mother had found the secret of the change, conquered all she could from her own body, and that she was now sitting there, surrounded by the pack, just putting up with each and every resistance of the old species. "The change is DONE. Everything is tooth and nail, ferociously after me, but it's over." A new mode of being of the cellular consciousness had appeared on earth as one day, in inert matter, there appeared a new mode of being called life—but this time it is "overlife": "The impression there is a way of being of the cells that could be the beginning of a new body; only, when that comes, the body itself feels it is dying." What would be the feeling of the first corpuscle to experience life? "The body feels it has reached the point of ... unknown. A very, very strange sensation. A sort of new vibration. It's so new that ... I can't speak of anguish, but it's ... the unknown. A mystery of the unknown." And there, what we call "death" is like the other side of the bowl for the former fish, and yet it is not "another world": "They are surprisingly one within the other! There is something there.... Is it possible? For overlife is both life and death together."

And then this cry of the breakthrough: "What appears to us as 'the laws of nature' is nonsense!..." Another world ON EARTH in which the old mortal laws of our bowl break down into ... something else? "I've just had a fantastic vision of the cradle of a future ... which is not very far. It's like a formidable mass suspended above the earth." But will the old pack let her go through to the end?

Mother's Agenda

VOLUME XII — 1971

The last turning point of Mother's yoga, and she comes out of it with this cry: "I have walked a long, long time. There was nothing but a constant cry, as if everything were torn away from me. It was the whole problem of the world."

And this *Agenda* is more and more strewn with heartrending little cries. It was not enough to have found the secret for herself, the others too had to understand, her own disciples like dominions locked in their egoistic power: "They have no faith! 'She is old, she is old,' an atmosphere of resistance to the change; 'it is impossible, impossible' from all sides.... We should not waste a single minute —I am in a hurry.... The reign of the Divine must, oh, must come!... If the entire Russian block turned to the right side, that would be an enormous support! The victory is certain, but I don't know which path will be followed to reach it.... We must cling, cling so tightly to the Truth.... They don't listen to me anymore." She is 93, groping her way into the unknown: "I see more clearly with eyes closed than with eyes open, and it is a physical vision, purely physical, but a kind of physical that seems more complete. The consciousness of the cells is what has to change, all the rest will follow naturally! I have the feeling I am on my way to discovering the illusion that must be destroyed so that physical life can be uninterrupted—death is the result of a distortion of consciousness."

Will she be heard? Will she be allowed to pursue her experience? "Only a violent death could halt the transformation; otherwise the body knows that the work will go on and on and on...."

And this cry again: "There will be a miracle! But what, I don't know."

February 1983
$12.50 (U.S.A. & Europe)
Rs. 78/- (India & Asia)
Paperback · 393 pages
ISBN 0-938710-05-2

Mother's Agenda

VOLUME XIII — 1972-1973

"Before dying falsehood rises in full swing. Still people understand only the lesson of catastrophe. Will it have to come before
they open their eyes?"
This is the year of Watergate, of Nixon's first trip to China, the
assassination of the Israeli athletes in Munich, the first oil em-
bargo. This is Mother's last lap. A lap strewn with heartrending
little cries and stunning visions. The end of one world, the beginning of another . . . whether we want it or not. "Sometimes, it is so
new and unexpected it's almost painful."
And I would ask her, "But is it a state outside matter?" "I don't go
outside of physical life, but . . . it looks different. But it is strange.
And PHYSICAL, that's the extraordinary thing! As if the physical had
split in two. . . . A new state in matter. And ruled by something that
is not the sun, I don't know what it is. . . . I am touching another
world. Another way of being . . . dangerous but wonderful."
How I listened to her little breath as she gasped for air, a breath
that seemed to come from another side of the world: "There is no
difference between life and death. It's neither life nor death, it is . . .
something. It is not the disappearance of death, you understand:
BOTH are being changed . . . into something still unknown, which
seems at once extremely dangerous and absolutely wonderful." And
what if "death" were merely the other, MATERIAL side of our human
bowl, the sunlit shore for a species to come? A new condition on
both sides of the world, in which life AND death change into . . .
something else? "I am treading a very thin and narrow line . . . ."
And then this cry, this entreaty: "Let me do the work!"
On November 17, 1973, she passed away—why?

March 1984
$12.50 (U.S.A. & Europe)
Rs. 78/- (India & Asia)
Paperback · 468 pages
ISBN 0-938710-07-9

English cassette available with Vol. 13:

*A cassette containing Mother's conver-
sations in **English**. Approximately 90
minutes of recording. Side 1: April 13,
1962 (the 1st turning point); May 18,
1963; May 5, 1973 (the Mantra). Side 2:
April 7, 1973.*

The Mind of the Cells

An Essay

by Satprem

Written to give the reader a succinct and comprehensive view of Mother's full experience in the cellular consciousness of her body, this book describes one after another the main features of her discovery, as well as the different kinds of difficulties and "cellular habits" she had to overcome. One learns about "tactile vision," "the substitution of vibrations," and "the training of the cells"; the author even explains what is meant by "descending into one's body"— and perhaps how to do it.

Using numerous extracts from the *Agenda* to illustrate its development, the book goes through each and every aspect of Mother's endeavor—including the lack of comprehension of her disciples—and shows how it all converges in a sort of evolutionary evidence: that *indeed* Mother opened up in her body the door to another being after man, a being whose physical functioning is different, whose handling of circumstances and of the world is different—a being who enjoys an incredible physical freedom: the fairy tale of our species.

November 1982
$6.95 (U.S.A. & Europe)
Rs. 48/- (India & Asia)
Paperback · 217 pages
ISBN 0-938710-06-0

Mother's Log

noted by

Satprem

Mother's words from 1950 to 1973 concentrated in their essence, and without commentary.

This short book, entirely made up of Mother's words, is an attempt at condensing in 250 pages the 3,000 pages of her *Talks* at the Playground plus the 6,000 pages of her *Agenda*. Satprem did so by picking out in each of Mother's conversations the "essential cry," as it were, much in the manner of a scientist jotting down a few words in his log to retain the essence of an experiment in progress. The result here is a sequence of short sentences, with dates, that present Mother's experiences in the order they happened—and that order is certainly deeply relevant. Here, the issue is not explanations and logic, but the possibility for the reader to go into the experience himself by feeling the main lines of force—and perhaps by finding unexpected paths and coordinates, for Mother's map is not finished once and for all. A book that speaks to the heart.

Mother

A Biography
by Satprem

This trilogy written by Satprem after Mother's passing in 1973 recounts her life from the external point of view, but it also gives us insights into what led Mother, at the age of eighty, when she had already achieved every possible spiritual realization and conquered all the inner worlds, to put *everything* into question because one small link was still missing: the plenitude of the material body and life in *this* world. She faced the question squarely, as she always did, and was gradually led to "descend into the body," down into the genetic code and the "consciousness of the cells," which ultimately holds the key to our human condition on earth. And she found the secret—in the cells—the Power that makes us what we are and can remold the laws of our being, much in the same way the first thought transformed the nature of the ape. We can be part of this evolutionary process, if we want—that is Mother's discovery.

VOLUME I, **The Divine Materialism** concerns Mother's life from her birth in Paris in 1878 to Sri Aurobindo's departure in 1950. It recounts her spontaneous early experiences as a child, her friendship with the great Impressionist artists of the time, her first lessons of occultism with Max Théon in Algeria, her journeys to India, and her meeting with Sri Aurobindo. From 1926 on, she will be "Mother" for an increasing number of disciples and devotees. The book follows her in her multifaceted daily work in the Ashram, her minute attention to the needs of each and every seeker, and most of all her life and relationship with Sri Aurobindo.

December 1980
$6.95 (U.S.A. & Europe)
Rs. 80/- (India & Asia)
Paperback · 355 pages
ISBN 2-902776-05-5

VOLUME 2, **The New Species** recounts Mother's life from 1950 to 1968. In the first part, from 1950 to 1958, she attempts to find some receptivity and open a few consciousnesses to the new Possibility in the Ashram population (especially among the young). It is the period of her *Talks* at the Playground. She then withdraws to her room to do the work of transformation in herself. It is the long and arduous "descent" into the mysteries of the human body, through the various "layers" that keep us subservient to the so-called laws of nature. She finds the key in the cells —the "mind of the cells."

June 1983
$8.95 (U.S.A. & Europe)
Rs. 70/- (India & Asia)
Paperback · 486 pages
ISBN 0-938710-03-6

VOLUME 3, **The Mutation of Death** evokes her last five years, from 1968 to 1973. The most critical and poignant period. It is as if the secret were there, available to all—she had found the key —but some degree of participation and *understanding* from the human element around her is necessary for the process to spread, for what is at stake is an evolutionary transition of the species. But this will be denied to her: she will find no comprehension among her disciples, and tragically her door will be closed to Satprem, her confidant. Six months later, in November 1973, she passed away, leaving many questions for us to answer, and a luminous hope.

Man After Man

An interview with Satprem
by Frederick de Towarnicki

Frederick de Towarnicki, a French radio commentator and interviewer, went to India in 1980 to interview Satprem. The interview was later broadcast on French radio, and this book is its integral transcription.

Satprem recounts his past and retraces his journey from the time he was a child in Brittany gazing out at the ocean to his meeting with Sri Aurobindo and Mother, who gave his life its meaning. We follow him in his adventures through the Guyana jungle, Brazil, Africa, Egypt, and on the byways of India as a mendicant Sannyasin: a life of search to find the meaning of life.

He finally settles down near Mother, realizing that hers is the real adventure. He will become her confidant and follow her in her physical attempt, he to whom we owe the possibility of reading the *Agenda*.

In this interview, remarkable for its simplicity and matter-of-factness, Satprem explains at length and simply Mother's work in the cellular consciousness and how her discovery indeed leads to the next evolutionary being on earth.

By the Body of the Earth

A Novel

by Satprem

A book about the travels of the soul, which are also called reincarnations. A "perpetual story" which unfolds in three cycles (after many others) or three lives; three islands located in "this country or that," apparently in India, but Egypt is there too, as well as the frozen lakes of Norway. And a character, Nil, ever in search of "something else"—a new state of being on earth outside the Machine and the laws of the mind—who has burned everything to make his quest; he sheds the robe of the world for that of a mendicant *Sannyasin*, discovers another, vaster consciousness, a cosmic one, with new perceptions, but finally realizes that although he may have found free air up above, he has lost the earth. And each time, life after life, he finds the same circumstances again—only worse each time—and also the same actors and an eternal lover, Mohini, Batcha, his mate through every cycle, whom he burns each time in order to grasp the ungraspable other thing: "three times you came; three times you killed"; as if this long journey were meant to lead him to an impossible point at the heart of himself, the same knot of destiny, where a man has to choose between catastrophe once more and the emergence into another level of consciousness. Until the day when, in the depths of night, before the funeral pyre of his beloved, Nil finds the "other thing," the "powerful light" of the next cycle, and understands at last that freedom is not necessarily found above, beyond this world, and that we are the children of Heaven "by the body of the earth."

1978
$5.95 · Paperback · 337 pages
ISBN: 0-06-013768-1

Gringo

by Satprem

The "Book of the Jungle" in reverse. Not a young of man returning to animal life, but another young of man living in a primitive tribe of the Amazon, who seeks an exit from the human tribe and the passage to "man after man." The story of evolution told as a legend and of the Elder of evolution, represented by the "queen" of the tribe, who takes Gringo into the past adventures of the earth—in Egypt, in Atlantis, and in the Arctic—and into the adventure of the future of the earth. Each time, he must break the barrier set up by the keepers of the Law, whether the law of the old Initiates, the Amazonian tribe, the spiritualists, or even of the twentieth-century biologists. For every summit, once attained, becomes the obstacle to the next cycle.

Satprem here evokes the adventure he lived in the Guyana jungle as a young man and the adventure he lived with Sri Aurobindo and Mother in the future of the earth: a spell-binding odyssey, from the prehuman forest to the mysterious forest of tomorrow.

Sri Aurobindo

or

the Adventure of Consciousness

An Essay
by Satprem

The now classic work on Sri Aurobindo. Satprem describes the main aspects of Sri Aurobindo's yoga and its stress on making the traditional yogic realizations effective in everyday life. One learns about the working of the various psychological processes of the human being and how he can achieve higher—super-conscient—openings. Whole chapters are devoted to mental silence, the descent of the Force, the opening and growth of the psychic center. The development is clear and precise, taking the reader step by step through the process of yoga. The last chapter touches on the physical transformation and Mother's work in the body. Highly recommended as introductory reading.

February 1984 (New English edition)
$9.95 (U.S.A. & Europe)
Rs. 70/- (India & Asia)
Paperback · 400 pages
ISBN 0-938710-04-4

On the Way to Supermanhood

An Essay on Experimental Evolution

by Satprem

A book for those who want to *feel* the vibration of the new world. Although the development follows a certain line of logic, there are no explanations or demonstrations here; we are simply led into another world, we bathe in an atmosphere different from everything we have known, yet very intimate, as if we were reading about ourself, our true self, deep inside. It is the new man in gestation, the deeper possibilities that form a new way—"super" is a mild qualifier—of being here on earth, and which will eventually lead to the supramental creation announced by Sri Aurobindo.

A book of extraordinary power and beauty, which Mother regarded as the book of tomorrow.

Scheduled for 1984
ISBN 0-938710-11-7